Me, Myself,
and Men

SHARON ST. JOHN

Me, Myself, and Men

Copyrighted Material

Me, Myself, and Men

Copyright © 2020 by Sharon St. John. All Rights Reserved.

No part of this publication may be reproduced, stored in a retrieval system or transmitted, in any form or by any means—electronic, mechanical, photocopying, recording or otherwise—without prior written permission from the publisher, except for the inclusion of brief quotations in a review.

For information about this title or to order other books and/or electronic media, contact the publisher:
Sharon St. John
San Pedro, California
SharonStJohnAuthor.com
sshotsie@gmail.com

Library of Congress Control Number: 2019914535

ISBN: 978-1-7333030-0-2 (Hardcover)
         978-1-7333030-1-9 (Paperback)
         978-1-7333030-2-6 (eBook)

Printed in the United States of America

Cover and Interior design: 1106 Design

You can also contact Sharon at her social networking accounts:
Facebook—https://www.facebook.com/Sharon-St-John-Author
Twitter—https://twitter.com/sshotsie
Instagram—https://www.instagram.com/sshotsie/

*Only when you know the love of God
can you embrace the love of man.*

You must first believe that God lives within you.

*Dedicated to My Father, George St. John,
My First Love*

Contents

Intro	xi
The Beginning	1
The Teenage Years	15
The Twenties	45
The Thirties	107
The Forties	265
Outro	335
About the Author	339

Intro

Talking to some of my girlfriends and listening to all their problems and their theories on men, not to mention my own ideas about the male species, I have come to one conclusion: Some men are full of shit, and the sad part is that there is always a woman out there to take their shit. Women have made excuses for a man's bad behavior by making comments such as, "Men—you can't live with them, and you can't live without them." There must have been at least one woman out there who also felt that this was a stupid comment, and she came up with, "Men are like buses—you miss one, and you can always catch the next one."

In my journey, I've learned that both these phrases are stupid. Men are men, and they will get away only with what we as women allow them to get away with. When a child is not held accountable for their bad behavior, that behavior then becomes embedded in their personality. Most people will always claim, "This is who I am; this is my personality," as if that is an excuse for bad behavior. When people mature, their personality changes. And although there are no official guidelines on maturity, it is expected that, by a certain age, everyone should have a specific level of maturity. With that level of maturity comes ownership of your behavior, good or bad.

Some would say men are simple, but the simplicity of a man is difficult to understand. Men say they don't like drama or women who are "crazy." Now, what exactly *is* "crazy"? Is it the moment she says, "Where have you been?" Is it the moment she asks, "Can you take me out and spend some time with me?" Is it the moment she says, "What are we doing?" or "Where is this relationship going?" Is it the moment she says, "I deserve respect"? These basic questions will get a woman labeled "crazy" in the amount of time it takes to say the word "crazy."

Men say they want one kind of woman but can't handle her when they have her. They want someone who is self-sufficient and can bring something to the table besides her body. When they meet this woman, the relationship becomes a fight for power. Within that power struggle, the level of respect becomes a casualty of war. If she has to work overtime to get ahead on her job, she is accused of sleeping with someone at work. If she makes more money than him, then she thinks she is better than him. Small jabs at a woman's personal accomplishments can have a negative effect on her self-worth.

Ladies, there is nothing wrong with picking up the tab every now and then, but a man should always do his part. Most women, including myself, will take care of a man with the hope that, when he gets on his feet, he won't forget who helped him when he was down. When that doesn't happen, we feel used. It may take some time, but we as women have to let a man be a man. If that means seeing him down and knowing you have the means to bring him up, we have to let him do it on his own. So many of us go into this maternal-instinct mode to protect the one we love. Sometimes people need to hit that brick wall in order to appreciate the lesson that had to be taught.

It is my opinion that, with men, tough love is the best love. When making the decision to commit yourself to another person of the opposite sex, fidelity is first and foremost. Men have the ability to convince a woman that she is the only one. I can say for sure that Adam made Eve feel that way, because she *was* the only one. But if Adam had had a choice, would he still have chosen to be with Eve? Did she convince him to bite that apple as revenge for his thoughts of infidelity? I sometimes wonder: *Did God really create men first—and, if so, why?* Why are men chosen to lead when they can be so easily persuaded by the appendage hanging between their legs? I once heard one of my male friends say, "Women are demons straight from the semen." I guess he thought he was saying something profound, but what he didn't think about was the fact that semen flows from the *male* sex organ. In other words, if a woman has devilish qualities, it stems from the genes her father contributed to her whole genetic makeup.

Sometimes I wonder: *Was I a man in a former life?* Maybe I treated women really badly, and now God is punishing me by sending me all the wrong men. Ladies, when I find myself remotely interested in a man, I repeat my version of the Serenity Prayer: "God, grant me the strength to accept the things I cannot change about him, the courage to change the things that I can, and the wisdom to know when to walk away." I mention all of the above because these things, compounded with a woman struggling with her own self-worth, is a cocktail for disaster. A superficial man is like pointing a gun at the head of a woman with low self-esteem.

After reading my story, I want you to call me all kinds of stupid, but my hope is that you never find yourself in any of these situations. Having low self-esteem can cause someone to be trapped in their own mental prison. I pray that you recognize the signs of self-destructive behavior and will be able to uplift yourself or someone else before a lifetime is wasted chasing love down all the wrong roads. Each man in my life served a purpose, and I wrote this book in hopes of realizing that purpose in order to become a better me. My hope is to learn about myself through my journey with men, and then I will be prepared for what God really has in store for me. I also hope that the men I have written about learn something about themselves and that they will be able to teach another generation to be better people.

Here is my journey. This is a true story based on my recollection of events. Names have been changed to protect the privacy of those who were involved.

The Beginning

My earliest memory dates back to the year of 1976, and I was in my apartment in Brooklyn. The address was 250 Clarkson Avenue, between Nostrand and Rogers. I shared a room with my two sisters, Camielle and Lorraine. My brothers' room was around the corner and down the hall. All four of them shared this room. I remember the room well—it had posters of Bruce Lee and an odor only a pig could grow to love. The youngest brother, Gary, worshiped the ground my second-oldest brother, Andrew, walked on. He would sleep in his bed no matter how stinky and brown the sheets were.

My mother's room was directly across from the front door as you entered the apartment. I also had another sister, the eldest girl, Angela. She was married and lived with her husband and her two children, Yvonne and Marie, four blocks away on Lennox Avenue. She made me an aunt at a very young age. I was only five years older than my oldest niece, Yvonne. Everyone in my family can write a book of their own. Each one of us would have a chapter titled "Mother."

My mother's name is Gloria Reynolds, and she was born and raised in the country of Jamaica. She came here hoping to make a better life for herself and her children. She worked as a housekeeper by day and security guard by night. She sent money back home to Jamaica to her mother, who was then raising her six oldest children until my mother could afford to send for them. My younger sister and I were born in Brooklyn, New York.

My mother was an extremely beautiful woman. Her skin complexion was like smooth-flowing caramel. Her hair was jet-black, soft, and silky. She had legs fully proportioned to match her shapely hourglass figure. She would have no problems getting a man to notice her. Aside from being beautiful, she had her own problems. Her mother never revealed the truth to her for 55 years as to who her real father was. He turned out to be a white man, who, my grandmother says, raped her. This would explain my mother's jet-black silky-smooth hair and beautiful skin complexion. The hair was a good thing for my mother because she wanted all of her children to have "Good hair." She made good on this promise to herself by marrying a Chinese man and conceiving six of his children.

Somewhere along the line, she must have strayed, because my oldest brother had a different father, and I have a different father. My sisters were all blessed with light skin and good hair. I had to get my hair straightened with a hot comb or a chemical relaxer to give the illusion of good hair. I was also of the darker-skin complexion and was often called a "cousin" instead of a "sister" by strangers. As a young girl who started having children at an early age, my mother was probably taught that, in order to keep a man, a woman should keep quiet.

I am not sure how true the story is, but for as long as I can remember, I was told about my mother's husband, Willie Reynolds. I remember him as a handsome man who took more pride in his clothes than in his kids. I knew his love for dice was stronger than his love for his children or his wife. To see this man, you would never think that he was capable of lying next to his firstborn and touching her as he would his wife. If mothers today would see or hear of this, the man would probably be sent to meet his maker or have plenty of time to think about it in jail. The mothers from back in the day, who started having children as early as fourteen, such as my mom, would turn their backs and pretend it never happened. The sad part is that women like my mother continue to have children with these predators just to keep their man.

I am not sure if that's my mother's story, but I know she made a whole lot of mistakes. One of her major flaws was her child rearing. She always came out swinging if someone tried to hurt her children. She didn't consider what *she* was doing as hurting her children. Unfortunately, children, just like men, sometimes need to stand on their own two feet. She lacked the ability to tell her children when they were wrong, especially her sons. She also displayed favoritism among her kids, which nearly ruined the relationship among the siblings. The separation among the children because of the different fathers was the worst. Thank God, we get older and a little wiser than our parents. My brothers and sisters never made me feel different because of my hair, skin color, or because I had a different father.

My father, George St. John, was born in Brooklyn. He was a distinguished man with a certain presence about him. The way he walked, the way he spoke—it was like being in the presence of royalty. Somehow, he maintained his down-to-earthness. You were able to talk to him about anything. This man was knowledgeable about almost every topic. He was heavily into politics and law. I think this is probably where I developed my interest in the criminal-justice field later on in life. My father also had a private side to him. He took many trips out of the country, and he would never say when he was leaving or when he would be returning. In between trips, he made time for me and my siblings.

I remember, when puberty set in for me, things were crazy between my mother and me. My father made arrangements for me to come to Brooklyn every weekend just to get away from that situation with my mother. We would discuss topics like life and why it is the way it is. We never arrived at an answer, but it was always a good conversation. The topic of boys was never mentioned in detail, because I had not yet realized that I liked them. They were fun to play with, but other than playing kickball or flipping on old mattresses, I had no use for boys. Looking back there were many questions I wish I could have asked my father. I remember many quotes and phrases he would use then that I didn't quite understand as a child. He would always say, "Whatever happens to you in your life, be it bad or good, you have only yourself to blame or take credit for it, because you allowed it to happen." He would also say, "Pride is comfort to a fool." When he would take me out to dinner, he would open doors, including the car door, and pull out the chair for me to sit at the table. He would say, "If a man can't do these simple things for you, then you don't want to be bothered with him." I listened to what he was saying, but I had no clue what he meant by any of it. Once I got older, chivalry became one of the sexiest features in a man for me.

My father was what most people would call an atheist. This is someone who believes there is no God. When we would go to bed at night, my mother would say, "Don't forget to say your prayers." My dad would say that we should be praying to *him* because he is the one who provides for us. I always thought that was funny. My mother would get upset because she didn't want him to teach us that there was no such thing as God. After a while, it was never discussed anymore, and my father's belief was his own.

My mother and father had a relationship that I accepted as normal. People will say it was strange, but they were very open with one another in front of us. When my mother started getting gray pubic hairs, my father would take the tweezer and pluck them out right in front of us. My mother would literally be lying on the bed with her legs spread apart, and he would be lying in between her legs fully focused on getting every single gray hair he could find. I remember he asked me if I wanted him to marry my mother, and I said "No." I didn't know why I didn't want him to marry my mother, but I know he never mentioned marrying her to me again. I am not even sure if she wanted to marry him. I just knew I liked things the way they were. My father never lived with us, but he was there every night, and when he didn't come over, he was on the phone. There were nights when we would be asleep and wake up to find him standing over us, just watching us sleep. It always made me so happy to see him standing there. It was a *safe* feeling—almost like an extra blanket on a cold winter night.

I am not sure whether it was good parenting skills, but we never witnessed an argument between them. My mother would play games with him, like having one of us girls answer the phone and tell Pop she'd gone out. Sometimes she would get dressed up while he was there, acting like she was waiting for someone to pick her up. He would sit there and wait patiently, and then when he would leave. As soon as he left, she would take her clothes off and go to bed. We knew it was a game she was playing, and it was funny to us to watch.

My father, on the other hand, would act like he had another girlfriend by the name of "Gwendoline." He would sing this song—"Oh, Gwendoline, my Gwendoline, the only woman who loves me." Every time he sang those lyrics, it would drive my mother crazy, but she would never discuss it in front of us. She would just say, "George, don't sing that song in my house." My sisters and I were the only ones who knew that Gwendoline was my mother. He would sing it only when he wanted her to do something that she didn't feel like doing at that moment. He would say things like, "My Gwendoline would have done it for me." Sometimes my mother would go along with it, and other times it backfired and my father didn't get his way.

I knew that, when something was really bothering my mother and she wanted to talk to him in private, she would call him into her room and close the door. I remember she had a rocking chair in her room that he always sat in whenever he was there. She would sit on the floor in front of him with her head resting on his leg. I remember hearing her ask for money from that position. There was always something about that position that gave me an uneasy feeling. A woman bowing down to her man just was not a concept that I could accept then—and, definitely, not now that I am older. That image still upsets me. They managed to stay together 29 years and were never married.

Whether some parents know it or not, how the mother and father figures interact with one another has an effect on how a child perceives all relationships. I learned from my mother to stand by your man, come hell or high water. They taught me that there is a time and place for everything. They also taught me that a little game-playing is harmless, if done in the right way and with respect. I also thought there was no need to be married, because my parents never were—and they were happy. This was the biological component that set the stage for my thinking on what a relationship should resemble.

At the age of nine, my mother decided, for some reason still unknown to me, that she could not do the mothering thing anymore. She came to the conclusion that putting her children in a foster home would be a good idea. It was a sad, sad day. We got into a livery cab, which took us to the Angel Guardian Home Agency in Queens. There we sat until a social worker came in and explained once again that this was a temporary situation and that my mother could get us back whenever she was ready. My mother was also trying to explain that she was coming back to get us once she got on her feet. A tall woman walked in, with two other big girls. We soon found out that they were her biological daughters, who she believed could do no wrong. She seemed really nice at first. She promised my mother that we would be well taken care of.

My mother was standing there crying, telling us to *be good* and that *this was just for a little while.* My sister Lorraine was crying because she didn't want to leave my mother. My other sister, Camielle, was just trying to be strong. I remember being very angry and confused because I didn't understand why we were the only ones going to a foster home. I later found out that two of my brothers, the two younger boys, Michael and Gary, were also placed in a foster home.

We were taken to Queens, New York. This lady lived in a house on a quiet street filled with houses that resembled each other. She had a dog, a Doberman; I can't remember his name. This dog had constant diarrhea. We were not used to living in a house, with a dog, in a quiet neighborhood. It took me weeks to get used to the sounds of crickets at night. This woman had no husband. All she had was her two daughters, Susan and Sharon. I really tried to like this lady and her daughters in the beginning. I tried to get used to our living arrangements.

She had a bunk bed placed in her oldest daughter's room for my sisters and me to sleep in. My sister Lorraine and I shared the bottom bunk, and my sister Camielle slept on the top. Although we lived in an apartment in Brooklyn, we all had our own beds. Sleeping together was torture for me. My mother raised us to bathe at least twice a day and change our clothes when we came home from school. Ms. Velasquez, that was her name, would not let us bathe twice but only once a day and forget about changing clothing. She took us shopping at the local Salvation Army around the corner on Linden Blvd. She just had her way of doing things, and it was her way or no way.

She later took in a foster boy named Ronald. Once Ronald got there, things became worse. Ms. Velasquez became more mean than before. We would come home from school, and Lorraine and I would be chained to the gate in the rear of the house, with the very playful, diarrhea-having Doberman. He would run around in circles, many times stepping in his own bodily waste, and then he would jump on us while we were still chained to the gate. Camielle and Ronald would be inside doing chores. I can only assume that my younger sister and I were so full of energy and questions, chaining us to the fence was the only way she could deal with us after school. I don't know what made her stop chaining us to the fence, but it didn't last long.

There was a time when Camielle made rice better than Ms. Velasquez, and when we brought it to her attention, she put us all on punishment. Our punishment was to stand on one leg in the corner until she said we could move. She was very strict about the times meals were to be served. Dinner was at 5 o'clock sharp—after that, nothing was to be eaten. She placed a bell on the refrigerator, and if ever she heard that bell go off, it was in the corner for you. She made us eat wheat germ on our cereal every morning. Yuck!

Many nights, she made us roll her hair. This was the only time we could pay her back for being so mean to us. We would put mounds of gel in her hair or pull her hair real hard just to get back at her. I constantly complained to the social worker of our treatment in this home, but my complaints often fell on deaf ears. My sisters called me a tattletale and said mommy was going to be mad at me for not being good. An entire year went by, and the lesson I learned more than anything else was that everything that looks good on the outside is not always good on the inside. My mother later told us that my father somehow found out where Ms. Velasquez lived, and he used to sit out front of her house, watching over us. This was the perfect *Don't judge a book by its cover* situation. The outside of her house was so beautiful, but it was the inside that was the devil's playground.

The morning of our visit with my mother and my older sister Angela, Lorraine and I were in bed arguing because I said I was going to tell mommy what was going on. Ms. Velasquez came in and grabbed me by the arm and scratched me. Then she started saying all these mean things about my mother. She said my mother was jealous of her because she had a house. She said we were poor and that we'd never had anything. When we arrived at the agency, I was so happy to see my mother, my sister, and—to our surprise, they brought my brother, Gary. I could not hold it in any more. I told my mother what she was doing to us and what she had said about my mother. When Ms. Velasquez returned to pick us up from the visit, Angela and Gary completely lost it. They went ballistic. They were trying to fight that lady and her daughters. I remember my sister, Angela, yelling at Ms. Velasquez, saying, "If you had a man, then you wouldn't be such a bitch." I really didn't understand why she said that or what that had to do with us.

Needless to say, Ms. Velasquez no longer wanted us in her home. I believe we went back that night, and, first thing the next morning, we packed our things and waited for the social worker to pick us up. We were eventually picked up by the social worker and we said goodbye to Ronald. I often wonder what happened to Ronald and if he remained in her home. I don't think about Ms. Velasquez or her daughters that much, except when I drive past her house as an adult. They were my first lesson in dealing with people from a different walk of life. Later on, Ms. Velasquez became that image of a single mother raising daughters on her own. She became the poster person for me of a bitter woman living without a man in her life. I think she took her frustration out on us for not having a man in her life or in her home.

On the way back to the agency to meet our new foster parents, my sisters would not speak to me. They made me feel like I had done the wrong thing by telling. My mother met us at the agency, and this time, she stayed to meet our new foster parents. We waited for a long time. I thought no one wanted to take us. The social worker kept saying it was difficult to place three children at the same time. She felt it would be easier to separate us. My sisters really hated me now. It was entirely my fault—if only I had just kept my big mouth quiet, we would not be here.

Finally, the social worker came out and said she'd found someone, a couple from Long Island. It was an even longer wait for them to get there. A heavy-set woman and a tall man walked in. The first thing I noticed was the woman had on a wig, and the man was dressed really nice. The social worker said, "This is Mr. and Mrs. Pruitt." My mother shook their hands and pled with them to take care of her babies. They, too, promised to look after us, but they went a step further and gave my mother their home phone number, which was prohibited. The biological parent was not supposed to know the phone number or the address of the foster parent. All visits were to be made at the agency-site location. This time, there was no display of emotion or tears—just a simple "goodbye," and we were off to our new location.

Freeport, Long Island, was my new home. I decided that, whatever happened, I would not say anything because I didn't want to be moved again or have my sisters hate me for the rest of my life. Living with the Pruitts reconfirmed my need to be an only child. They had eight biological children of their own. Most of them had children of their own. She also had four other foster children. The house was not as nice as the Velasquezes', but it held a lot of people. There was a total of eight foster kids and three of her own, adult, children who still lived at home under that roof—one of whom had two kids of *her* own.

The upstairs had four bedrooms and a half-bathroom. The first floor had the master bedroom; next to that was the kitchen, the full bathroom, a dining room, and living room. The basement was an open area with one more bedroom, a bar, a piano, and the laundry room. The kitchen was the most important room in the house.

All meals were served communal style. Mr. Pruitt sat at the head of the table, while Mrs. Pruitt sat to the immediate right of him. No one was allowed to eat unless someone blessed the food. I had never experienced this. They made the entire family sit down to eat together and talk about their day. It was weird at first, but I quickly became accustomed to it. I liked the idea of having the man at the head of the table and the woman right by his side. I guess that is our rightful place, being that we were formed from the rib of man.

Living with the Pruitts was my first experience with attending church. Daddy, Mr. Pruitt, rarely went to church with us. The entire three and half years that I spent with these people, we never missed a Sunday in church. I even joined the junior choir. I learned that my father's views were frowned upon and that nobody found his comments funny at church. Being so young, I never understood how people could get up on Sunday happy and carefree, sing praises to the Lord, and, as soon as church was over, they were back to talking about people. "Girrrl, did you see what Mrs. Durden had on today?" they would say behind her back. "The pastor's wife must not be giving him some anymore," they would utter. They would complain that the pastor's sermon had not been delivered in his usual up-tempo spirit.

I knew firsthand that Mrs. Pruitt suffered from this Sunday bi-polar personality as well. Every Sunday, like clockwork, I was sent outside to pick a switch. I was never beaten by my mother or father therefore, I had no idea what a switch was. Anyone who has grown up in the South or had parents from the South knows how to pick a switch. You should never come back with some small twig from the ground. You better get something that resembled a small tree limb—or your beating would be even worse. I became so used to getting a beating on Sundays that I had my crying speech down to a science: "Ma, I won't talk in church again! *Ouch! Ouch!* Ma, I am sorry! *Ouch! Ouch!* I won't do it again!" Finally, to make it stop, I would say, "I love you, Ma, and I won't be bad no more!"

The punishment was always the same. You could go outside, but you couldn't leave the yard—which was just as good as saying, "Don't go outside." Everything that was fun happened outside the yard. She always had her spy, her grandson Derek. He could not wait to get one of the foster kids in trouble. I think many of the beatings I received were because of Derek.

I always preferred to be outside in the backyard or on the front porch. Whenever I stayed in the house, I often came downstairs to hear Mrs. Pruitt and her grown daughters talking about how much they didn't like me. They talked about how they would keep Camielle and Lorraine any day over me. They mentioned that they thought I was ugly and was going to be a problem for my mother when she took us back.

I remember sitting on the stairs listening to their conversation about me, and out popped Derek. He ran into the kitchen and told them I was eavesdropping on them. This time, she let Derek pick the switch that I was going to get a beating with. I believe this is when I gave Mrs. Pruitt a reason to not like me. I told her she couldn't hit me, because she was not my mother. Why did I say that? She hit me harder than she ever had before. I just remember crying for my father to come get me. I felt hated by all adults, including my parents. My mother had left me there with these people who beat me all the time. My dad wouldn't come for me, because his belief was *If I can't do for all, I won't do for one.* I felt abandoned by my parents. I went from wishing I was an only child to wishing I wasn't a child.

I had become really good friends with one of my foster sisters, Vanessa. She was two years older than me. She was not attractive to the naked eye—at least that's what I heard everyone say. I remember Mrs. Pruitt and her daughter making jokes saying that we were lesbians. I didn't even know what a lesbian was at that time, so I paid them no mind. But there was something about her. She made me feel liked. She talked to me when nobody else would. Not even my sisters. My sisters thought I was going to get them kicked out again.

When Vanessa and I walked to school together, boys would notice her. Everyone said she wasn't pretty, so the boys had to know she wasn't pretty. Why didn't they notice me? She was knock-kneed and dark skinned, and she had big breasts. What did they see in her? I didn't have those big old things in front of me. I was small and petite. The other kids said I had big buck teeth. The fact that I actually *had* fallen in the yard and chipped my left-front tooth didn't help matters, either. I thought I was okay looking, except for my teeth. At that age, everybody's teeth were too big—at least that's what I told myself. I thought, *One day, I will grow into them, and I will be prettier.*

The boys weren't very nice back then. On the way home from school one day, this homely looking boy grabbed Vanessa's breast. He had the face only a mother gorilla could love. It wasn't just that he *grabbed* them—he twisted them in opposite directions before he let go. She gave a good chase, but when she caught up, he threatened to slap the shit out of her. I thought, *How could he have grabbed her breast and then cursed at her?* At that moment, I wanted nothing to do with breasts. I began to sleep on the floor. Chest to the ground. I was going to make sure that my breasts never grew. I wanted to make sure no one thought it was OK to grab me by my breast and threaten me with being slapped because I didn't want them to touch me. At the age of twelve, I'd begun to notice that boys weren't that bad. Well, at least—not *all* of them were bad.

There was one boy who I thought was cute. His name was Pat. He had slanted eyes, with bow legs and muscles. I never let him know I liked him, but Vanessa did. She wrote him a letter telling him how much she liked him and wanted to be his girlfriend. She later told me she snuck out the window at night to meet him around the corner. That's when she said it: She said she kissed him and he sucked on her breast. My little body became hot, as I listened to her tell me the story. I could see it as if I'd been standing right there when it happened. That was my first experience with the human emotion called "jealousy." I actually began to hate her. Then I started to hate him, because he liked her back. Vanessa and I eventually stopped speaking, but she never knew why.

I didn't care: I'd made a new friend. Bria was in foster care, just like me. We were the same age. She was very pretty. She was light skinned, and that was always a plus with the boys. She had medium breasts, which was cool because none of the boys would want to suck on them, at least that's what I thought. Bria had one thing I didn't have—hips and a big butt. The boys would go crazy when she would walk past them. I was shaped like a #2 pencil. I was still wearing T-shirts, and she was already wearing a bra. Boys would say that it looked like she had a basketball in her pants. Bria never liked the attention she received from boys. Vanessa, on the other hand, loved it.

There was nothing Bria could do with that thing except wear clothes that made it look smaller. She loved long skirts. She said they didn't hug her butt, so they made it look like it wasn't there. We got along because she didn't like the boys I liked. She had a different taste in boys. A lot of boys liked her, so the girls didn't like her. She tried to pretend that it didn't bother her, but I knew better. She used to make stupid comments like, "If they are going to call me a hoe, I might as well be one."

I knew—even back then—there was no way I was going to let what someone else thought about me determine who I was. Bria and I remained friends because she was good to me. I shared everything with her that I experienced living with the Pruitts. One time, I was in the house, sitting on the stairs, and one of Mrs. Pruitt's sons, Jerome, came over to visit. He was cool, and he never treated me like her other kids did. He used to always give me a big hug and kiss on the cheek. He used to say how pretty I was and called me his "little chocolate kiss." He walked into the house through the side door, where the stairs that led upstairs were located.

I said, "Hi," like I normally did. He asked me why I was sitting on the steps in the dark. I said, "Because Ma won't let me go outside." He said he would talk to her for me and asked for his hug. I stood up to hug him, and he hugged me back, but, this time, he kissed me on my lips. That felt weird, but it got even worse for me: The next thing I knew, he had his tongue in my mouth. I pulled away, and he just looked at me like I was crazy and walked around the corner to the kitchen. I ran upstairs to my room and sat in the closet in the dark. I thought that was the most disgusting thing I had ever experienced. After that, every time Jerome came over, I would hide. No more hugs for him.

I guess he thought I was like Mary. She was the eldest foster child. She had been there the longest. She was Puerto Rican. She had a cute face, but she was on the heavy side. For two of the three and a half years I spent in the Pruitt residence, Mary was sleeping with Mrs. Pruitt's eldest son. There was at least fifteen years' age difference between them. Mr. and Mrs. Pruitt pretended they knew nothing about it. She would have lost her ability to take in foster children had anyone found out. That would have been a major blow to their finances. They were receiving $1500 per foster child each month. Meanwhile, we were allotted only $21 per month for personal items. We were never given that money, either. The foster-care system was a hustle for the Pruitts. Her son was about to ruin all of that for them.

Mary was getting out of hand. Every night, I could hear her and the Pruitts' son arguing because she wanted to spend the night in his room. There was one night I woke up to use the bathroom, and he had her pinned against the corner of the door. She was crying, begging him to let her in. I watched as he took his right elbow and jammed it into her stomach several times until she crumbled to her knees. Then he pushed her into the hallway, slammed his door, and locked it. She sat there, bawling her eyes out in front of his bedroom door. After that night, he moved into the room in the basement. The affair lasted a little while longer, until he finally moved out.

Watching a grown man treat a young girl like that and Jerome putting his tongue in my mouth made me find older men disgusting. I knew I would never date an older man. There was no need for me to waste time with the thought of an older man, because I could barely get the attention of young boys. Every boy I liked, they liked someone else. They seemed to like me, but only as a friend. I did everything to get them to notice me. I played kickball and did flips on old mattresses with the boys, but nothing worked. I was hopelessly stuck in the friend zone.

Teenage Years

My mother finally decided to come get us back from the foster care system. She bought a house deeper into the Village of Freeport. The address was 99 Shonnard Avenue. It was located on the corner of Shonnard and Remson Avenue. It was a red-and-tan, three-bedroom, one-bathroom house. Camielle had her own room, and I was stuck sharing a room with Lorraine again. Our room was set up with canopy beds, twin chests of drawers, and a television. The canopy looked pretty, but it felt like you were sleeping in a coffin. We eventually took it down, and it made the room look bigger.

Camielle's room was small. In fact, it was smallest of the three bedrooms in the house. She had a captain bed. That meant only that it had two drawers on the bottom of the bed. She had a small dresser, and her television sat on top of that. My mother's room was the largest of all three. She had two walk-in closets with strings attached to the light fixture in the ceiling of each closet. My mom had two chests of drawers in one closet and still had room to hang all her clothes on both sides. The other closet she used as storage. We thought she was weird because she had two televisions and a radio all playing at the same time.

The rest of the house was unfurnished. It had three doors leading to the outside. The back door was off the laundry room next to the walk-in pantry. I never even knew what a "pantry" was until we got this house.

The other door was on the side of the house. When you entered through this door, you could go straight to the basement or walk up three steps to enter the kitchen. The kitchen wasn't that big, but you could fit two apartment-size kitchens in it. The dining room was big enough for a long table with matching china cabinet. It also had a window with a bench-like seating area. I loved that window—you could actually sit in it. You couldn't even *stand* near the window in Brooklyn.

I remember when they were working on the roof of the building in Brooklyn, large pieces of wood and debris would fall from the top of the roof. A large piece of wood broke the glass, and all I saw was blood pouring from my arm. I must have passed out from the sight of all that blood, because the next thing I remember was coming to in the hospital with a doctor standing over me with a large needle in his hand. I know my mother was there, but I wanted my Pop. They held me down so this man could stab me with that big needle. He did the worst stitching job on my arm to close the wound from that piece of wood. Kids in some third-world countries would have done a better job sewing my arm up than him. Every time I look at my arm, I remember to never stand too close to a Brooklyn window because you never know what might come through it.

The window seat in the house on Shonnard Avenue had three large separate windows. There was plenty of sunlight. The side of the house faced Remson Avenue—a street with no houses on it, so it was like we had our own street. It was like an extension of the backyard. This house was a mansion compared to what we were living in Brooklyn or at the Pruitts'. My mother had done well by her girls for once.

I was still embarrassed to bring my friends there, because we didn't have furniture. The grass wasn't cut, and it was almost as tall as me. I finally let my friends come over one day when we went with Bria to the house of a boy named Chance. He lived around the corner from my new house. They loved my house, no furniture and all. They just kept talking about how big it was. I told them I was embarrassed, but one girl said to me, "At least you *have* a home." Bria said, "At least you are with your family," and she was right. I was so happy to be out of foster care. No more Derek, Jerome, Sunday beatings, and no more grown-ups sitting in the kitchen talking bad about me. After four and a half years, I was finally back with my family. I had survived foster care.

We didn't all survive those years when the family broke up. Michael and Gary ran away from their foster home. They started living on the streets. I am sure they stole things and gambled to survive on the streets. They couldn't stay with my mom because she was living in my dad's house on Eastern Parkway in Brooklyn. At least that's what she said. Michael learned fast, and he met and started sleeping with an older woman who took him in.

Gary was different. He relied on friends. He ran the streets during the day and slept wherever he could at night. At the age of 14, he went to my mother and asked her if he could stay with her at Uncle George's, and she told him "No." ("Uncle George" is what they called my father.) She told him that she couldn't bring him into that man's house. Soon after that, my brother was shot in the head at the McDonald's on Flatbush Avenue in Brooklyn. I was told he'd been caught in a crossfire. A 14-year-old's life meant nothing to his mother or to McDonald's, because they cleaned up the blood, moved the body, and continued to sell their all-beef patties, special sauce, lettuce, cheese, pickles, and onions on a sesame seed bun. They notified us of his death when we were still living with the Pruitts, but we were not allowed to attend his funeral service. The irony of it all is that he died on my father's birthday. On January 9 of every year, my mother didn't know what to do. Should she be happy, celebrating my dad's birthday, or sad for the loss of her baby boy?

My older brothers and sisters never forgave my mother for the death of my brother. His death did not affect me or Lorraine as much it did the others, because they'd grown up together in Jamaica, whereas we were little and just getting to know them. I just knew I had a brother I was never going to see again.

I was still attending Roosevelt School District, and I was about to graduate from Theodore Roosevelt Elementary School. Before graduation, there was a prom. Most of the girls in the sixth grade were asked to the prom, but not me. Bria was asked by a boy named Sean.

I wanted to go with a boy named James. He decided he wanted to go with another friend of mine named Tawana. It was getting close to prom day, and I still had not been asked by anyone. I thought to myself, *I'll just go by myself, then. All my friends will be there. Why do I need a boy to ask me?*

I made the right choice, because, at the prom, the boys all stuck together, and the girls stayed together on different sides of the room. It was as if everyone had come by themselves, anyway. The girls danced in circles among themselves, and the boys stood by the walls in the auditorium and bopped their heads to the music. I made it through that night without feeling awkward about not having a date.

Graduation came and went and it was now time for me to attend high school. I wanted to stay with my friends in Roosevelt, but because I'd moved further into Freeport, I was supposed to attend Freeport School System. The Roosevelt School System didn't find out that I had moved, so, I attended Roosevelt Junior Senior High School for the early part of seventh grade. I walked almost 45 minutes each way, to and from school, stopping to pick up Bria on the way. The high school was something out of the movies. The halls were dark, and the classrooms were 90% empty. The cafeteria looked like a combination of scenes from the movies *Fame* and *Lean on Me*. There was loud music, gambling, and dancing. Students ran down the hall throwing garbage cans filled with trash at classroom doors, where some students actually attended class. I attended some classes, but the teachers were afraid to show up most of the time. Many classes were canceled for that reason. There were several occasions when things really got out of hand. Someone actually rode their motorcycle through the hallways and down the stairs, causing students to scatter, trying to find a safe place to stand without being hit.

While all of this mayhem was going on, the school actually had time to find out that I was living outside the Roosevelt School District jurisdiction. I had to leave Roosevelt High, effective immediately. Freeport School System was different because they had a separate junior high school. The seventh- and eighth-graders attended John W. Dodd Junior High. *This school is so clean*, I thought to myself. Roosevelt High

School had predominantly black students. This school had a little bit of everybody. They had buses that picked some students up because they lived a certain distance from the school. I had to walk because the school was only ten minutes from my house.

Nobody at this school would speak to me except a little white girl named Kim and her friend, a black girl named Diane. I sat with them at lunch, and they showed me around the school. They even came to pick me up from my class just to walk me to my next class, so I wouldn't get lost. Once we became really close, Diane told me she'd been adopted because she had been raped by her uncle ever since she was a little girl. She told me she tried to kill herself by taking pills and that her mother blamed *her* for what had happened and didn't want her around. This reminded me of my mother staying with her husband, the pedophile.

Diane was a pretty girl who was very quiet. She didn't speak about boys too much, and she didn't care about clothes or doing her hair. She just was who she was and appeared to be comfortable in her own skin. That's what I liked about her. Nothing seemed to faze her. If a fight broke out, she would never run to go look like the rest of the kids. She would act as if it wasn't even happening. We remained friends throughout junior high school, and prom time came around again. Diane was asked to the prom, and she accepted the offer. I waited to see if anyone would ask me, but nope—not a chance. This time, I decided I wasn't going to go by myself.

The girls in this school talked about everybody. If you didn't have the latest gear, you were considered a "nobody." I tried to match my clothes and make my outfits look different every time. I even wore some of Camielle's clothes, but nothing worked—the girls didn't even want to get to know me. The boy who asked Diane was also considered a nobody, according to junior high standards. This is when I came to the conclusion that something was wrong with me. Some girls were asked by boys who'd graduated the year before. That was a big deal, because these boys were in high school now. They'd come to the school and just stand outside until we were dismissed, just to talk to girls coming out.

Triangle Park is where everyone would go to talk or watch a fight. I must admit—watching fights was fun. It was always some girl from the north side of Freeport versus some girl from the Freeport projects, the south side. I didn't like the project girls. They weren't nice people. All they did was dress nice and fight, but they were dumb when it came to classwork. They would always try to cheat off my paper. One girl, Latoya, asked me if she could cheat off my paper. I wanted her to like me, so I said "Yes." She did cheat and passed the test, but after the test, she never spoke to me again.

One day, girls from Roosevelt came up to the school to fight Latoya and her sister. Roosevelt girls ran deep, and I knew most of them. When the girls from Freeport saw that I knew the girls from Roosevelt, they hated me even more. I didn't care—I used it to my advantage, because the girls from Roosevelt let it be known that if anybody messed with me, they would come back to kick their butts. I wish they would have beaten one of these boys up and made him take me to the prom.

On the day of the prom, I was at home watching everybody outside, all dressed up and taking pictures. I went into the house and cried. I knew no one asked me because I wasn't pretty, like the other girls. My butt didn't look like I had two cantaloupes in my pants, and my breasts didn't look like I had two grapefruits in my bra. I'd convinced myself that things would be better in high school. *The boys will be older and wiser. Think again, Ms. Sharon! This stupid little bunch of idiots want nothing to do with you.* The boys my age or a year older wanted a girl in the eleventh and twelfth grades. The boys in eleventh and twelfth grades wanted girls in college.

What the hell was wrong with them? Are their testosterone levels out of whack? What makes a man pursue the un-pursuable? They just were not satisfied with the girls who wanted them. The girls they were after wanted *men*—college men with money and cars. I still had high hopes that someone would find me attractive.

My sister Lorraine had no problem meeting boys. She started seeing this boy named Sheldon, who lived up the street from us. Everyone called him Romeo Boy Ski. He was the smooth-talker type. He would make you laugh like there was no tomorrow. One night after my mother went to sleep, we snuck Romeo in, like we had on many nights before. I would play lookout while they would talk or do what they do—which wasn't much, considering Sheldon always brought his high yellow friend, Rob, with him. All he talked about was his private area and how his penis was black and big. I hated for guys to brag about what they had in their pants. When he got angry one night because we were teasing him, he pulled it out. He had lied about it being black *and* about the size. To top it off, he had two big yellow balls. We made sure he would never live that down.

While we were laughing at Rob, I heard something. "Lorraine, I think I hear mommy," I said.

"No, she is knocked out, and I closed her door," Lorraine said.

"Okay, but I heard something." I went and sat on the bottom of the stairs; sure enough, she was walking down the stairs.

"Where is Lorraine?" she asked

"In the kitchen," I answered with a quaver in my voice.

"What are you all doing?" mommy asked.

"Nothing," I said, as innocently as I could sound.

She walked past me, and I tried to make noise so Lorraine could hide the boys, but it was too late. She saw them, and the chase pursued. Lorraine and I sat on the stairs and watched as my mother chased these two boys through the kitchen, dining room, and living room. They ran in circles about three times, and Rob finally wised up and ran out the front door. Romeo wasn't as bright, because his stupid butt ran into the pantry, leaving him with nowhere to go. My mother grabbed that door handle like she had the strength of The Bionic Woman. She snatched Romeo and began to scratch him up. His dumb ass finally broke away and ran out the front door.

But Romeo didn't let this situation stop him. He either really liked my sister, or he was just determined to try and get some. A few days later, while my mother was at work, we had some boys over. Lorraine had a friend named Jordin, who was tall with beautiful jet-black eyes. Jordin was in our room with a boy named King (she had a major crush on him), and Lorraine was with Romeo on a cot that my mother kept in the corner of her room.

I was in Camielle's room, soon to be my room, with a boy named Kyle. I ended up with Kyle by default. He was the odd man out, and so was I. He was short and very unattractive. He resembled the Ewoks from the *Star Wars* movies. His personality is what made him stand out. He was funny and very popular. I guess that meant something to me back then. I just wanted someone to like me. I thought that he would if I let him feel me up. He said he wanted to sleep, and he lay down on the bed. I lay next to him, and he said, "Get comfortable." I had no clue what he meant.

Then he said, "Take your pants off." I thought, *Oh, my God, is this going to happen?* As I was removing my pants, I kept thinking, *I don't like him.* But I also thought, *Kyle is popular, and, if he were my boyfriend, I'll be popular, too.* As he climbed on top of me, I saw his body moving, but I didn't feel anything. I'd heard other girls talk about doing it, and now I knew they were lying. *This doesn't hurt and there is no blood*, I thought. I was always told there was supposed to be blood and pain.

When it was over, which was about five minutes later, he got up and said he was ready to go. I think my mother had the same idea, because she came home early. I ran to her room to get Lorraine, and we hid all the boys in Camielle's room, which was the room closest to the stairs. We knew my mother wouldn't go into her room because it was normally dirty. We stood at my mother's room door talking about anything we could think of while Jordin snuck the boys down the stairs, one by one. I am certain Jordin and Lorraine went all the way and lost their virginity that night also. Romeo gave Lorraine a hickey on her neck that night. She was so light-skinned that it was hard to hide. Pop was the first one to notice it.

"Lorraine, come here," he said. "What happened to your neck?"

She wasn't prepared for the question, so she said, "I got hit in the neck with a basketball." Romeo's nickname was unofficially changed to "Basketball Lips" by my father.

Kyle and I became very good friends, and we never discussed what had taken place in the room that night. Somehow, I think he knew he was my first. He would call me just to talk. He used to tell me about this girl he met and how much he liked her. I didn't mind hearing about another girl, because I didn't like him like that. However, becoming friends with him did earn me some cool points with the project kids. He told me this girl was playing hard to get.

I said, "Kyle, my mother would say, 'Show me your company and you tell me who you are.' Maybe she's scared to hang out with you because of the company that you keep." Kyle hung out with older guys, the drug-dealing guys, who had no respect for the female gender. He said he was bored and that he and King were going to come over, and we would finish talking about it then.

I called Jordin so she could be there, because I knew she would want to see King. Then Bria called me to say that she was also bored. They arrived one after the other. Bria walked in, and her face hit the ground.

"Sharon, how do you know him?" Bria asked.

"He's my friend—why?" I asked.

"Sharon, you didn't tell me you knew Bria," Kyle said.

"I didn't know I had to tell you," I said to Kyle. "Why?"

"Bria, can I talk to you for a minute?" Kyle said, not answering my question. Bria and Kyle went into my room. They were in there for a long time. King filled me in on the story. Bria was the girl Kyle was going crazy over. I thought it was so nice that my homegirl and my homeboy liked each other. I'd never told Bria—or anyone else—what had happened between Kyle and me. Why mess up what I thought was a good thing?

I, on the other hand, still had issues. I was in high school, and I didn't fit in anywhere. I was fourteen going on fifteen and still had never had a boyfriend. I had strictly friends, all of whom called me "Little Sis" or "Cousin." There was this guy named Luke in the tenth grade. Luke was a tall, chocolate, fine brother who could dress his butt off. He turned many heads, from freshmen to seniors. I would always get bored in math class, so I would take bathroom breaks and roam the halls. Every day, like clockwork, he would be in the hallway with this girl named Kiana, hugging and kissing on her. Kiana was in the ninth grade with me, and we even had some classes together.

Freeport High had two levels. The second floor had two hallways separated by classrooms in the middle. Luke would meet Kiana in the east hallway, and, by the time I came out of the bathroom and made my way around to the west hallway, he would be there, hugging and kissing a sophomore by the name of Somaya. I don't know how he did it, but he kept that up for two years, until Somaya graduated. Luke and I formed a bond because of his cheating ways. Luke went on and eventually married Kiana, but that did not stop his cheating ways. Luke lusted for a woman who was very pretty, slim, with a nice butt. He married a woman who was cute in the face but thicker in body. This is a perfect example of men not knowing what they want.

I used to see Luke after school, hanging out with his friends, and he would smile at me. His friends would ask him if he knew me, and he would say, "Yeah, she is mad cool." Luke was the reason most people in high school knew me.

Around this time, my mother decided it was costing her too much money to travel from Long Island to Brooklyn every morning to work, so she moved in with my father. Camielle would spend her nights with her friends or her boyfriend. He was this white guy she'd met in high school.

The school sectioned itself off by race or nationality. The black and Hispanic students hung out at the duck pond or the front of the school. The white students sat on the floor in the main lobby of the school. That's where you would find Camielle, and she never admitted to anyone that I was her sister. She was funny like that, and it made me feel like she was ashamed of me. I never told Camielle how that made me feel, because I didn't think she would care. I couldn't focus on that too much because I was more focused on trying to get boys to like me.

Lorraine and I stayed in the house by ourselves for a while; no one even noticed. My mother still paid all the bills; all we had to do was go to school. Camielle moved out for good when she started college in the city, so I took her room. My oldest brother, Patrick, moved in with us in the absence of my mother. Patrick became the reason that all of Freeport knew me and my house. Patrick was a weed smoker, and he was very generous with his weed. If you enjoyed getting high, Patrick enjoyed getting you high.

Luke and his friends Javon and Ryder liked to hang out with my brother, so they were at my house a lot. It was my fifteenth birthday, and I decided to try smoking some weed. That was the worst feeling I'd ever had. Some of my friends were drunk, and some were high. Old English beer was the drink of choice back then. I wish I would have gotten drunk instead. I just remember laughing a lot and moving in slow motion. We were all sitting in the living room, and someone said, "Look at Sharon—she looks like a horse." I kept laughing, but I'd heard it loud and clear. I eventually went upstairs and looked at myself in the hallway mirror to see if I did look like a horse. To my surprise, it was the truth. It was like I couldn't control my mouth. My lips kept opening further and further, and my smile grew wider until every tooth in my mouth was exposed. I was too high to cry, and I couldn't control my smile or laughter, but I knew at that moment that I would never smoke weed again.

Nights like these went on all throughout high school. Bria came over and met the guys, whom we now called "the fellas." The number of boys and girls hanging out at my house increased dramatically. There were days I would come home and see people in my house I'd never imagine would be there. They were all coming over to visit Patrick, who was a couch potato and enjoyed the company. More than anything, Patrick just had a good heart, and he wanted everyone around him to be happy and enjoy themselves.

I hated when the females started coming around. These were the girls who didn't like me or Lorraine because they thought we were sleeping with the guys they liked. Little did they know, I still had not gotten one boy to kiss me, let alone sleep with me, again. One girl even said, "You guys are cool. It's not like what I thought it was going to be over here." I never asked her, but I did wonder, *What the hell did she think was going on in my house?*

My house developed a nickname—"The Clubhouse." My mother somehow got wind of what was going on in the house. I think Pop snuck out there and went back and told her. We, of course, denied it. After all, we kept our grades up, and we went to school every day. Well, I had a habit of not going to school if it snowed or rained too hard, but I passed my classes. I wasn't walking that far in bad weather, and I hated taking the bus. My friend, Patty, was the only one who noticed my routine. She often made jokes about the weather and if she would see me in school the next day.

My mother didn't believe us, so she said, "If you want to be grown, you pay the bills." We thought she was just playing, but she showed us. She paid the mortgage, and the mortgage only. We had to buy food and pay the electric bill and the phone bill—*and* buy oil to heat the house. Patrick paid what he could, but he complained every step of the way. We decided to get jobs. Lorraine was taller than me, and we looked nothing alike. We really had absolutely no features that would even hint at the fact that we were related. The fact that we had different last names was also great. We went job hunting together, and no one would suspect a thing. We told people we were cousins instead of sisters.

Lorraine was legally too young to work regular hours, so we had a hard time finding jobs at first, until we went into Burger King in Merrick. The boys at the burger station liked Lorraine, so he spoke to the manager, whose name was also Lorraine, and she hired us. We pretended to be cousins until Lorraine turned 16; by then, it was too late to fire her. Lorraine the manager turned out to be a coke head. That's what we called people who sniffed a lot of cocaine. She ended up getting fired. The manager who took her place tried to have Lorraine fired, but the store manager liked the way we worked, so we kept our jobs.

The bills got paid, and we shopped like crazy. We even got her friend Jordin a job with us. That was the most fun I ever had. Every night, we all walked home together. A few of the guys who also lived in Freeport would walk with us over the bridge and across the Long Island Railroad tracks. Most of the girls our age were too proud to work at Burger King or McDonald's, so they didn't have money like we did. The other girls were sleeping with older guys to get their money. That was not for me, although, it did seem easier than working. I saw how those guys treated those girls like property or spoke to them as if they were children. I could not give a boy/man that type of control over me.

I guess having my own money made boys notice me more. At school, the boys started saying things to me now, and it felt nice to receive a compliment now and then. On the days when Jordin, Lorraine, and I didn't have to work, we would walk up to Dodd Jr. High, like all the other cool kids did, and just hang out. There was this boy who caught my eye. He was brown-skinned and had very bowed legs. I found that very appealing in the male of the species. I hadn't seen him before, and I knew he didn't go to the high school. He eventually noticed that I used to watch him all the time, and he came over and introduced himself. He said his name was Lahmeek. That wasn't his real name.

All the guys in the late 80s thought being in the Five-Percent Nation was everything. They called themselves "Gods." It was stupid, but I went along with. They used to get real upset and saw it as disrespect if someone other than their mother called them by their "government name"—the one given to them at birth. A female who dated a so-called "God" was called an "Earth." An "Earth" had to obey her man. She was told what to wear and what she could eat. None of it made any sense to me. I saw it as just another way for boys or men to put themselves above women, instead of seeing them as their equal.

Lahmeek invited me to his apartment in the projects. He made small talk for a little while, and then he asked me to take my clothes off. I was scared shitless. I didn't want to seem like a tease, but I was not ready for this, because I had only just recently met him. I did what he asked because I wanted to appear mature, but he saw right through me. He took his clothes off as well and stood behind me. He reached around me and opened the closet door, which had a full-length mirror hanging on it. There I was, standing in the nude looking at myself in the mirror. I had never looked at myself naked like that before, and it made me nervous, so I moved out of view.

He sat on his bed, which was positioned in front of the mirror, and admired himself. I looked at all that he had to offer, and I guess he saw the horror on my face when he said, in a soft tone, "Don't worry. I know you can't handle this. You can get dressed, and I will walk you to the cut." As we were leaving the apartment, a shorter version of him entered. Lahmeek introduced him to me as his cousin, Emory. I started seeing Emory a lot more up at the junior high school and in the mall, at the pizza place. When he finally spoke, he embarrassed me by telling everyone within earshot that he knew me from coming out of the apartment with Lahmeek. People started saying that I'd fucked Lahmeek, but Lahmeek kept it real, and he told everyone that nothing had happened.

One day I was at the pizza place when Emory walked in. I tried to leave as soon as possible, for fear he was going to try to embarrass me again. Instead, he came over and apologized for doing what he did. He did say he still believed that I fucked Lahmeek, because he knew his cousin wouldn't bring a girl to the crib and not fuck. I saw him in a different light after he apologized. He was short, but he was confident. I knew I was starting to like him, and I think he liked me, too. It seemed as if everywhere I went, he was right there, telling me how much he liked me. Emory always said that, but, in the end, he would say, "Why don't you come to my house?" This always made me think he just wanted to see if he could get in my pants, because he thought his cousin had gotten some.

Something in me wanted to believe he really liked me for me, so I reluctantly went to his house. It wasn't really a house but a really small, dark apartment on Merrick Road, a very busy street in Freeport. The building had only two apartments in it, and there were no other apartment buildings around it. When I first went to his house, I met his mother, brother, and sister. They made me feel like it was all about me. His sister, Nia, would call me all the time, and we would go to house parties together. I even went shopping with his mother on occasions. His brother and I became really close, too. His brother would try to tell me what Emory was doing behind my back, but I didn't believe him because he was known for lying all the time.

I continued to go over there, and one day when his mother, sister, and brother weren't home, we went into his room. I stopped dead in my tracks, and I wondered, *Why would he bring me in here? All this time he was telling me how much he liked me, he's had the name "Dora" carved into the wood of his bunk bed.* Everywhere in this room were the words "I love Dora" or "Dora-n-Emory 4 life." When I asked him about it, he just said, "It's old. If you don't believe me, ask my mother." Something about that statement made me believe him. On that day, something in my young mind made me say to myself, "I have to make him love me like that." I wanted *my* name all over his walls, doors, and clothes. That's what people did back then. It was cool to have a sweatshirt with "Emory luvs Sharon" on it. *What better way to make him love me than to have sex with him?*

There was no kissing—just take your pants off and put it in. He must have thought that I was very experienced because he just changed positions as if it was so natural. I remember he turned me around on my hands and knees and was doing it from behind. That was my first experience with doggy style. He was going in and out, really fast, and one time he slipped, and it went in the wrong hole. It went right in and came right out. I had never felt pain like that in my life. He just said, "Sorry," and we stopped. I thought I was not going to be able to walk home after that. We never spoke about that incident again.

On my way home, I wondered if he loved me now and if he was going to carve my name into the wood of his bed. I continued going over to his house, having sex with him, waiting for that day when he would say, "I love you." There were many occasions when I would go to his house, and he would be coming out with other girls, all of whom I knew. He always had an excuse, like they were visiting his sister or his brother. When I would ask his brother and sister, they would always say the person was there visiting them. The final straw came when I went to his house, and he was walking out with a girl with whom I'd become close—a girl I'd brought over there with me. This was my first lesson with backstabbing bitches, who will steal your man in a heartbeat.

After that day, I had nothing else to say to him or her. He tried to explain a few weeks later by saying that he did it to prove that she was not really my friend. At age fifteen, I think I was smart enough to comprehend the words "She is not your friend"—if he would have just said that. Emory really hurt my feelings, so I decided to get back at him by sexing his best friend, who lived across the hall from him. I was willing to sacrifice my body in the name of payback.

I went next door, but I couldn't go through with having sex with his neighbor, whose name was Kareem. I'd met Kareem through Emory on my many trips to Emory's house. Sometimes when Emory wasn't home, he would tell me to wait for him at Kareem's house. So, it wasn't a weird situation with me knocking on his door. I guess I should've expected that he would tell Emory that he could have knocked boots if he really wanted to. ("Knocking Boots" was another expression we kids in the 1980s used for having sex.) Emory had the nerve to call me a hoe when he found out. I knew I was not a hoe, because I was only fifteen, and I'd slept with only two people, but one didn't count.

After Emory, I decided not to think about boys for a while. In actuality, I don't think the boys were thinking about me. One day in Northeast Park, which was around the corner and down the block from my house, I was surrounded by boys I liked but who liked other girls. It seemed as if everyone from Freeport was in the park that day. Lahmeek came over to where we were sitting and asked if I wanted to go for a ride on the scooter. I felt so special that he had asked me, in front of all my friends, so I jumped at the chance. I thought everyone would be envious of me, so I made sure people saw me getting on the scooter with him. We rode out of the park, and he went toward the back of the park, which was called Lovers Lane. It was really dark on that street at night, and people would park their cars back there and have sex.

Further up the street on Lovers Lane was a grassy, woods-like area, beneath the water tower called "The Reservoir." As he pulled into The Reservoir, I started thinking, *What the hell are we doing here?* He told me to get up, which I did, and then he said, "Take your clothes off," which I refused to do. He started cursing me out and calling me an ugly bitch; then he told me to walk back to the park. After that moment in his apartment and when he stood up for me when Emory embarrassed me, I thought he was a good guy—until he did that.

As I was walking back toward the park, I saw Emory, Kyle, Kareem, and some other people walking toward The Reservoir. As we passed each other, they were all laughing at me. They all knew what he'd been planning to do. They thought I was going to give it up right there in the open, and they were supposed to come over there and watch. I couldn't even go back into the park because I was so ashamed; I cried all the way back home.

When I got home, it was like God sent my brother Michael a telegram that his little sister needed help. He called and said he wanted us to come to Texas to visit for a week. The timing was perfect—we were able to get out of work, and I was able to get away from the drama of that day in the park. The trip to Texas was just what I needed to get over the trauma of what had happened in the park.

When we came back, I focused on work and school. I worked the drive-thru a lot, and I got to know a few of the regulars. There was this guy, Jacob, who probably didn't know how to cook, because he ate there every night, at least every night that I was working. One night, I finally asked, "Do you know how to cook?" He gave a half smile but never answered the question. This guy was always greasy. His hands were black, and his nails were dirty. He drove this old Monte Carlo with tinted windows, so you couldn't see in. He had a loud radio system in that old car. You would hear him coming from blocks away.

One night, he switched things up and decided to come inside instead of using the drive-thru. After he placed his regular order, he asked for my number and asked if he could take me out sometime. I kept turning him down every time he asked. He had two strikes against him from the beginning. One, he was older than me. How old, I didn't know, but definitely older, which went against my rules. His second strike was that he looked dirty all the time. He looked as if he worked on cars all day long, slept in his clothes, and woke up to do it all over again. I thought, *I need to try something new, and this could be good. The boys my age don't like me, so, maybe I should try something different.*

I think the fact that he was pursuing me made the difference. I never had anyone display how much they liked me and wanted to take me out. I didn't find him attractive, but he was the only one who found me attractive at that time. I don't know what made me finally agree to go to the movies with him, but I did, and we had an okay time. I thanked God that, when he came to get me, he was all clean. He almost looked like a different person. It turned out that we had fun together, so I kept dating him. I don't really recall having sex with him too much, because all he ever did was come in and go to sleep. I didn't mind because I was sick of sex. Sex didn't bring me joy at all. Jacob really showed me that he liked me for me.

I never wanted for anything, and I didn't have to ask for anything. If he didn't like my shoes, he would just give me money to buy a new pair. At this time, my niece, Yvonne, had come to live with us, and Jacob always made sure she had money in her pocket. He even gave my sister money. I thought he was the sweetest person on Earth. I gave him a key to my room, just so he could be there when I got home. He introduced me to his family and his daughter. His family called me their "little Sharon." It was so nice to have someone like me like this. People would tease me for being with him, but I didn't care, because I knew he was special.

We had a healthy situation going between us, until I started feeling sick all the time. He made me go to the doctor to make sure everything was okay. When I finally went to the doctor, he told me I was pregnant. I was scared to death. My mother was not the type of mother you can go to with a situation like that, and my dad would have been disappointed in me. I knew I didn't want a baby at seventeen, and I thought, because we were so close, that he would want me to keep it. When I told him the news, he looked me right in my face and said, "It's not mine."

I was shocked, disgusted, and totally confused by what he said. He told me because I had all those guys hanging out at my house all the time, it could have been one of theirs. I wasn't going to argue with him, and I knew I didn't want to be someone's baby mother, so there was only one thing to do. I called the one person I could always depend on, Bria. She came with me to this place in Queens called Choices. They didn't ask any questions, and they got me emergency Medicaid to pay for the abortion. Jacob and I never spoke about that situation; we just acted as if it never happened.

I needed more money, so I decided to get a full-time job during the day and attend school at night. Jacob would either drop me off or pick me up from school every night. I became friends with this girl named

Tabitha, and, on some nights when Jacob wasn't available to pick me up, we would walk home together. She would tell me about her sister Shaniece's boyfriend, who was beating on her while she was pregnant. I would say things like, "He's a real piece of shit to even beat on a woman, let alone a pregnant woman." This was our nightly discussion until one night, when she actually said his name—"Jacob."

There was no way there could be two skinny, brown-skinned men with a blue Monte Carlo riding around in Freeport. I was so pissed off, because here I was with this man for one and a half years, and Tabitha was telling me that her sister was pregnant by him. I was never really happy about having that abortion until that night. I couldn't wait to get home from school that night to question Jacob about it. The only explanation he offered was that he was drunk one night, and it happened, but that he didn't want to be with her. We talked all night about it, and I eventually forgave him for cheating on me. I believed his version of the story until the night I paged him; normally, he would call me right back. When the car pulled up in front of my house, I went outside like I normally would, only this time when the window rolled down, it was Shaniece, asking me what I wanted with Jacob. I was finally able to put a face to the name of the person in the stories I'd heard about in night school. The only thing I could think of to say to her was, "Tell Jacob to come find out what I want."

Two hours later, I heard a tap at my window, and I knew it was Jacob coming to plead his case. I was now in touch with a new emotion, called "rage." I also became fully aware that what's done in the dark will eventually be shown in the light. I went downstairs to open the door, and as soon as I saw his face, I completely lost it. I grabbed him by the throat and pushed him against the wall, trying my hardest to stop him from breathing. My brother, Patrick, had to pull me off of him. I knew I had to leave him alone before I did something I would later regret.

This grown woman would try to run me over with his car when she saw me walking in the street. She kept coming to my house, trying to get me to come outside. Apparently, Jacob was messing around with someone else who was stalking Shaniece, and she naturally thought it was me. Something had to be done, and so I told Jacob he'd better talk to her before she got herself in trouble. He promised he would, and I guess that, somewhere in their discussion, he felt the need to ask her to marry him, and that's what he did. I didn't care, because it got her to leave me alone. What bothered me was that he really thought he could still be with me, because he gave some lame excuse about marrying her for the kids. I'd had enough bad luck dealing with boys, and I didn't need that kind of bad karma following me, so, no thank you, Jacob.

I was 18 years old and living the single life. I was surrounded by my friends, the fellas, Bria, and my homegirl, Astry. Astry had family issues of her own, so my mother allowed her to move in with us. She stayed in my little room with me and slept on the floor. She started dating a guy, Reg, who hung out with Truth and Kareem. Yes, the same Kareem who lived across the hall from Emory. We were older now, and all was forgiven, as far as I was concerned. Truth was like a big brother to me. He had a crush on Bria, but she was still in love with Kyle. Kyle and Bria were now the parents of a beautiful baby girl.

I really don't know how this happened, but I think it was because we all hung out at my house—Kareem expressed that he had feelings for me. Kareem no longer saw the girl who was trying to make his friend jealous by using him. His feelings were right on time, because it had been almost a year since Jacob, and I was tired of being alone. Some nights, when Astry and I were asleep, you would hear pennies, quarters, or small pebbles hitting the window, for one of us to come and open the side door. Reg and Astry on the floor beside my bed, Kareem and I on the bed, and Truth on the floor by the door. We would stay up all night talking shit or snapping on each other.

Kareem had dark-chocolate skin complexion, with a nice body, compliments of the juvenile detention center. He was my first Bad Boy. He had a knack for stealing cars, some right off the showroom floor. He had a Mercury XR4TI, that he drove around as if he paid for it. He took me to several dinners and movies in this car, and I blocked out the fact that I was riding in a stolen car. He was sweet and treated me with respect all the time. The sex was okay, but there was still no kissing involved. He now lived around the corner from Bria in Hempstead, and he would pick her up and bring her to my house on many occasions. I trusted Bria with my life. She was like a sister to me—even better than Lorraine was at times, so I thought nothing of it when she told me Kareem would stop by her house to visit sometimes. There were some nights that Reg and Truth would show up, and Kareem wouldn't be with them. Whenever I'd ask where he was, they would say they didn't know.

We later found out Kareem had gotten locked up for that same Mercury XR4TI. All I could do was thank God that I was not in the car with him when it happened. Truth and Reg would still come by to hang out, and there were times when Truth came alone. On one occasion he said, "Sharon, you are a good girl, and I don't want to see you get hurt, but did you really think that Kareem was going to Bria's house for no reason?"

I instantly started crying. *Not my sister,* I thought to myself. *She would never hurt me like that.* He just simply said, "Sharon, think about it." Kareem called collect later that day, and I couldn't wait to ask him about what I'd heard. I was hoping he would say that Truth was lying, but he didn't deny it. In fact, he said it had happened only once and that he was very sorry. I felt like such a fool, because by this time I had found out I was pregnant, and we were planning to keep the baby. I was taking two buses to go see him at the Nassau County Jail, and I was sending him money, bringing him socks, underwear, and magazines. How stupid could I have been?

I still didn't want to believe it, until I heard it from Bria. When I called her, she thought I wanted her to come over, but I couldn't look her in the face. When I asked the question, all I heard were her tears. She said she never meant for that to happen and that it had happened only twice.

I thought, *How could you not mean for it to happen, but you let it happen twice?* I didn't know who to believe: Was it once or twice? I decided that she and I had been friends way too long to let some stupid boy come between us. That's when she dropped another bomb on me and said she was pregnant.

I knew that I didn't want the child I was carrying after hearing that. How could I have a baby by a man who would cheat on me with my best friend—and impregnate her, too? I made a special trip back up to the jail just to tell him I was not keeping the baby. He begged and pleaded with me not to kill his baby. Those words fell on deaf ears. Bria made her appointment and did what she had to do—she was barely taking care of the daughter she already had. Truth was there for me, trying to help me deal with it all. He said, "You deserve better," and, with that, I made my appointment and went by myself back to Forrest Hills, to have another abortion. I started receiving letters and cards from Kareem, expressing his love for me. Until that point, I'd never had a boy tell me that he loved me, and it felt so good that I forgave him.

The next thing I knew, he had convinced me to come see him at his new place of residence, Green Correctional Facility in upstate New York. I had to get up at 4 o'clock in the morning to take the train to Penn Station and then catch the subway to 59th Street and Columbus Circle. I waited at Columbus Circle for a crowded bus filled with other women and children traveling the three-hour ride to various correctional facilities. On one trip, there was a woman on the bus who was traveling with her two-year-old son, which wasn't odd, until she started breast feeding him. Being breast-fed when you are that old has to do something to the male psyche. I remember thinking, *What kind of man is he going to be when he gets older? Is he going to want his women to cater to his every need? Is he going to be a breast man, talking only to women with big boobs?* All the way up to the jail, I kept thinking about that little baby.

When I finally saw Kareem, he was bigger than ever. When he hugged me, I thought he would crush me, but at the same time, I felt safe in his arms. He promised that if I stayed with him for the rest of his bid, there would be no more secrets.

Everything was going great. I made a few more trips to the jail and sent a lot of packages. Bria and I worked out our differences, because, by this time, she was now sleeping with Truth. She would even try to tell me about her sex life with him, but I didn't want to hear that—he was my brother in my eyes. I remained faithful to Kareem for a year and a half, while he was locked up. My friends, at the time, gave me a party because they said they knew that they could never have gone that long without having sex. Sex didn't mean that much to me, and every time I'd had sex, it was to get someone to like me. I had developed a really good rapport with his mother and nieces. She said I was the only female who'd ever stuck by her son when he went to jail.

While out shopping for Kareem's next package that I was going to send him, I ran into this girl from the neighborhood named Bel. She asked how Kareem was and said to tell him that Tiani had the baby.

I said, "Why would he care if Tiani had her baby?"

This bitch smiled and said, "Because the baby is his."

I wanted to snatch her pie-face ass up off her feet. I also knew enough not to shoot the messenger. Tiani was a chick I hated, and she hated me. So, not only did she fuck my boyfriend, but now she may possibly have his baby. There was no way I would take him back under those circumstances. I quickly realized that someone having a baby—when they are supposed to be my boyfriend—is a definite deal breaker for me. I thought, *First Jacob and now Kareem both cheated and made a human being as a constant reminder.*

I made my last trip to Greene Correctional Facility, just to tell him to kiss my ass and go to hell. He continued to write, because I wouldn't accept his calls. In every letter he wrote, he tried to convince me the baby wasn't his. "That baby could be anybody's," he would write. He wasn't even smart enough to deny that he slept with her just to reinforce the fact that the baby couldn't be his. "I fucked her in the hallway, on the stairs, in Bel's building," he wrote. I guess he thought that would make things better. I stopped opening his letters, and eventually they stopped arriving.

About a year or so later, Kareem finally came home from jail. He showed up at my house trying to convince me that I was still in love with him and that he was not letting me go. "You were the only girl who has ever stood by me, and for you to do that, you have to give me a chance." I told him that he'd blown any chances he had left with me and that I was not going backwards. Why do men never realize what they have until it's gone? Besides that, by that time, I had no feelings left for him anyway.

Once again, I decided to take a break from boys. My mother had just moved back in with us, and she brought my dad with her. When I was sixteen, my dad suffered a stroke and never fully recovered. My mother quit her job and became his full-time nurse. When she came home, we thought all hell was going to break loose. There was no way she was going to stand for a bunch of guys hanging out in her house all the time. It was a little hard at first, but I had to remind her that I was 19 years old and I was grown. She eventually gave up on trying to mother us and focused on taking care of my father.

She soon learned to love the fellas as if they were her sons—in fact, they called her "Mummy." We became a family—the 99 Shonnard Avenue family. We talked about everything and shared all of our sexual experiences with each other. Javon and I were the closest of all the fellas. Some would say he resembled Michael Jordan, but he was dark like Wesley Snipes. There was nothing I couldn't tell Javon. He knew all about the drama with Emory, Jacob, and Kareem. He even offered me some advice with the Kareem situation—nothing that I didn't already know—but he tried. My friend Astry used to say, "I think Javon likes you." I would always tell her to shut up—that that was not a possibility. We were just friends, and that was that. She would say, "Friendship is the best foundation for a relationship." I would reply, "Sex can be the demise of a friendship, and that's not worth the risk."

Javon and I continued to hang out, and I guess Astry's words stayed in my head. I started looking at Javon differently. I had been alone for a while now, and other boys/men were not trying to approach me in the streets. We were so free with each other that I just came out and asked him if he liked me. Javon was shy when it came to kicking it to a girl, but he used his humor to break the ice. I think I shocked him when I asked the question, so he went straight for the punch line: "Sharon, you can't handle all this dick," in a very cocky tone of voice. "Well show me what you working with, then," I said, laughingly. He was not shy about his anatomy, and it was as if he'd been waiting for the day he could whip it out and show me. The penis looked pretty damn good to me, although, I hadn't seen a penis in a couple of years. I was sort of intimidated, because it reminded me of Lahmeek's penis. I had never actually touched a penis before it went inside me, so I just wanted to touch it.

When we finally did it, I actually felt him inside of me. It was a weird feeling to see him moving up and down and still feel the motion of his penis, going in and out. I was trying to remember if I'd ever felt anyone else going in and out. His body started to jerk, and he pulled his penis out; white stuff squirted all over my room wall. We looked at each other and just started laughing. That was the beginning of our newfound friendship.

Astry and Reg were still messing around, but Javon was a little uncomfortable with us all being in the room together at night. Some nights I would go to his apartment, which he shared with his sister and brother. I don't think they liked me, in fact, I know they didn't like me, because they told Javon I wasn't cute enough. He didn't allow them to change his mind. That was a major plus in my book.

Our friendship was exactly the same, except now we were having sex. I was truly happy dealing with Javon, and I would talk about him to anyone who would listen. Before my niece, Yvonne, came to live with us, every time she called I would talk about the fellas, especially Javon.

She was five years younger than me and more like a close friend than a niece. Even at the tender age of twelve, her body was shapelier than mine. She was so cute and—I thought—innocent. When Yvonne came to Freeport, she met, of all the people in the world, Kyle. Just in case you don't remember, Kyle was my first unspoken sexual experience and my friend Bria's baby daddy.

I later found out that Yvonne had given Kyle the honor of taking her virginity, at age twelve. Who was I to say anything? She was my niece, not my daughter. I tried to keep her away from him as much as possible by letting her hang out with Javon and me. I remember there were times when she would call and say she was bored, so I would ask Javon to take her to the movies or something, just to get her out of the house while I was at work. She also started hanging out with girls who didn't like me or my sister Lorraine. They had her smoking weed and drinking. We had to fight a few girls because of things Yvonne told them we said, which were lies. When she turned fourteen, she thought she was so much wiser and ready for the world. Javon said that he'd tried to talk to her about her behavior and hanging out with those people, but I don't think she was listening. He told me he would keep trying to get through to her.

My brother was still living in Houston, Texas, with his new wife and newborn baby girl. I wanted to go see my new niece, and I offered to help his wife with the baby. Michael agreed to pay for me to come for a two-week visit. A few days before I was going to leave, I gave Javon a key to my room to be there to receive my phone calls if Astry wasn't home to let him in. Later on that same day, Astry and I got into a big argument because I couldn't take her sloppiness. I was so mad that I threw her out of my room; she slept in the extra room in the basement. I left for Texas, and the trip was great.

Upon my return, everybody appeared happy to see me, including Astry. Javon told me that he missed me, and that felt good to hear. Yvonne told me she'd hung out with Javon and Ryder a lot while I was away. I thought that was nice of Javon, but he hadn't told me about them hanging out when I'd called from Texas, and he didn't mention it when I came home. When I asked him about it, he said that they only went to the mall and that he took her to his house. He said his sisters liked her, and they thought she was so pretty.

Javon and I were approaching our two-month mark as more than friends. Lately, it didn't seem as if we were friends with benefits, because we weren't having sex anymore after I came back from Texas. He never wanted to spend the night, and he always had to go home for some reason or another. I never wanted to go to his house because his brother and sister made me feel unwanted and uncomfortable. I was thinking it was because Astry was in and out of my room, but she had decided to move out and leave New York altogether. I think she felt guilty because she had become friends with Bria, and now she was sleeping with Kyle. Once again, yes—this is the same Kyle. All I can say is popularity went a long way for him, and he was very funny. You can take the ugliest guy, give him some money and a reputation, and he can get all the women his heart desires.

Back to Astry: the day she was leaving, all packed and ready to go, she said, "I know you are still mad at me for everything, but I love you, and there is something you need to know." I thought she was going to say *anything but* what she actually said. She said, "Javon and Yvonne were fucking in your bed while you were in Texas." She said she'd come home one night and my door was locked, so she used her key and walked in on them.

Was I hearing what I thought I was hearing? How could my own family do this to me? She was my favorite niece and also the person I confided in about Javon. As all of these thoughts were going through my mind, Astry said, "Sharon, I am sorry, but I won't let them play you."

I hugged her and thanked her for being my friend. Astry left, and I waited all day for Javon and Yvonne to come home. Oh, yes, I did let him take her out that night, because I was feeling sick. He even called me to tell me they were at his house, and he would bring her home later. I didn't want to confront him over the phone, so I decided to wait. He finally brought her home about 11 o'clock that night. He didn't come inside, but he told her to tell me that he would call me later.

I didn't know how to ask her if was it true. All I knew was that I was angry. My anger wasn't over Javon, because that was a short fling between now ex-friends, but more because she disrespected me, and I was the reason she was even living with us. I was in my room, and I heard her talking to my mother across the hall. I got up, went into my mother's room, and asked her in front of my mother, "What did you and Javon do tonight?"

This little 14-year-old bitch looked me right in the face. She said, "None of your business" and kept talking to my mother like it was nothing. Her response alone told me that everything Astry had told me was true. In that moment, I knew how it felt to have tunnel vision. All I saw was Yvonne, and the rest of the room went black. I had a hot metal object in my hand, and I slammed it violently into the side of her head.

When I came back into the light, my sister was grabbing me and pulling me off of her. My sister later told me that the hot metal object was a small portable heater my mother had sitting on the dresser. In the midst of all the chaos, I learned of one more betrayal. To me, it was almost the ultimate betrayal. How was I supposed to process the fact that my own mother knew all along that her 14-year-old granddaughter was sleeping with her daughter's boyfriend, under her roof? She allowed Javon to come over while I was away and use my room to have sex with her granddaughter.

When I looked into my mother's room and saw her consoling Yvonne, I felt real hatred for both of them. I heard that little bitch get on the phone and call Javon to come get her. Would you believe the bastard came back to pick her up? She spent the night at his house that night. She had a better relationship, at 14, than I'd ever had in my 19 years.

They were together for the next six years from that night. Somehow Javon and I found a way to remain cordial, but Yvonne and I could not regain any sort of family bond. In fact, we had several physical fights, all of which I was trying to hurt her just like she was a bitch in the street. Javon and I had a few conversations during the course of their relationship, and I told him she wasn't ready for that kind of relationship, no matter what she was saying. Somehow, to Javon, my advice translated into me being jealous. At least that's what he told her. On several occasions, she let it be known that he'd said I was jealous of her. He told her that I was mad because she took him from me and that she looked better than me. During several of our verbal altercations, she let it be known that she thought I was ugly. This man-boy had been my best male friend at one point, and he knew my insecurities with my looks—he betrayed me. She was my family, and she was calling me "ugly" to my face.

I felt as ugly as they said I was. I was feeling like nobody was ever going to accept me looking like the lead of a number 2 pencil with teeth. I probably was a little envious of her, because she did have nice-sized breasts, small waist, a big butt, and a beautiful face. I was also fully aware of the difference between envy and jealousy. I knew jealousy was wanting what someone else had, so, by definition, she was jealous of me, because she wanted what I had with Javon, and she took it. I also knew that she couldn't take what didn't want to leave. Javon may have been dealing with his own self-esteem issues, and Yvonne may have given him that boost of self-confidence he needed. That, to me, was something to be envious of. I wanted someone of my own to give me that boost of self-confidence.

I was back to being alone and hating it. Everyone knew what had happened between Yvonne, Javon, and myself, but no one knew that I was pregnant by him during all of this. Were these guys trying to leave their mark on me, like a dog peeing on a tree? I knew I couldn't be that chick who had a baby from a man who'd cheated on her, with her niece, so I terminated another pregnancy. In the end, Yvonne cheated on Javon several times, and he had to admit that I was right—she was too young.

The Twenties

I had stopped going to night high school after the Jacob situation, and I had gotten a full-time job in a lighter factory. The owner made me a manager, and I got her to hire all of the fellas from around the way. It took one person to ruin it for us all. My homeboy Bengi—or "Rap," as we called him—threatened to beat her down in the church parking lot. It was shortly after that she slowly started letting us go one by one. My sister Camielle saw I was doing nothing and going nowhere fast, so she had me enrolled at Drake Business School in Manhattan.

I loved going to that school because I met new people and saw life from a new perspective. The school itself was predominantly filled with Black and Hispanic students. The females were pretty, with long hair and very curvaceous. The Black guys all wanted Spanish mommies, and the Spanish guys stuck to their own kind. I didn't fit anywhere, so I ended up in the friend zone with all of the guys in class, again.

I gave up and studied hard to get my GED to become a legal secretary. When the semester was over and I'd passed my GED exam, I decided to go to college instead. I wanted to make my father proud of me even if he wasn't able to speak the words. In January 1991, my sister Lorraine and I were enrolled at Nassau Community College. Our first semester was hard for me. I had no job and no one to depend on. If it hadn't been for my friend Regina, I don't know how I would have made it to school every day.

I wore my hair in a ponytail every day because I couldn't afford to get it done. I had no clothes for the winter because all I wore at Drake was business attire, consisting of slacks and dress shirts. I told people that I didn't like wearing a coat, but the truth was I didn't have the money to buy one. I wore a light spring jacket all that winter long and had only two pair of shoes to my name. I tried with all I had to get a job, but it was hard with my class schedule. I was happy that it was winter, because no one notices your winter gear like they do the summer gear. As the weather started to break, I got nervous because my secret would be out that I had no fly clothes.

The girls were rocking short haircuts or finger-waves hairstyles, and I still had a ponytail. My sister had a job as a waitress, so she stayed fly, but she wasn't the type to share her fortune. I was not cut out to be a waitress, because I had what most would call "a bad attitude," so I remained unemployed. I stayed to myself in between classes, or I would wait in the Union for my sister and Regina.

The Union was the cool place to be, where everyone would gather to just hang out. The Who's Who of NCC would hang out in there. People would come in and out of the Union with the latest wears. I would sit in the corner and watch, hoping for the day I could participate in the fashion show. There was this guy who always came in there with his girlfriend. I thought they looked so cute together, because they were either dressed alike or very similar to each other.

Day after day I looked forward to seeing them, but one day she didn't show up. I thought it was odd, but then I just didn't see her anymore. He was still hanging out in the Union, but now he was with his homeboys and still dressed to impress. He was medium height with coffee-light-and-sweet skin complexion. He wore glasses that made him look educated, with bowed legs that gave him a sexy walk. His smile was bright, with perfect teeth. I would sit and watch him from across the Union, as he sat by himself. Everybody who was a regular in the Union would speak to each other, so I would say "Hi," and every now and then, he would give me a dry-hi in return. A dry-hi is that "Hi" that someone would mumble under their breath.

My sister became friends with this girl named Michelle, who started dating a guy from Lakeview, who was popular in the Union. He brought attention to our little clique. The really fly girls didn't understand what we had that they didn't. Michelle didn't have money or clothes, either, but she was a cute girl, and she had her own car. Regina had a laid-back attitude, and she was just so cool to be around. My sister was funny, just like me. I think because none of us was caught up in the superficial stuff, we just knew how to have fun being ourselves. We all spoke our minds, and the conversation wasn't always about the latest designer or hottest shoes on the fashion scene. The guys seem to like that about our group.

On the way home one day, Lorraine said some guy was asking about me in the Union. For the life of me, I couldn't think of who that could be. I thought maybe it was someone from one of my classes who wanted to borrow my notes.

She said, "No, because he asked if you had a boyfriend."

I was always in there, and no one tried to talk to me except to ask about one of my friends or my sister. I think she was shocked that someone asked about me as well, because she hadn't bothered to get his name. On the inside, I was excited to know someone was checking me out. The next day when I went into the Union, Mr. Light-and-Sweet came and sat beside me. As he sat down, he said, "Did your friend tell you I was asking about you?"

My heart started racing, and all I thought to say was, "That was my sister." My mind was wondering, *When did he start checking for me? Why was he checking for me?* I didn't even compare to his last girlfriend. I was sitting there wearing an old crop sweater with even older jeans, and my shoes had a hole in the bottom.

He said, "My name is Darnell, and I have been watching you for a while. You are not like the other girls in here." He explained that he was from Amityville and that he was majoring in liberal arts for now. We exchanged phone numbers, and I couldn't wait to call him that night. I knew I had to play it cool because I didn't want to seem desperate. At least, I didn't want *him* to know that I was desperate.

To my surprise, he called me before I had a chance to play myself and call him first. I took it as a sign that he really liked me for me and that it wasn't just a ploy to get close to my sister or friends. We talked for hours that night. I found out that his girlfriend had moved to Atlanta to attend school there. I learned that his mom had recently passed away and that he lived with his father in Amityville. He had his own car, which he called "Buttercup." He worked as a manager at Modell's in Sunrise Mall in Massapequa, but he hated his job.

I didn't want the fact that I didn't have a job to be the reason he wouldn't want to continue to talk to me, so I told him I was waiting to hear from this store in Roosevelt Field, called Topaz. I'd applied to the stores in the mall that had all the fly clothes, but I never got a call back. I assumed they didn't want to hire me because I didn't have "the look." In those stores, it was always the light-skinned girl with pretty hair working there. If she was brown-skinned, she had to have a really nice shape, with white features. By "white features," I mean thin nose, pretty hair, thin to medium lips, and not too thick in the hips. I was hired by Stern's Department Store, where mostly old people shopped, instead. I didn't care, because I didn't have to shop there. All I needed was my check, so I could go to the stores with the fly clothes.

Darnell noticed I was buying something new every week, and I think that made him like me more. I made good on a promise to myself that I would buy nice clothes and shoes once I found a job, and I had a lot of catching up to do. We were talking for a few weeks at this point, and I think he felt more comfortable about me.

That's when he told me he had a daughter. He didn't see her too often because he didn't get along with her mother. I didn't care, as long as he still wanted to be with me. After he told me about his daughter and I didn't have a reaction to the news, we became even closer. Until this point, we were just talking on the phone and in the Union, so when he asked if he could come to my house, I was ecstatic.

His first trip to my house was an absolute disaster. My mother had just taken up a new hobby—drinking—just because. Darnell and I were standing in front of the house, side by side, leaning on his car, when her window flew open, and she began screaming, "Sharon, come inside! You look like a whore standing in front of the house."

I didn't feel embarrassed because I was too pissed off. To top it all off, my niece, Yvonne, decided to show her ass that night as well. We didn't have our usual fistfight, but it was an ugly display of negative words slung back and forth that Darnell shouldn't have been privy to. I don't think I could have apologized enough for what happened.

Despite all that he'd witnessed, Darnell did come back to my house, and we had sex for the first time. The sex was plain and ordinary, but if that is the way he wanted it, I was willing to do whatever it took to please him and keep him. In those days, it was a big thing to have a man trick on you, meaning "spend some money." It was cool for a guy to say he bought his girl something really nice, because that meant he had money.

For a man, you were *the shit* if you got a woman to trick on you. I always said, "I ain't tricking on no damn man." Well, Darnell, made me eat those words. Everything he said he wanted, I got. I wanted to him to come see me, so when the car had problems, I would pay to have it fixed. I no longer cared about buying fly clothes for myself, because whatever Darnell wanted came first.

Darnell and I continued to have occasional sex, until the day I found out I was pregnant. The phone calls were less frequent, and there were no more visits. He said that he was not ready for another baby; he didn't believe in abortion, so he wouldn't help me pay for it. I had spent all my money on him, and I knew it would take me a while to raise the money for the abortion.

I thought about all the money I'd spent on him, paying his phone bill and his father's phone bill—not to mention the $600, 5-CD disc stereo system and $200 beeper I'd bought him. He had to have a new pair of sneakers every week, some costing upwards of $120 per pair. There were times when I would give him my entire check and leave myself broke. I gave him my entire refund check from financial aid in the amount of $975. I wish I could say this was in the name of love, but it was from a place of desperation and low self-worth.

One time he came with me and my friends to the mall, and he saw this polo shirt that was $95 before taxes at Macy's. He knew I had a credit card, so when I told him that I didn't have any money to buy the shirt for him, he threw his hat on the floor and stomped his feet as if he were a child who'd just been told he couldn't have any candy. My friends looked at me like I was crazy, so I had no choice but to stand my ground. I knew that, if they hadn't been there, I would have bought that shirt. We left the mall, and he pouted all the way home.

He called later to apologize for his behavior and somehow convinced me to come to Sunrise Mall the next day for lunch. I took the bus to Massapequa, where we had lunch at Wendy's and somehow ended up in Macy's again. I did end up buying him a polo shirt—not the one for $95 but one for $75. Darnell had me wrapped around his little finger.

All this money spent in a matter of four months, yet I could not find the money to terminate this pregnancy. My plan was to hide the pregnancy from everyone, so I went to school and work as if there were nothing wrong. It was difficult because I was tired all the time, so I told people that I was having a hard time sleeping at night. When I started showing, I wore long or big shirts over my pants so I could keep my pants unbuttoned. I started to develop that ridiculous walk, but I was still able to get up on my own. I was showing a lot, and nobody noticed anything.

It was funny because I knew I didn't want to have the baby, but I did like how it felt to be pregnant. It finally hit me that I was going into my fifth month and that this baby might become a reality. When I first felt the baby moving, there were no words to describe that beautiful feeling inside except "butterflies dancing in my stomach."

Darnell and I remained friends, although the relationship had faded away. I realized that we had entered the friend-zone when I found myself listening to him tell me he'd met a girl named Jennifer, from uptown, and how much he really liked her. I was actually happy for him, and I gave him advice on how he could get her to like him back. We never had the discussion about why *we* couldn't be together, even though I was carrying his baby.

One day my sister Camielle came by to visit and barged into my room while I was lying in bed, with my stomach exposed. She just said, "Hello" and went right back out of the room. Later, when she got home, she called me and asked me directly, "Are you pregnant? All these months, and she was the only person who noticed. I was never able to lie to her, so I told the truth. She asked me what I wanted to do. I said innocently, "I am not ready to have a baby, but I have no choice because I have no money and no insurance."

The next day she called and said, "You have an appointment for next week. Tell mommy you are going to house sit for me, and you can stay the week."

I immediately called Darnell to tell him what my sister had done. His response was, "It is your body. Do what you want, but I'm still against it."

He was right—it *was* my body and my baby, and I would be doing both of them a grave injustice by continuing this pregnancy. The following week, I was examined by the doctor. He said that, if I had waited one more week, I would not have been able to terminate the pregnancy. The hospital set it up so I could get emergency Medicaid to pay for the procedure.

The next day, I was admitted into the same hospital that I was born in, Kings County Hospital in Brooklyn. I was in a room with another girl having the same procedure. She scared the hell out of me by the way she was acting. We were both five and a half months pregnant, so I thought I was going to be like that. This procedure was nothing like the usual D & Cs that I'd had in the past. They had to extract the amniotic fluid and replace it with saline, causing death to the fetus. Then they gave you a needle just under your navel to induce labor.

I was in labor for two days. The nurse finally came in and said that I must walk. I remember pacing the floor with my IV pole leading the way. I had an urge to move my bowels, so I went to the bathroom. As I began to push, I felt something just fall out. I was scared to look down, so I pushed the button on the wall for a nurse to help. She came in right away and told me to bend over, while she cut the cord and removed the baby from the water. She wrapped it up in some paper and put it in the trash. As if it were second nature for her, she said, "Get back in the bed; you should feel another contraction—then push out the afterbirth." It happened just as she said, and as I lay there, I thought, *It is finally over.*

The nurse refused to tell me what the sex of the baby was for fear it may have an effect on my mental state.

I went back to my sister's house the day after and called Darnell to let him know it was over. He was really concerned and offered to come to Manhattan to pick me up. We didn't speak often after that, but whenever I felt the need to talk to him, he would call out of the blue, almost right on time. Darnell eventually left Nassau and went to Atlanta to attend one of the Black colleges. While on a short vacation to Atlanta a few years later, I ran into him, and—just as I thought—he looked good and was doing fine. There were no hard feelings between us.

I was still attending Nassau, but I was off for the summer. As usual, everyone was in the park—Bria, her little sister, and I. Her sister had a friend by the name of Tical, who had a brother he felt should meet Bria. My mother had converted the front porch into a bedroom on one end and a small living area on the other end. I decided to take that room because it gave me more space and more privacy. Bria had moved in with me after she was released from her foster home, so we converted the small living area into her bedroom. Tical set it up for them to meet at my house.

When Wyatt showed up, he had two friends with him: Leo and Damon. When I saw Leo, I thought he was so sexy. His eyes had this Chinese look about them, and his nose was thin and pointed. He was tall, with perfect skin and perfect teeth. Leo had his eye on my sister, Lorraine. Damon was cute, but I was more attracted to Leo. Damon was cool and showed interest in me, but, as always, I think it was because both he and I were the odd man out. Wyatt had just rented a house in Lakeview, so we decided to go see his house. When we got to his house, Leo decided to leave and go home because Lorraine hadn't come. Bria wanted to stay with Wyatt, and Damon used his car to bring me back home.

Damon and I ended up sleeping together that night. The next morning, I was ashamed of myself for having sex with someone I barely knew. He made me feel as though we'd known each other forever, and, I guess you can say, "It was on from there." Wyatt's house became party central. Every night, after everybody had drunk and smoked themselves into a stupor, Bria and I were left to clean up the house. There were some nights when we were not there, and Wyatt would call to ask if we could come over to clean up. That was cool the first two times, but, after that, I started feeling like they were fucking the maids. I stopped going to Wyatt's house for that reason.

Damon started coming to my house more often. He would bum a ride from someone or get Leo to drop him off. He didn't have a job, so we didn't go out very often. He always told me about the job he *used* to have but never mentioned anything about the job he needed to get. I listened to it for a while, but then I started dropping hints that he needed to get a job. He caught what I was saying to him, and he really made me believe he was looking for work. I remember his friends would tease him because he never had money to buy his own cigarettes or beer. I should have suspected something, because when we first started hanging out, I had to page him on Leo's beeper.

Wyatt and Leo had formed a rap group, so they performed at several clubs in the city. Before almost every show, they would go shopping to get some new gear. Damon was one of those guys you would see onstage with no purpose, but he was in front of the crowd, so he wanted to look good also. They had a big show coming up, and I wanted him to look good onstage as well. Me being me—wanting to prove that I was a good girlfriend—I took him shopping and maxed out my Macy's credit card. We had become really close, and he had also gotten close to my family. I was never the type to care about people meeting my family or me meeting theirs.

I remember the first time I met his mother. We were at his house, fresh from having sex, and she walked into his room without knocking. There were no "Hello's" or "Nice to meet you's." She just commenced to yelling, "I told you I don't want any of these nasty little girls in my house." I was beyond embarrassed and just wanted to get out of that house. He started yelling back at his mother, and that made me even more uncomfortable. The worst part was, we had to wait for someone to pick us up to take us back to Freeport. After that, we spent all of our time together at my house. He would be waiting at my house for me when I came home from work at night. I loved our relationship, and I thought I was falling in love with him. He really showed me how much he cared about me: I was in a car accident with my sister and Bria's little sister, in Wyandanch. When we came home from the hospital, he was right there, waiting with open arms. I'd really hurt my back in that accident, so I decided to sue the driver who hit us.

On my first doctor's visit, they made me take a pregnancy test, which turned out to be positive. I was shocked, and I thought, *Here I go again.* But Damon was so happy. He already had a daughter, but he didn't really have a relationship with her mother. He said that had happened while he was drunk one night. He told me my baby would be special. We were so close that I never even considered aborting the child. Whenever I needed to do something, he would borrow his homeboy girlfriend's car, just to take me. It was to the point where he would take public transportation to see me, and he hated the bus and the train.

Then, it was almost as if he lived with me, because he was with me every night. His friend was arrested, and his girl started letting Damon hold the car at night, while she was at work. I did get a little suspicious, but he assured me that she was just a friend he took to work at night and picked up in the morning. I didn't argue because he would drop her off and come straight to me. I never questioned it again.

He still hadn't gotten a job, so when he got a beeper of his own, I questioned that. He claimed he'd found it, and his cousin had let him borrow the money to turn it on. I wanted to believe that was true, so I let it go.

It was November then, and everything was going fine. My birthday was around the corner, so to speak, and I couldn't wait to see what he would get me. My birthday has always been my special holiday. I didn't really celebrate Christmas or Valentine's Day. I believed if someone truly loved me, their gift would reflect that they were thinking of me, and only me, when they purchased it. For my birthday, he took me to Leo's brother's football game, and we went to his house. I was very reluctant because I didn't want to relive the first embarrassing moment with his mother again.

We went upstairs to his room, and he gave me a box he had hidden in the bottom of his closet. The box was from Victoria's Secret. I opened the box—it was a purple negligee; the tag said, "Large." I was all of 119 pounds and stood 5-foot-4 inches tall. *Who the hell was he thinking about when he bought this shit?* A few minutes later, his mother made us leave, saying something about "I don't want anything happening in my house."

This time I was more than happy to leave her house, because my gift sucked. I don't understand why men buy lingerie as a gift. That is more for their pleasure than mine, and, by the way—I never wore it. I also never asked him why he'd bought a freaking "Large." When his birthday came, which was also in November, I gave him $150.

Now it was approaching Christmas, and I paged Damon; he didn't call back. I paged him three times—he never returned one of them. *There goes his Christmas gift*, I thought to myself. It was now 11 o'clock, and some girl called back, asking if someone had paged Damon. Naturally, I thought it was his homeboy's girlfriend or just one of his homegirls. I didn't feel I had to be jealous because he had homegirls just like I had the fellas. When I asked who she was, I thought she would say a familiar name. She replied, "I am Gia, Damon's girlfriend."

Then she asked me—as if *I* were the other woman—"Are you messing with Damon?"

I don't believe in answering this types of question from anyone, so I hung up on her. I immediately called his house, which I never did, because his mother was a witch. (For the record, I really wanted to use the B-word, but I do have some respect for the fact that she is his mother.)

He answered the phone immediately, knowing it was me, because "Gia" was on the other line, telling him she'd just spoken to me.

The only question I wanted answered was, "Who is 'Gia' to you?"

Lord knows I was shocked when he said, "Gia is my girl." I just hung up the phone, because there was nothing left to be said. The next day, she called me again, telling me how long she'd been with him. She told me she'd just had an abortion for him. I was just listening to her talk and not offering any information about me and Damon. I learned that she had been with him just as long as I had been with him, only she'd had an abortion, and I was still pregnant.

I learned that it was her pager, and she'd let him borrow it. Damon knew I was pregnant, and he pretended to be so happy, knowing the whole time that she was pregnant, too. My baby was not special, because, in fact, she was pregnant before I was. I was so hurt and confused. How could a man spend damn near every moment with me for five months and then turn around and call someone else "his girl" in the end?

I called Damon and told him I didn't want anything from him except a ride to Brooklyn to have the abortion. There was no way I was going to have his baby now. I was four months pregnant, and I had to have the same procedure as with Darnell's baby. Gia kept calling me, trying to get me to meet with her and confront Damon. I was not into doing things like that. Besides, once he said she was "his girl," there was no need for a confrontation, because he'd made his decision. Damon kept his word, and he borrowed that girl's car to take me to Brooklyn. I would not speak to him the entire ride to the hospital.

When we arrived at the hospital, it was normal—a formality, really—for them to run a sexually transmitted disease test on you before the procedure. The nurse came back and said that I was carrying the bacteria that can cause gonorrhea. That had to be treated before I could terminate the pregnancy. I had to ask her several more times to explain. I had to be sure, because what I heard her say was that *I had gonorrhea*.

She explained it several times that I did not actually *have* gonorrhea—I had the bacteria that *causes or develops into* gonorrhea.

I didn't care how many ways she explained it. Whatever it was, I knew Damon had caused it. He was waiting in the hall; I don't know where I found the strength, but I grabbed him by the throat and pinned him against the wall.

I was really trying to kill him right there in the hospital waiting area. I had my thumb pressed firmly against his Adam's Apple, trying to cut off his air supply. The nurses came and dragged me off of him. I never hated anyone as much as I hated him in that moment. It was that moment when he realized just how much I cared for him and how deeply he'd hurt me. Everyone called me "Shotz," so he just kept repeating my name and saying, "I'm sorry."

They gave me some antibiotic, and I had to reschedule my appointment for the following week. All I could think of was getting this baby out of me. This baby had more determination than I thought, because it was refusing to leave my body the following week. The nurses came to me on the second day and said I had to start walking around to help bring on the labor. I remember walking the halls, dragging the IV pole beside me, and thinking to myself, *Why, God? Why can't you send me someone for me?*

On that day while lying in bed, I felt an uncomfortable pressure, like a really bad gas pain in my stomach, and as I pushed out what I thought was going to be a loud fart, it just fell out onto the bed. I pushed the button for the nurse, and before she entered, I sat up and pulled the sheets back to see that it was a boy. The nurse rushed in and told me not to look and to lie back down. She explained that people have a hard time handling this type of abortion when they know the sex of the baby.

I felt nothing but relief. Damon and Leo came to pick me up from the hospital the next day. I made sure I told him it was a boy. I knew that was what he wanted, and I wanted him to know how much he'd messed up. After 200 "I'm sorries," and "Please forgive me's," I forgave him. He did anything and everything to remain in my good graces. I am a very forgiving person, so I tried to act as if it were all behind me.

Everything was fine for about a week or two. Then Yvette, Bria's sister, called me. She had just gotten married and was being introduced to her new in-laws. "Barbara" was her husband's cousin, who loves to talk about her boyfriend, Damon. *Is this déjà-vu?* I thought. Barbara was the so-called homeboy's girlfriend who was letting him borrow her car.

When Yvette told me the story, I almost felt bad for her. He was disrespecting her on every level, by having me in her car the way he did. She came to Yvette's house that following weekend, and they called me. I don't understand some women—as soon as I got on the phone, she wanted to meet me. She actually thought that I would let her pick me up, from my house, to go and confront him. My answer, of course, was "No."

I didn't know that chick from Adam, and she could have been some lunatic trying to set me up to get jumped. I did, however, confront him, and this time, *I* was his girl, and *she* meant nothing to him. He was swearing up and down that he was just using her for her car and that he had been faithful to me. He even said he hadn't even spoken to Gia since the last incident.

I fell for it hook, line, and sinker, because Yvette showed me a picture of Barbara, and I felt confident in my position. I also saw someone who may have been struggling with the same affliction as me—low self-esteem. A month later he said he was thinking about moving to Washington, DC. He said his uncle was going to hook him up with a job working at UPS. He just needed me to help him purchase his ticket to get there. He made all sorts of promises on how he would call often and visit on weekends. He tried to sell me on the idea that, maybe once he got settled, I could consider moving there, so we could be together.

About a week later, I received an unexpected call from Gia. She was very polite and acted as if we'd been friends for years. She just wanted to know if I'd had any contact with Damon since everything that had happened. I declined to answer any of her questions, because I owed her no explanations about my personal life. She advised me to calm down and said she was just asking "woman to woman," because men lie, and she needed to know the truth before Damon and she moved to Baltimore, Maryland, together. She said Damon had told her that he'd never seen me again or spoken to me since that time.

This was the final nail in his coffin, as far as I was concerned. He'd once again denied me, as if I meant nothing to him. From what I heard about Gia, she was light-skinned with pretty hair, and that may have been the deciding factor. I told her what she wanted to hear, which was that I had neither spoken to nor seen him. I was expecting him to come over later, and when he did, I told him about my conversation with Gia. He tried to lie his way out of it by saying, "She is lying, and I am going to DC with my uncle."

At that point, it really didn't matter to me where he went, just as long as he went away from me. What better way to get rid of him than to send him to Baltimore to be with Gia? I learned from her that their agreement was that he could move to Baltimore with her, if he paid his own way down there. I gave him the $150, and it was the best $150 I've ever spent. There was a weight lifted off my shoulders once he was gone.

Two weeks after I'd sent him on his merry way, I received another phone call from the happy couple. I guess things weren't so beautiful in paradise.

I have no idea what either of them were thinking when they called me. She got on the phone, telling me to come get him, because she doesn't want him anymore. Then he snatched the phone away from her, saying that he'd made a mistake and that he wanted me to send for him, so he could come home to be with me.

That, sure as hell, was not going to happen, I thought.

I was holding the phone, listening to them argue with each other. Then I heard a lot of tussling, and the phone disconnected.

A few months later, Gia called me while Damon was at work to say she regretted bringing him down there with her. We spoke as if we were old friends. She told me how he hated her rice, and she hated how he left his dirty clothes lying around. She told me she was pregnant, and everything about him was getting on her nerves. We laughed, and she said how she hoped the baby didn't have his long head.

Damon never knew about that conversation—or the last one I'd had with her almost a year later, when she couldn't take it anymore. She said they were coming home, because he couldn't keep a job, and he didn't help with their daughter. I heard from Leo that they broke up when they got back to New York. She went home to her parents, and he moved back in with his mother. To my surprise, he didn't try to reach out to me, and we never spoke again.

I am sure by now that most women are calling me an outright, stupid bitch.

I was not that damn stupid this time.

In August, after the first incident with Damon, I began talking on the phone with this guy, Dave, whom I'd met at a cookout in his honor. He had just come home from basic training in the Army, and it was his birthday. We didn't get along at all when we first met. He had this arrogant attitude about him. We argued so much while I was there that I left the cookout and went home. The *real* reason I left the cookout was that I heard him say something about my teeth behind my back. His comment really struck a chord with me, because the feature I hated most about myself was my big, crooked teeth. I never grew into them, like I thought I would, as a child.

A few weeks later, Dave's best friend, Jonathan, told me he wanted my phone number. I wasn't about to give him shit, after the things he said.

Why would he want my number? We didn't even like each other!

I remember telling Bria about him and what had happened at the cookout. The mention of his name sparked a memory for her. She reminded me of a story she once told me about a guy who'd tasted her essence under the boardwalk in Long Beach. Dave was that guy.

I really didn't want to have anything to do with him after hearing that. Every time I saw Jonathan, he would tell me that Dave had asked about me. *Why does he keep asking for me, and what does he want to talk to me about that's so important?*

I finally gave in and told Jonathan to give him my number.

When he called me, it seemed so natural talking to him. I tried not to get caught up in that, because *everyone* had given me that same, natural feeling thus far. He was very respectful—nothing like the person at the party. He was so easy to talk to that, when I told him I was still dealing with Damon, he was very understanding. He said he just wanted to see how I was doing every now and then, and so he called every two to three weeks.

I began to look forward to his phone calls. I started to confide in him about certain things between me and Damon. He never took advantage of the troubles I was going through with Damon. He went out of his way to make me feel better and laugh again. I sent Damon to Maryland in March of 1993, and Dave called me in May to check on me. I was free to go out with him—more to the point, I *wanted* to go out with him. I felt he had more to offer in a relationship than anyone else I had dated in the past.

To be honest, I think he had more going for himself than I did. Dave was two years younger than me; he was in the Army Reserve, working as a security guard, and had his own apartment. The apartment was not in the best of neighborhoods, but it was his. Looking at his life and what he had accomplished made me check myself. I was 22 years old, living with my mother, and not working because Stern's had gone out of business. I was still in school at Nassau Community College, and at that time, it felt as if that's all I had going for me.

Anyway, our first date was a movie, and then we went back to his apartment. It was in desperate need of a woman's touch, and I was determined to be that woman. We talked for most of the night and fell asleep in each other's arms. We spent almost every night together after that. Sex was better than I ever imagined it could be. This young guy taught me so much about my own body. He showed me that sex was not just about someone getting on top of you, sweating and panting until they released. He showed that changing position was not a freaky thing to do but that it naturally enhanced the sexual experience.

More than once, our bed would be against the wall when we started going at it, and, when we were done, the bed would be in the middle of the room. We would just lie there and laugh, trying to figure out how the hell the whole bed had moved and we hadn't felt it. He would pat me on my back and say, "Girl, you got the Mott's." There was a commercial that proclaimed Mott's applesauce as the best applesauce on the market. He used the phrase as a way of telling me that I had a good sex game in bed.

I never talked to my mother about anything, but he made me want to run home and say, "Good God, mommy, he is the best."

My first climax was with him giving me oral pleasure. There was something about him that was more than just being handsome and confident. I fell head over heels in love with him, secretly. Until this point in my life, I hadn't told anyone that I loved them. He made me want to shout it from the rooftops.

He also had a strict, no-nonsense rule about women and relationships. On one occasion, there was this girl who showed up at his apartment, banging on the door and windows, yelling all sorts of crazy things because he told her he wasn't going to see her anymore. I understood why she was acting like that, because he was something special, and she wanted it back. I never found out what she'd done to mess things up with him, because he would never say. I didn't push to find out because her loss was my gain.

He gave me the keys to the apartment within the first week of us dating, and I cleaned that place from top to bottom. His father even made a comment about how clean the apartment was and that Dave should keep me because I was the type of girl that he needs in his life. I didn't really move in, but I did have a lot of things there. He had a few female friends, which, again, I didn't have a problem with, because I hung out with mainly guys myself. I had a problem when I would come home from school; his female friends would be there, and they wouldn't speak to me. Then they started hanging up the phone on me when they would call the house. I spoke to Dave about it, and he took care of the problem right away. I thought to myself, *This is how a relationship should be. Your woman should come first, and respect is due to her, from all.*

Then what seemed to be the curse of my life happened again: I found out I was pregnant. He already had a daughter, but she lived in North Carolina. I was just about to finish school, and I just could not have a baby now. Dave said—only one time—"Don't kill my baby," and he never spoke on the subject again. I did what I thought was best for me and had an abortion. I told Dave after the fact. He was so upset that he didn't speak to me for seven days and eight nights. I would call him, and he would just hang up on me. When he finally took my call and I tried to explain why I did what I did, he seemed to understand.

I thought we had made up, but he called and asked me to stay at home because he was going to stay at my house that night. The reason he gave was that his father wanted to use his apartment now that it was clean. His father is what most would call a dirty old man. He liked young girls, and he couldn't bring them to his house, because he lived with his mother.

I couldn't wait to see Dave, but he never showed up at my house.

He called that next morning and said he'd stayed at Jonathan's house instead. After school that day, I went to the apartment to pick up some things. I had a habit of always knocking before I used my key, in case he wasn't dressed, because I often brought my friends over, as I did that day. When no one answered, I proceeded to use my key, but the chain was on the door from the inside. I started knocking on the door, and a girl in her nightgown came toward the door. I told my friend to go ahead without me, because I didn't want her to think anything negative. I had spoken so highly of Dave, and I didn't want to look like a fool. I didn't get upset, because I knew his father had used the apartment the night before, so I assumed that she was there for him.

She opened the door and walked back toward the bedroom. I introduced myself, and she hummed under her breath, as if she'd heard my name before. I became a little suspicious, so I asked her directly, "Are you here for his father?"

"No, I am here for Dave. He went to the store to buy me some cigarettes," she said, as she lay across the bed.

Wait—did I just hear her right? I must be confused, I thought.

I sat there and looked around the apartment that I had cleaned, the new sheets that I'd bought, and the new television that I'd bought. Then I re-focused on the girl lying in *my* bed, on *my* sheets, and watching *my* television, like *I* was a *guest* in *her* home.

I had to be sure, so I asked the only question that came to mind: "Do you know who I am?"

As the words slipped from my lips, the visual scene played out in my head. I imagined me dragging her across the living room, out the door, down the stairs, and banging her head on the cement pavement. The sound of her voice brought me back as I heard her answer:

"Yes, I know who you are."

As I stood up to make my vision become reality, I heard keys turn the lock in the front door. As he entered the apartment, he didn't even flinch. He walked past me into the middle of the bedroom and said, "April, didn't I tell you not to open the door for anyone?"

He proceeded to give this disrespectful bitch her cigarettes, turned to me, and said, "You can leave now."

He placed his hand in the small of my back and ushered me to the door, as he asked for his keys back. I was very much still in shock, so I said, "Well, I want my television."

He told me flat-out "No" and escorted me out of the apartment. As we entered the hallway, I asked him, "Why?" Is she who you want now?"

As I said those words, I remembered the girl who was banging on the doors and windows. "It's my way or the highway. You shouldn't have killed my baby," he said simply, in a cool, almost-scary calm manner. I pleaded with him: "Tell her to leave, so we can talk. You said you understood why I had to do what I did."

He said, "You have to leave before my girl gets mad."

How had she become *his girlfriend* in seven days, I asked myself.

Although he never said it, I always felt like it was because she was prettier than me. I constantly compared myself to the women whom the men in my life chose over me. Somehow, I always felt like I came up short in comparison. He stood there, staring at me, with a blank look on his face, as if to say, "I am waiting for you to leave."

Just like that, it was over, and all I wanted was my television.

I left and walked around the corner to Javon's job. Yes, the same Javon who'd slept with my niece. Javon saw how hurt and upset I was, so he came back to Dave's apartment with me to get my television. Dave, of course, wouldn't let us in, but he said he would bring it to me later that night. I used the television as an excuse to keep calling. A week or so had passed, and I was still calling, but he wouldn't take my calls. I was calling Jonathan all the time as well, but he would just say something like, "Dave is asleep" or "He just left." I knew it was a lie, but I kept calling anyhow.

Regina and I went up on the Drive, in Hempstead, to meet up with Big D, and there he was, all hugged up on April, in front of everybody. I felt so low—all I could do is leave with whatever pride I had left. I couldn't even hang out with our friends anymore. I couldn't take any more, so I called my brother Michael in Texas and told him that there was nothing left for me in New York. In one week, he sent me some money, and I started packing to kiss New York goodbye.

Two days before I was set to leave New York, Kareem stopped by. After all this time, he still felt he had a chance with me, and he was going to try to take it. I don't know if he ever truly loved me, but I do know that he was grateful for the love that I showed him. I let him down easy, and we spoke as friends. He told me, once again, that Tiani's baby wasn't his, but he had fathered a little girl since he had been home. He said he wasn't with his daughter's mother, and he explained he was having a hard time finding a good woman.

I suggested that he stop hanging out in these little hole-in-the-wall spots and going to clubs trying to meet a good woman. I told him he should slow down on hanging out and settle down with his daughter's mother. He wasn't listening to me; instead, he switched the subject back to me and the reason I was leaving New York. I didn't go into details, but he knew something was up. He said, "If you are going to Texas running away from your problems, it won't work. "Problems go away only when you deal with them head on."

I was trying not to hear him even more than he was trying not to hear me.

We changed the subject, and he helped me finish packing. The next day, my friends gave me a going-away party. No one cared about why I was leaving—they just cared about having a reason to drink and get high. My heart was broken, and the only way to mend it was to get away.

It took me two days to get to Texas. I traveled the cheapest way possible—Go Greyhound. I took a tour of the coast by changing buses every two states. In Louisiana, they made all the passengers get off the bus and sent in the dogs to sniff for drugs. I was good and tired by the time I arrived in Texas.

My plan was to get my license, get a job, and buy a car. I figured eventually I would get my own apartment. My brother had different plans for me. He decided I was best suited as a babysitter for his kids. He had two girls and one son. His youngest daughter and son were both autistic. His oldest daughter thought she was second-generation monkey. She would run and climb up your leg straight to the top of your head before you could say, "Don't."

They were beautiful kids, but it was very difficult watching them. The autistic kids couldn't speak, and I never knew what they wanted. Little Mikey sounded as if he were trying to learn the alphabet and got stuck on the letter "E." He would sing that letter all day. Re-Re couldn't speak, but she communicated a lot better. She would grab me by the hand and swing it in the direction of whatever it was that she wanted.

This routine with his kids was way too much for me. I had to refocus on what I'd come there for. My brother would never get up in the morning to teach me how to drive. Instead he suggested that I take the car in the morning on my own. That is exactly what I did.

I taught myself how to drive in his Toyota 4-runner. I started realizing that Texas was not the place for me. He had a beautiful home, equipped with five bedrooms, three full bathrooms, a huge kitchen, a den, two living rooms, and a gigantic playroom. This house was something that most people dream about. No one in their right mind would want to leave here—except me.

I told my brother that I was unhappy and wanted to go home, and that's when he decided to take interest. He made his wife take me to get my license and show me around. It all came too little, too late; my mind was made up. I was ready to go on the first thing smoking back to New York.

I called home to tell my mother and sister that I was coming home, and that's when Lorraine told me that Kareem had been shot and killed. She said he was at this club in Jamaica, Queens, called the Q-Club. The only thing she could tell me was that it was over some girl. I could hear her voice, but all I could see was his face, when we last spoke. I remembered the last words we said to each other. Maybe our words to each other were not so much advice—but a premonition. He was right, I should have never tried to run away from my problems. I was crying, because I wished he would have listened to me and stayed out of the clubs.

I was gone three long months, and everyone was still doing the same thing. Because Dave and I had the same friends, they informed me that April and Dave were now living together and that they were expecting a baby. At that point, I decided not to let him know that I was back in town.

I focused all my attention on bettering myself. I got a job and bought my first car. It was a box-style, brown Maxima. It was so old that it was a *Datsun* Maxima. The man who sold it to me said everything was working fine on the car. They always say a woman should bring a man along when she is buying a car. I didn't listen to that piece of advice. I brought my friend Regina with me.

I learned that lesson the hard way. That car had no heat, and I had to drive with gloves and earmuffs on inside the car. When I took it to the mechanic, he said the car didn't even have the heating coils. During the summer, it had no air conditioning, and it had the nerve to have leather seats. I lost five pounds a day driving that car, sweating like crazy. I said to myself, "I can live with all of that, except not having a radio."

The radio required personal attention. You had to turn the car on and off three times in a row, but on the third try, you had to put it in drive and then turn the radio on. It was a pain in the ass, but it was my car. There were days when I just wanted to drive that car and park it in the living room of the man who'd sold it to me. But that car got me from point A to point B, safely. I was proud of that old car, because I worked and saved up all $1200 to buy it.

By the time I got my first car, my sister was on her third car, all courtesy of my mother. I will admit that my mother hurt my feelings a lot with her obvious display of affection for my sister over me. I had to accept the fact that she loved my sister more than me, but it gave me motivation. I was motivated to show her that I didn't need her or anything from her. I continued to work hard, fully determined to save my money to buy myself a better car. My hope was to find a decent man and move on from the past.

Before I knew it, five months had passed, and I had no male prospects. I felt I needed a change. While I was in Texas, I'd listened to a lot of Toni Braxton; she even got me through my road test. I thought she was very pretty, with the sexiest haircut. Out of respect for Toni, I had to do it. I cut my hair off and started getting my nails done regularly. I changed the way I dressed and made sure I looked good every time I went outside.

A few more months passed, and, one day, Lorraine came home and said she'd seen Dave at UPS. She said, "He asked about you and wanted your number."

I'd figured he would find out that I was back in town through our mutual friends. I tried to play it off like I didn't care when she told me, so I said, "I hope you didn't give him my number."

She replied, "I did give him the number. I didn't know that you would not want him to have your number."

Two days later, he decided to call and said Jonathan told him I was back in town, and he'd heard I'd cut my hair. "I just wanted to see how you were doing," he said. I tried to play hard-to-get at first, but soon, I gave in. I wanted him to see my new haircut and all the changes I'd made in my life, including my new (or not-so-new) car. On the day I agreed to meet him, I wore a mini-skirt. I'd never really liked my legs, so I didn't wear skirts very often.

When I saw him, I knew that love just doesn't go away because you want it to or because it's easier that way. I looked at him, and something inside me couldn't hate him more. He told me how much he loved my new haircut. He told me that I'd better go home—before we both did something we might regret. I took that to mean he was pleased with what he saw.

We started talking and calling each other the way we used to. He told me all about the breakup with April and how it felt to be the father of a new baby girl they'd named "Blue." Eventually, I ended up back at his apartment, and the sex was even better than I remembered.

But I'd gone back on my word, and I was disappointed in myself. I had made a promise to myself that, once I was done with someone, I would never go back to them. *Maybe the second time will be a charm*, as they say, I thought to myself.

We had such a good time hanging out. We drove that car to Sylvia's in Harlem, and it was funny because we prayed the entire way there and back that the car would not break down on us. We went to see plays on Broadway, and he made me feel really special. Things were okay for a while. He would drop me off at work and pick me up later. I worked a lot, so he had my car more than I did. The days when I finally got to drive my own car, people would ask me for the guy who owned the car. Some guys would actually say, "Oh, you must be *wifey* to be driving my man Dave's car." That shit used to piss me off so bad, because I didn't recall Dave ever giving me any money toward that car. I paid for gas, I paid for maintenance—as a matter of fact, I paid for everything.

Dave was no longer working; Ms. April wasn't working, either, and their daughter's first birthday was coming up. I thought to myself, *Sharon, do the right thing, and support your man. Blue is his daughter, and for that reason alone, you should love her.*

I had just gotten a Sears card, so off to the store we went. The "new softer side" of Sears had all this cute stuff for little girls. I almost maxed out my card doing the stand-by-your-man thing. I bought the cake and balloons for a party that they were giving—a party that I couldn't even attend. April didn't want me to be there, and, of course, Dave couldn't miss his daughter's birthday, so I did the right thing and stayed home.

Every time he had to pick up his daughter, April had something to say about me being there. I was tired of her broke ass calling all the shots as to who can ride in my car—especially *me*. I told him he was not taking my car unless I was going with him from now on.

A few weeks passed, and his daughters were all in New York. Yes, I said ". . . his daughters." He had three girls. I was so happy for him because all he wanted was for his girls to meet each other. Once again, he let April dictate who could ride in my car and convinced me to wait at home until he got back with the girls. We were going to take the girls to have their pictures taken together in Green Acres Mall. When Dave pulled up, I noticed that his oldest daughter wasn't there; only the two little ones were in the car. As I was getting into the car, Blue started crying, saying she didn't want me to go. The next thing I knew, his other daughter was crying, too. Now they were both crying and yelling in unison, "Daddy, no, we don't want her to go."

My feelings were beyond hurt. It took everything I had not to break down and start crying myself. I told him to just go without me and enjoy the day with his girls. All I could think about was how ungrateful those little bitches were. Then it dawned on me: *They're just little girls.* Then the other side of me took over again, and I thought, *Those little bastards—if it wasn't for me, they would be sitting on the damn bus, butt naked, talking shit. How dare they say they don't want me to go in my car?*

I had to think rationally and calm myself down. I waited for Dave to call me later, and I politely let him know that this would be the last time his daughters would ever ride in my car. He knew I meant it, too, because I was so calm about it. He understood why I felt that way, and we continued our relationship. We even decided to move to Virginia together. He had a cousin who lived there who was going to hook him up with a job. He went down first, and I was going to move down later.

Now my weekends were spent renting cars and traveling back and forth to Virginia. I loved Virginia because it reminded me of Long Island, but better. I found an apartment in Alexandria, but I needed a co-signer. Dave's credit was shot, because he'd stopped paying rent and all his other bills when he stopped working. My brother Michael had agreed to co-sign for me, but I had to get a job to prove I would be able to pay the rent myself. I couldn't let him know that I was moving with a man, because he would not have that.

I applied to the Manassas Police Department, but I failed the lie-detector test. Of all the stupid questions to ask, they asked me if I'd ever taken anything from my workplace. I said "No," but I knew I had taken several items from various jobs that I'd worked. That is an unfair question—everybody takes something home from work. I managed to find a job in a department store down there. I told them I had to tie up some loose ends in New York, and then I would be able to start in two weeks. Within that time, Dave decided he didn't like Virginia anymore. So, I gave up the apartment and never went back to Virginia for the job. I was mad as hell because I'd wasted all that money on rental cars every weekend for nothing.

We were back in New York, and because he'd given up his apartment, he had to stay with Big D. Big D's apartment became the hangout. One day the house was filled with nothing but guys, Bria, and me. I just remember Dave calling me into the bedroom and telling me to go home. He said it was too many guys, and I shouldn't be in their faces. He said one of the guys told him I was looking at him and that they could have me if they wanted to. That was such bullshit, but I went home anyway. He later told me that, when men are hanging out, women should be in the kitchen or in the bedroom. He made such a big deal about that every time the guys came over that I would just get up and leave. Regina stayed in the room with the guys, and, because of that, he felt she was loose, so he started calling her "a jezebel." He made her feel so uncomfortable that she stopped coming to Big D's house altogether.

Dave wanted to live like he did when he had a job. He wanted to hang out with his friends and drink every weekend, and still have on nice gear. There I was, on that stand-by-your-man bullshit again, because he would be so sad when he couldn't hang out with the boys that I would give him money and the car to go enjoy himself. When I didn't have the money, he wouldn't speak to me for days. Dave started changing, and his attitude was totally different.

We were barely having sex anymore. I would call looking for him at night, and Big D would say he never came home that night before. I heard that he was messing with some young girl on Terrace Avenue. I believed everything I was hearing because he wasn't around to tell me different. One day, I went by to visit Big D, and, while I was there, the phone rang, and Big D told me to get it. When I answered the phone, it was some girl asking for Dave.

I didn't get upset. I told her he wasn't there, and I tried to take a message. He must have been expecting her to call, because as soon as I hung up the phone, he walked in the door. All he said was, "Good—I need to borrow the car. I have to go back to Hempstead."

I told him he could not take my car but that I would drop him off. This fool had the nerve to tell me that it was *his* car and that *he* was dropping *me* off. In the car, I asked him about the rumors I'd heard and about the girl on the phone.

I was not expecting his reaction. He reached over with the back of his left hand and smacked me so hard across the middle of my face. My lip started bleeding, and I was so shocked that I couldn't cry. I couldn't talk, and I couldn't think. All I thought was, *This nigger has to die.*

I looked around, and all I saw was a tree. Somehow the car ended up pointed in that direction with my foot on the gas. I had my seatbelt on, but he didn't. When the car hit the tree, Dave hit his head. I wanted him to die at that moment, but instead all he had was a small bump and a headache. I told him to get the hell out of my car. He was the one in shock now. He couldn't believe that I'd driven the car into a tree. It was winter time, and he would most certainly have to walk back to Big D's house in the freezing cold. My car was already on its last leg, but now it was missing the bumper. I picked up my bumper, put it in the back seat, and drove straight home.

I didn't hear from him for weeks. I was starting to forget what his voice sounded like or what he looked like. I hated him and loved him at the same time. Then I received a phone call from Nassau County Jail. Dave had gotten caught and arrested for possession of crack. I learned that he'd started selling crack when he lost his job. I put on my superwoman cape and flew out of the house, trying to get bail money and a lawyer.

My first visit to the County was okay, until I left, and my muffler fell off the car. That didn't even bother me, because I was happy. He said all the things I wanted him to say on that visit. By the second visit, all that had changed. He was back on that "April won't bring my daughter up here to see me if she finds out that you have been up here."

He didn't have to tell me twice. That was it for me and going up to the jail. I thought, where the hell was April when he needed that lawyer? Did he call her when he got arrested?

He ended up doing next to no time in jail, because of me. He still managed to come home on some bullshit. I didn't see or hear from him when he came home. I found out he was home only because Big D told me. When I finally saw him, he wanted to hold the car. He offered no explanation as to where he had been or why I had to find out through Big D that he was home. He said he had a job interview. I agreed to let him borrow the car, because I was going away for the week to see some friends in Atlanta. I didn't tell Dave who I was going to see. I thought, *Why should I? He didn't care enough about me to even tell me he was home from jail. If he did care, he would have asked who I was going to see or who was I going with.*

Maybe it was best that he didn't ask, because he hated the person I was going to see. After Darnell left Nassau, there was one other guy who found me attractive. His name was Sire, and he was also from Hempstead. We used to hang out in the library, because Sire didn't like the Union. He was a cute brown-skinned boy who stood about six feet tall and wore his hair in dreadlocks. I hated the way his dreads looked. It wasn't nice and neat like some of the guys wore their dreads. He would say that *that* was not the real lock—that's just fashion.

After Damon, I dated both Sire and Dave. Read my words carefully: I said I *dated* both guys, not *slept* with both guys. People tend to get the two mixed up. We hung out, ate dinner, and went to the movies on occasion. There wasn't even any kissing involved. I never lied to either of them, and they both knew about each other at the time. Dave stepped his game up, and Sire played it safe and cool. I chose Dave for that reason.

With all the shit I was dealing with messing with Dave, I knew I had made a bad decision back then. I was going to Atlanta to see a friend but also to make right a wrong. While in Atlanta, I realized I hadn't made a mistake. I realized that I should not have dealt with *either* of them. I was looking forward to seeing Sire and spending time with him to make up for how I'd treated him when he was in New York. I loved the time we'd spent together in the library. Our dialogue was filled with witty banter and snappy comebacks that made us both laugh all the time.

I think Sire had his own get-back plans, because he spent almost no time with us when we were there. We had one brief moment where Sire finally got what he wanted all along. He would tell a different story, of course. He said that I treated him like a dude and used him for sex. When I returned to New York, I just never called him again. I guess I could see why he would feel used, but all he wanted to do was argue while I was there, during the brief periods that he spent with us. That constant bickering was a turn-off for me; besides that, he was too far away *and* not what I was looking for at that time. I don't even know why I slept with him. I think I just needed to feel some sort of connection with a man, and I knew that, at one point, he'd liked me.

The day I returned, Dave called to inform me that my car had broken down in Hempstead on the side of some store. When I asked where the car was, this fool said he left it there. I'd been gone a *week*, and he'd left my car on some street in Hempstead, by a store. I had had enough of Dave and his shit. I had committed myself to Dave, but I had sex with Sire, and I am not a cheater. I always felt that if I had to cheat on a man, then, mentally, I was already checked out of that relationship. The car wasn't worth saving, and neither was my relationship with Dave, so I junked them both. The light at the end of the tunnel was that at least I got $100 for my car.

Dave and I didn't end the relationship in the traditional way of saying it was over. We just never spoke again for months. During that time, I still showed support for Wyatt and Leo's rap group. They had a show, and the after-party was at a club in Hempstead. My friend Regina and I got there early, so I sat at the bar waiting for them to show up. At the end of the bar was a tall, handsome guy. He wasn't really dressed for the party, so I thought he knew somebody who worked there. He was flirting with the bartender as he ordered a drink called a "B-52." I had no idea what the hell that was. I listened as that caramel-colored, picture-perfect guy gave the bartender instructions on how to make the drink.

She couldn't get it right, so she gave him the bottles, and he did it himself. I moved closer, because I wanted to see how it worked. I watched him pour the Kahlua, Bailey's, and Grand Marnier, layer after layer, using the back of the spoon, and then he briefly lit the drink on fire. While he was puckering his lips to blow out the fire, I imagined him puckering those lips to give me a nice, soft kiss on my soup coolers. I always thought my lips were too big for my face, so I used to bite my bottom lip, so no one could see how big it was. After he blew out the fire, he drank it in one gulp.

He noticed I was watching him, so we began to talk. He said he had to go but that he would come back. I didn't believe him. Why would he come back to talk to someone like me? After he left, I was still sitting at the bar, and the owner asked me if I wanted to make some money that night. I agreed to work the coat check and get paid instead of standing around looking stupid. Two hours into the night, still checking coats, someone came to me and said their friend wanted to dance with me. When I looked up, it was him. He really did come back, to my surprise. He had changed his clothes and was standing there looking like the perfectly wrapped Christmas gift. I was making my way over to him like I was a thirsty dog, and he was a puddle of water. He was beyond fine. He gave a new meaning to the word "gorgeous." As we were dancing, I realized I didn't know his name.

When I asked his name, he looked at me strangely. He said, "You don't know who I am?" I assured him I did not know who he was or his name.

He replied, "My name is Floyd." He was still looking at me as if his name was supposed to ring bells. All that I cared about was that this beautiful man was here and dancing with me. Regina was like, "Sharon, who is that? He is cute," she said.

I was sounding like a teenage girl when I said, "Girl, I know."

"Did you give him your number?" she asked.

"I sure did," I replied.

"You can't let something like that get out of here without giving him your number," Regina said, laughing.

I was thinking, *Is he really going to call me or not?*

The next day, he really did call me. He asked me to go out with him, and I jumped at the opportunity to see him again. He told me he was at work and would send his friend, Howler, to pick me up. He said he would meet me at Howler's house. I can't remember where we went that night, but it must have been a good date because we hung out a lot after that. Howler was picking me up night after night, and I never questioned why it had to be that way. One day, while waiting for Howler to come pick me up, Dave called. I told Dave not to call me anymore, because I was seeing someone else now. I was only too happy to say that to him and tell him all about Floyd.

Floyd's name rang several bells for Dave. Floyd turned out to be the baby father of the crazy chick who'd been outside Dave's apartment, the first night I went out with Dave. Floyd was also known for having a lot of money. Dave said that he sold drugs out of state. I didn't believe Dave. I thought he was just jealous because I wasn't waiting around for him anymore. Floyd couldn't have been a drug dealer because he worked in Howler's mother's restaurant in Queens. I thought, *What drug dealer does that?*

I had been to the restaurant a few times and seen him with the apron on myself. I couldn't wait to see Floyd to ask him about everything Dave had told me. Howler never came to pick me up that night, so I called Floyd to find out what had happened. He said he couldn't make it that night. Sexually, I was ready to be with him, so I offered to come to his place by cab. Floyd said he stayed with his grandmother and that she didn't like women in her house. This was the reason, he said, that he'd never invited me to come over.

We talked on the phone for the rest of the night and agreed to see each other the next day. I woke up that day looking forward to seeing Floyd. I was in the middle of picking out one of my prettier outfits when my homeboy stopped by. We were close friends, so I decided to tell him about Floyd. As soon as I said his name, he interrupted me by saying, "Floyd-Floyd!"

"Yes—why? Do you know him?" I asked.

"Shotz, that is my cousin's baby father and fiancé. They live together up the street," he added.

Floyd literally lived seven blocks away from my house. I was crushed after hearing this. This man lives a few blocks away, with a fiancée and a baby. I was mad as hell, so I told him all about Floyd and me and how we'd met. I told him how Floyd used to come over and just lie in bed with me, because I wasn't ready to have sex with him. My homeboy laughed when I told him Floyd would masturbate and cum on the floor. All the pieces were starting to fit together—this is why Howler had to pick me up all the time and why I couldn't go to his house.

I called Floyd while my homeboy was standing there, and he denied living with her but said they did have a baby together. He kept denying everything, until I put my homeboy on the phone. He also admitted to everything Dave told me about him being a drug dealer, except now he didn't sell drugs anymore. He called me "Little Miss," as he offered a lame "I'm sorry." It was cute at the time, but as he said it then, I hated to hear it. I left his ass alone, immediately. I was happy I'd found out before it was all too late for me.

I had to refocus my life again, because I'd allowed another man to come in and wreak havoc. I still wanted another car, and that was my main goal in life at this point. I found a job in Lynbrook as a file clerk, and the bus ride alone was killing me—not to mention the boredom of the job itself. It wasn't bad when the weather was nice, but when it rained or snowed, it was terrible. I would sometimes take the train, but most of the time I took the bus, because I was too lazy to walk to the train station every day. It was a 25-minute bus ride or a 15-minute train ride, then another 10-minute walk from the train or bus stop on Merrick Road to the office building. I took this hike every day faithfully, because it was a means to an end.

One day, while I was waiting for the bus near my house, Howler drove up. I hadn't seen him since that mess with Floyd. Howler was really nice and funny at times. His laugh was childlike. He had fashionable dread, as Sire would say, pigeon toes, and a big belly. His looks were a different story. I didn't like to talk about people in that manner because I was no beauty queen my damn self, but Lord have mercy. Howler offered some truth to the word "evolution."

Howler became a really good friend. He started picking me up almost every other day to take me to work. Some days he would bring me lunch from the restaurant. All my friends knew I had a love for monkeys, so we secretly nicknamed him "Howler Monkey." He thought it was cute because he knew of my love for monkeys, but everyone else knew it was because of his looks.

I thought Howler and his girlfriend had it going on. She actually had her own business next door to the restaurant where Floyd worked. Howler and I became acquaintances through Floyd, but we developed our own friendship, because I found out he knew my sister, Camielle. Camielle and Howler had run track together back in Roosevelt High School. Camielle said he was a cool guy and a good person.

I hung out with him, but just as friends, because I was in no way attracted to him. I would ride with him to Queens every now and then, or we would go to the movies, as I did with many of my homeboys. He started saying things like he missed me when I couldn't go to hang out with him. I paid that no attention because I didn't want to give the wrong impression. During the time I was hanging out with Howler, Dave would call from time to time. One night, I heard a knock at my window, and it was Dave and his friend Jonathan.

"Why would you come here in the middle of the night," I asked, "through the window?"

"Just open the door, and I'll explain," he said.

When I went to the door to let him in, Dave had tears in his eyes. I knew something was wrong, because he was actually crying in front of me. He didn't give me any details, but I knew it was something serious. He said he needed a place to stay for a little while. I couldn't turn my back on him, so I told him he could stay. Dave stayed with me a couple of days, and he noticed that Howler was calling me. I made sure he understood that we were just friends and that there was nothing sexual between me and Howler.

I made sure Dave understood that there was nothing sexual going on between *him* and me, either. Although he didn't deserve it, he had entered "the friend zone" in my book, and I was not going back on my word again. I still didn't understand why he'd come to me. As far as I knew, Dave and April had gotten back together. He said he couldn't share the secret of what had happened that night with April. He knew he could trust me no matter what happened between us.

Dave left my house when he felt things were safe for him, and like always, I did not hear from him again for a long time. A few weeks later, I received a collect call from Dave, saying that April had had him arrested, and he needed me to get him a lawyer. Some of his friends gave me the money, and I retained a former football coach turned lawyer. He suggested that it didn't make sense to post bail, because the most Dave would get is three to five months.

Dave decided to stay in jail, and I didn't want him do time all by himself, so I started going to the jail to visit him. "Please remove all jewelry, belts, and shoes," the officers would say. I think the officers got off on degrading visitors. They loved to see two women come damn near to blows over a man in jail.

"Sign in, Miss," said the tall white man with ring around the collar in his dark-blue uniform shirt.

They made it a point to push the entire sign-in log in your face, which allowed you to see the name of the person who'd visited before you. This would always cause confusion in the visiting room. I became one of the correction officers' joke of the day, because I saw April's name on the list.

"Dave—what the fuck was she doing up here!" I yelled.

"She brought my daughter to see me, and you need to calm down," he said.

"Was she thinking about you seeing your daughter when she had you locked up?" I asked, still screaming.

He ignored my question and asked, "Sharon, did you put money on my books?"

"Did you ask Ms. April if she put money on your books?" I asked, as I got louder and louder.

The corrections officer came over and said that we had to tone it down.

"By the way, Miss, you were told to remove all jewelry, and you are still wearing your nose ring. I have to terminate your visit," he said.

I walked out of that room embarrassed and mad as hell. *Why the hell did I just take two buses up here to listen to that bullshit?*

When I finally made it home, the phone rang as I walked in the door. "Collect call from Dave. Will you accept the charges?" the operator said.

My stupid ass responded with no hesitation. "I will accept the charges, operator."

"Sharon, I need you to be patient. You know I need to see my daughter, but April won't bring her up here if she knows you are coming up here to see me."

"Oh, please, not this shit again!" I screamed into the phone receiver. "Dave, fuck you and that broke bitch April, and don't fucking call me again!"

I hung up the phone and called the operator to place a collect-call block on my phone. I wanted to pack my things and leave New York again, but I decided not to let a man chase me away from my home again. I sat in my room feeling used. Was I some sort of toy that he picked up when he was good and ready? I felt like he'd played me, and I knew he would never be given the opportunity to play me again.

I had graduated from Nassau Community College and decided to continue my education, so I enrolled in John Jay College in the City. School and my work hours began to conflict. The hours they wanted me to work did not coincide with my school hours. There was no way I could make that commute every day. I eventually started looking for another job. God is good, because the week they fired me, I found another job working at a shelter for homeless families. The job was per diem—another word for "part time" or "on call," so my hours weren't steady.

I didn't even know these shelters existed, because they were located in residential neighborhoods, amid the regular homes. They had many houses located throughout Nassau and Suffolk counties. I worked only at the houses in Hempstead and Roosevelt. They had a communal kitchen, living room, and dining room, and each bedroom was named after a famous person. The house in Hempstead housed eleven families and was called the Edna Moran Inn. The house in Roosevelt housed eight families and was called the Rosa Parks Inn.

I was eventually taken on permanent as a salaried employee as the Evening Supervisor Assistant of the Edna Moran Inn. We housed single mothers with their children, single fathers with their children, and husbands and wives with their children. The women in the house were a bit jealous of me, because I was the youngest person on staff, and it appeared that I had something going for myself. That made no sense to me, because I was a paycheck away from being where they were my own damn self.

I got along with the ladies for the most part, but whenever there was a male living in the house, the women would flip the script on me. They would tell my boss crazy stuff, like I was sleeping with this guy or that person's husband. Now, I know I lacked self-worth, but what in the hell would I want with a man living in the shelter? If he had them living in the shelter, what could he possibly do for me? My self-esteem was low, but not rock bottom. My boss saved my job many times, because all I wanted to do was fight all those idiots in that house for just assuming this was a possibility.

The only person who did not act funny toward me was a girl named Crystal. To me, she was the spitting image of Jada Pinkett Smith. She even had the short haircut with the petite body frame. Crystal came to the shelter because she'd caught her daughter's father making love to another man, in their bed. She never trusted another man after that point in her life, and she would only date women.

I didn't understand how someone so pretty could be with a woman. She used to ask me if I ever thought about being with a woman. I didn't even have to think about my answer, because the thought had never crossed my mind. I just didn't see the point in being with a woman. She would also say, "Don't knock it until you try it." I knew that would definitely never happen in my lifetime.

I met her girlfriend a few times when I would sneak her in for Crystal. She was dark-skinned, heavy set, and not that easy on the eyes, but she was one of the sweetest people I have ever met in my life. The saying is true: You can't judge a book by its cover. At first sight, you would think, *What the hell is she doing with her?* But soon after meeting her, you would think, *She would be a fool to let her go.*

All I wanted was a man to love me and treat me like Dina did Crystal. I guess love is love, and you can't control that. I was still in the process of learning to love me. At least that's how I framed it when I had no man and no prospect.

This job did put some money in my pocket but not enough to buy myself a car, so I had to get another job. I took a job at Chase Bank in Jericho. I worked days at the bank and nights at the shelter. I became a workaholic. I was so focused on getting the money for my car that I rarely saw my friends anymore. I had managed to save almost $4000. I had enough to put some money down on the car of my dreams, the Acura Legend. I would look in the paper every day at the price of an old model Legend. I knew I couldn't afford to get something brand new, but I knew I had to have the Legend.

One day, while waiting in the rain at the bus stop, getting ready to go to the day job at the bank, I saw Howler Monkey. He stopped and gave me a ride to Jericho. He was driving a brand-new convertible red Mustang. We started talking, and I told him that I wanted an Acura. He said he had a guy who sold cars that he buys from the auction in Philadelphia. He said he could get me a good deal. I thought, *Great! I won't get beat like I did when I'd bought the Maxima.* I told him how much I had saved, and he said he could double my money for me so I could get a better car. When I asked, "How?" he said he had a man who could flip the money for me. It all sounded really good at the time, but I was a little skeptical. I told him I would have to think about it.

That day at work, all I thought about was his offer. I could finally stop taking the bus, and I could stop working so hard. I had changed my hours at the shelter to overnights, and I'd taken on a job in the evening at Hempstead Honda, as the night receptionist, part-time. I was now working three jobs just to buy a car. After two more weeks of working like a dog, I quit the Honda dealership. It was getting to be too much for me. Howler's offer was sounding better and better every day. He had been giving me rides on a daily basis during this time. He even took me to some guy who was selling an Acura Vigor for $4500, and he also had a 1994 Acura Legend for $10,000. Howler said if I gave him the $4000 I'd saved, he could have $8000 for me in two weeks. I didn't ask any questions about how his friend would flip my money, because I figured some things are best left unknown.

He drove me to the bank, and I withdrew all my money. We were really cool with each other, and I really trusted him. He used to do all sorts of favors for me. When I would get my paycheck from the shelter and the bank, he would drive to Valley Stream for me and deposit my checks in my credit-union account. On a few occasions, I gave him cash to deposit in my account, and if he spent the cash, he would deposit his tenant's rent check in my account, after he'd signed it over to me, of course. We were just cool like that.

Things went on like this for a little while. Around three weeks had passed, and I was calling Howler to find out the status of my money that his friend was supposed to flip, but Howler would never call me back. I would have people take me to his house, but he would have his girlfriend tell me he was not home, even though I would see the car in the yard. I started leaving threatening messages on his voicemail, saying I would call the police and report him for stealing my money. I guess when he heard the messages, he decided to call me back. He had some excuse about getting robbed, but he could still get the money to me in two more weeks. I gave him the benefit of the doubt and agreed to wait two more weeks, in the name of friendship.

At this time, my job at the shelter had switched from giving us checks to direct deposit. I didn't get paid when everyone else got their first direct deposit, and the main office said there was a problem with my bank. I immediately called the credit union to find out what the hell was going on. They told me I had a block on my account, because there had been some fraudulent activity. I explained that I had not been to the bank in months and that those checks could not have been mine.

That's when it hit me: Howler had been depositing his tenant's checks in my account to replace the cash he'd spent. Again, I found myself calling Howler like a madwoman. His explanation for this was that he didn't know the checks he got from his tenants were bad checks and that he would give me my money back. He went so as far as to say he'd thrown the tenant out, because the same thing had happened to his girlfriend's account. I fell for that as well as the lie he told me about having all my money in two days.

The bank finally cleared my account, but I definitely changed all the PIN codes on my accounts. Two days came and went, and still no money or Howler Monkey. I was back at his doorstep every chance I got, when I was able to get a ride. One night, I finally caught up with him at his home because his daughter answered the door and she didn't know to lie to me about his whereabouts. He said he had my money and he would come by later, when his girl came home with the car. I don't know why I just didn't get my money right then and there, and, as you can imagine, "later" never came.

I didn't know what to do at this point. All my money was gone, and I'd feel like a fool if I told anyone what was going on. It was one thing to get played by someone you were sleeping with—but by someone whom you'd given the name "Howler Monkey"? That was too much embarrassment for one person to handle. I kept going to work and calling Howler every day. Then one night, while lying in bed feeling sorry for myself, the phone rang, and, finally, it was him. He said he'd had an argument with his girl the night he was supposed to bring me my money, and she'd run out of the house and got into an accident. He said she completely totaled the Mustang.

"What the hell does any of that have to do with me?" I screamed into the phone.

He said he was waiting for the insurance check to come in, so he could pay me my money. He said he would have the insurance company make the check out to me; that way, I would get my money off the top.

"I want all my money, Howler, and I am not playing with you this time! I want my $4000—the cash you took when you deposited those bogus checks in my account, and the $1900 you ran up on my cell-phone bill!"

Three days later, he showed up at my house with a check from State Farm Insurance Company in the amount of $10,000. It was made out to me, just like he said. He said I could deposit it in my account and just give him the rest after I take my money. I felt relieved that I'd finally gotten my money back after all these months. A portion of the check had cleared, just like he said it would, and I gave him his share of the money, because I'm not a vindictive person. I wrote a check for my cell-phone bill, and I left the rest of the money in my account. My intention was to continue to save my money the old-fashioned way and buy my car eventually. I was through with Howler Monkey, or so I thought.

The following week, the bank manager called to tell me they wanted their money back, because the check was counterfeit. My natural question was, "Why would you clear the money before you found out if the check was bogus?"

"This is the bank's policy," he said, with a stern voice.

The bank seized my account and took what little money I'd managed to save during that time. I was trying to get in touch with Howler, once again, but received no response. I tried to explain that I didn't have the money and that I'd given it to the guy who owed me money. The manager said, "If you don't return the funds, I will call the police on you."

I was scared to death after hearing this. I started calling the U.S. Marshall, FBI, and Nassau County Police to find out what I could do about this situation. They said they couldn't help me and that I had to sue him in civil court. I really think they misunderstood what I was asking. I decided to file charges against Howler. I went down to the First Precinct in Baldwin and explained the situation as well as I could at the time.

That police officer suggested that I check my bank account at the credit union to be sure he had not tried to deposit counterfeit checks there, also.

It turns out that the police officer had hit the nail right on the head. There were at least three checks he'd cashed in the amount of $4500. That was part of the reason they froze my account. The bank gave me copies of the back of the checks, which proved that I did not sign those checks. This man was actually forging my signature.

The Nassau County Police officer suggested that I write down everything that had taken place from the time I'd met Howler. I wrote out a 13-page statement, with exact details of every incident that led to me giving him my money. The other bank manager kept calling me, and I kept telling him the same thing: "I don't have the money—I was scammed." I stopped answering the calls from the bank, because I was sick of talking about it, until I had no other choice. The FBI came knocking at my door.

I was at home babysitting for Bria, and my mother was upstairs in her room, wondering who this white man was downstairs talking to her daughter. I didn't have time to explain to her who he was, because I was busy explaining the whole story to him, from the day I met Howler. He explained that he actually was there to arrest me, but because I had that written statement prepared—and the fact that Howler had done the same thing to a guy in Roosevelt, to the tune of $75,000—he would look into the situation some more before making the arrest. He drove me to Staples and made a copy of the statement I'd written. He was really nice, and, by the time he dropped me off at home, I was calling him by his first name, Dan.

I thought that would be it for now, until the Nassau County Police Department showed up at my door to arrest me. I was scared shitless. They didn't put cuffs on me, but I did have to ride in the back of the police car. I couldn't breathe once they closed that door. I felt trapped. The officers rolled their windows down because they saw I was struggling to catch my breath back there. They kept saying, "Calm down; we don't have far to go. They took me to the Baldwin Precinct, where I'd filed the original complaint. They put me in the room and started asking all these questions. They said the bank manager had called in the complaint. I told them all about my conversation with FBI Agent Dan, and I thought they didn't believe me at first.

I was thinking one step ahead of them. Before I got into the back of that police car, I made sure to bring Dan's business card with me. Officer Carl called Agent Dan, and he explained that there was an ongoing investigation involving Howler. I was once again warned that I should be placed under arrest, but they were letting me go until further notice. Needless to say, I never heard from either law enforcement agency again. The bank manager also never called me again. I also never saw Howler Monkey around town again. I did eventually find out that he'd been arrested and sent to federal prison.

I was back at square one, with no money. I could have kicked myself for what I'd let happen to me. I'd ruined my credit back when I was in college, but it was years later, and I decided to give it a try. I applied for a used-car loan with the credit union, and they approved me. No one could've imagined how happy I was. I went to the Acura dealership with check in hand and drove away with a brand-new (to me) used, green, four-door 1991 Acura Legend. I ordered my personalized plates in the name that Wyatt had given me, "SHOTS." I was so proud of that car.

I felt like I'd had the last laugh on Howler Monkey. He hadn't stopped me from accomplishing my goal. I drove that car with pride, and I wanted everyone to see me in it. I made sure I went around Dave's friends, so he would know I had a new car, and he was still bumming rides. I wanted Howler Monkey to see me most of all, but that was impossible, because he was in jail, where he belonged.

The car didn't help my personal life, because I still had no man. All my friends were on their third or fourth relationships—some, probably, on their fourteenth. Their boyfriends were doing things like taking them shopping, going to the movies, going out to nice restaurants to eat, or just having Blockbuster nights at home. My lonely ass was doing all of those things by itself. I must admit, I kind of liked going to the movies alone. I also spent a lot of time hanging with the girls: Angie, Regina, Racquel, Deidra, and Tina were my world apart from the fellas. I had nothing but work and my friends.

I thought hard about my life up to this point, and I was satisfied with what I had accomplished. I knew one day I would find the man for me. My twenty-fifth birthday was rolling around, and I was planning a big dinner with all my friends. I had never been to City Island, so that was the plan for my day. Everyone had new cars, and they were all lined up on the side of my house. I felt so special because everyone was there to celebrate me. Some of the people weren't really in my circle, but I was happy that they were there anyway. I was known to make a big deal about my birthday, so it was great that so many people had turned out to make a big deal with me.

We took off, and it looked like a funeral precession going down the parkway. When we got there, I went around the table taking pictures with everyone. I was like a kid in a candy store. There were a lot of couples there that night, but I didn't even notice or pay any attention to the fact that I was alone. I drank until my heart was content. I can't say I remember that night too well, but I do know I woke up with Eddie in my bed.

Eddie was a guy from around the way who looked like the rapper Common, but without the money to give him that polished look. I think I offended him because I couldn't remember what the sex was like—or even the fact that we'd even had sex at all. He asked me out to dinner that night after I got off of work. I accepted his invitation, but I wasn't sure about him. He lived in Hempstead, so I thought he knew Dave, and I just did not want to deal with someone else from that town. At dinner, I learned that he was really from Freeport, which was cool, but I'd had my share of guys from this town also.

After dinner we went back to his house, and I couldn't believe what I saw. *How can anyone live like this?* His room was in the attic, and it was filthy—not dirty, but *filthy*. It was a two-family house, and his mother rented both units. Her apartment was on the first level, and she gave her kids the second-floor unit. The bathroom and kitchen on the second floor were disgusting. They mostly used the back door to enter the house, because that is where the house split to separate each apartment. He actually entertained his friends in that breeding ground for roaches. They would actually come over to watch sports and play video games surrounded by that filth. This was our first date, and all I wanted to do was clean. He would allow me only to change the sheets that night, so he could get him some.

The sex was good, but I felt sort of dirty afterwards. Not dirty because I had sex in a filthy room, but because I really didn't know him. In the past, I normally spent some time talking to someone on the phone until I felt comfortable with that person. We didn't spend any real time talking and getting to know each other. We continued to hang out and have sex, and that was basically it. I finally had someone to go to the movies with and eat dinner with, so it was cool. He met my two criteria, which were that he had no kids and he had a job. He made very good money, but he drank and smoked most of it away, whenever he got paid.

None of that bothered me, until I thought I was falling in love with him. I don't know how or when it happened, but it happened. I think it started when he told me that he'd always liked me but thought that I was messing with one of the guys who hung out at my house. People always got things mixed up with me hanging out with so many guys. The guys just saw me as one of the guys, or little sis.

Back to Eddie: I cleaned that upstairs apartment like it was my home. I cooked dinner for him and his friends, and they all thought Eddie was lucky to have someone take care of him like that. He had no real sense of style, and he wore only earth-tone colors. I remember he was invited to go out with our mutual friend, which required him to get dressed up. He kept digging in his closet, coming out with all these old clothes, and none of them was a suit. I went to Roosevelt Field, to this store called Clappers, which sold nothing but the best in men's clothing. I bought him a $500 suit in his favorite color, brown, and surprised him with it. He reacted as if no one had ever done anything like that for him before.

His mother used to say that I was too good for her son. Watching his interaction with his mother made me very uncomfortable. He would say things like, "Shut the fuck up, Ma," and she would answer with, "*You* shut the fuck up. Your dumb ass needs to move out if you don't want to hear my mouth." It was said and done with love, but it was a lot to get used to. I only saw white kids on television talk to their parents like that. The saying goes, "How a man treats his mother is how he would treat his woman."

There was one time when his mother was calling him and calling him, and he would not answer his phone. She finally called me and said she needed a ride to the hospital because her tooth was hurting so bad, and she couldn't take the pain. She said she'd left him messages on his phone, but he wouldn't return her call. When I called Eddie, he answered and said he was on the block gambling with his friends. I told him what was going on with his mother, and he said, "She could take a cab." That should have been a lightbulb moment for me, but I totally ignored that statement.

There were so many signs that he was not the one, but I ignored them all, for the sake of love. He never really committed to being in a relationship with me, but I committed myself to a relationship with him. Some nights, after not going to his house for days, I would find another woman's underwear hanging across the love seat he had in his room. I would get upset, but he would just remind me that I was not his girl. What could I say to that? All I could do is leave upset and mad. Days later he called to apologize for hurting my feelings. I think I was wise enough to know better, but I still accepted his apology out of desperation.

This behavior went on for the next two years. He would hurt my feelings, and I would accept his apology and move on like nothing had ever happened. The really sad part is that I was now 27 years old and still had never been in a "cheatless" relationship. Even more sad was that I was willing to do anything to get Eddie to commit to me. When I met him, he was driving a little tiny red hatchback car. When he said he wanted a new car, I was happy for him. I know you think I was about to say that I bought him a new car, but no. I did the next best thing—I co-signed for his new car. My credit report had been cleared of all past debts, and my credit score was higher than it had ever been. I worked hard at clearing my credit and was determined never to have bad credit again.

I recall a run-in with a bill collector who was very disrespectful, but the experience was very eye-opening. She said to me on the phone, "It's not my fault you can't pay your bills." That was all I needed to wake me up and get my act together. I knew I would never have someone speak to me like that again. I felt comfortable with doing this for Eddie because he had a good job, so I knew he would be good for it. The fact that his mother and sister refused to co-sign for him was not a factor to me. I thought they were just being mean because of how he treated them. Thank God, they were wrong, because he was making his payments. He was really grateful to me for helping him to get that car.

I started spending the night at his house more often, almost like we were in a real relationship. On November 29, 1997, I was sleeping at his house, when I received the worst news of my life. My sister called me to tell me that my father had died. My dad had suffered a stroke when I was sixteen, and he never recovered. I never heard him say my name again. Although we laughed, it was sad to hear him try to speak. He lost the capability to form words after the stroke, and now, he called everyone "Dah-Woo."

He was funny during the first few years of his stroke, when he had the ability to walk. He would get confused as to where the bathroom was, and he would open my room door and try to pee on my friend, Astry, who was sleeping on the floor. He would chase you around with a bottle of hot sauce, as if it were a gun. If you tried to take it from him, he would try to fight you. He was such a strong man, even in his frail state. His condition worsened over the years. He became bedridden and developed bedsores on his back. I never knew what a bedsore was until it became a permanent mental picture in my head. One of them had gotten so bad, it looked like someone had used an ice cream scooper and dug a hole in his back. I still have the image of my mother using sterile cloths to clean them out and packing them with ointment-soaked cottonballs. As I write this, I can't help but cry, reliving this memory.

I told Eddie my devastating news, and he just said, "Sorry to hear that" and turned over and went back to sleep. I wanted him to hold me and allow me to cry in his arms. Because he didn't do that, I hated him briefly. Instead, I went downstairs in that disgusting bathroom and cried into a towel to muffle the sound. Although my dad was definitely in a better place now, losing him was still very hard. Eddie's lack of compassion made it that much harder. I sat in that bathroom remembering the times he'd taken me out to dinner and the things he was trying to teach. I knew, in that moment, why they say girls need their fathers. I wondered if I had developed daddy issues because of his stroke and his inability to be there for me. I believe that, if my father had never had that stroke, I would not have sought out self-validation in boys.

My mother made me feel inferior to my sisters at times, so I would like to think he would've been there to tell me every day that I was his beautiful princess. I wondered if I would have been in all these failed attempts at relationships if he'd been around? Would I have been sitting in that dirty bathroom, crying by myself, when the man I thought I was in love with was asleep upstairs? I realized how much I'd missed out on by not having my father in my life. I needed a break from Eddie because of the stress of losing my dad.

When my dad had the stroke, his eldest daughter, from his ex-wife, was given conservatorship. Yes, she was my sister, but she never liked me, and the feeling was mutual.

My father also had a son, whom he repeatedly called gay. I'm not sure if Pop was right, because I never tried to get to know his son on that level. We all knew Pop wanted to be cremated, and that wasn't a problem. The daughter handled his money, so she made the funeral arrangements. That wasn't the only arrangement she made. After the stroke, my father wouldn't allow anyone to handle him except my mother, so she told my mother as long as my dad was alive, she would pay our mortgage, so my mother could take care of my father. With my father's death, we found out the hard way that she'd reneged on that promise months ago. Our home was currently in foreclosure, and she never said anything. I believe her intention was for me to lose my home.

I personally feel that his daughter was the cause of my father's death. He didn't die from the stroke or the bedsores. He died from septic failure. His teeth started to rot away, and, when my mother asked her to make an appointment with the dentist for him, she refused to do it. Those rotten teeth caused an infection that poisoned his system, causing all of his organs to shut down. All of these things became major issues before my dad was cremated. While making the arrangements for the final viewing, my sister Camielle and I came under attack at the funeral home by his kids' fat cousin. She burst into the funeral director's office wielding a machete. My immediate reaction was to defend myself, so I grabbed the nearest thing to me, which was an antique adding machine he had on the corner of his desk. That thing was heavy as hell, but I picked it up and threw it as far as I could. I don't think I hit her, but she got the message that I was not going out like that. They dragged her out, and we called the police, but she was long gone.

As a result of that altercation, the funeral director refused to hold the service in his place of business, but they convinced him that they would make sure she would not be there. A few days later, she made arrangements for a limo to pick us up and bring us to the service, which was held in Brooklyn. I didn't think anyone from Long Island would show up, but to my surprise, all of the fellas showed up, including Eddie.

When the wake was over, I spent the night with Eddie, but it wasn't the same. The mind holds onto things that the heart is so quick to forget. Trust lives in the heart, and, therefore, it can be re-earned. Respect, for me, lived in my mind, and, therefore, there was no way to get that back. I had lost some respect for him the night I learned of my father's death. I began to distance myself from Eddie, but I knew I still had love for him.

I was preoccupied with trying to get my father's remains before his ex-wife got her hands on them. His ex-wife was known to practice voodoo, according to my mother and father, so there was no way we could let them have his ashes. I was also trying to track down a copy of my father's will. My mother finally told us that, when my father first had the stroke, his sister, Joyce, broke into his desk drawer and took the envelop that contained his will. She had the nerve to give me an envelope with $1000, at the wake. I thought, *You steal his will, which left me everything, and hand me an envelope with what amount to pennies.*

I didn't know where I was going to live. I had no money, and I barely made enough to afford my own apartment. During this time, Eddie had met and started dating this female from his place of work. He told me about her only because she started leaving her panties and personal products all around his room—the room that *I* kept clean. I didn't want my friends looking at me with the side-eye, so I kept her existence to myself. I guess Eddie had other plans for her.

My friend Tina had a New Year's Eve party at her house, and he showed up with Miss Gray Eyes on his arm. I felt disrespected, because he had to have known that I would be here, because Tina was my friend. I lost a little more respect for me, but my stupid heart was still telling me that I loved him. No one could imagine how embarrassed I was, because, up to this point, they thought I was with Eddie. Of course, I played it cool, so none would be the wiser.

When I was able to catch him alone for a few minutes, he apologized for introducing her like this, and he told me that he loved her. In fact, he told everyone that he loved her. Our friends were trying to be kind by saying things like, "She is nice, but you are better for Eddie." That didn't help me at all. *Why can't he love me?* I thought.

I took inventory of my past failed attempts at having a relationship, and I felt like I couldn't deal with life anymore. I retreated to my bed, and I did not eat solid food for two weeks. I barely drank water, and I think I took a shower only every other day. I seriously considered suicide. I was ready to make it happen when my friend Regina called and talked to me for hours. I still say she saved my life, because at that moment, when she called, I had a handful of my dad's medication. So, Regina, if I never said this to you then, here it is in writing: thank you.

The next day, I had a new outlook on life and how I intended on living it. Putting things in perspective, I knew I had to focus on getting a better job and finding a place to live. During the Howler Monkey days, I had applied for a position as a corrections officer in Nassau County. I was forced to withdraw my application because of the situation he had me in with the counterfeit checks. I called to make sure that I was in the clear to reopen my application for corrections and was given the green light.

During this time, I continued to work and act as if the fact that I didn't have a man didn't bother me. I kept my head held high at all events at which Eddie paraded his new woman in front of me. I had to listen to all the places Eddie was taking his new gray-eyed, half-Hispanic girlfriend to. I vowed to myself that I was going to make all those boys regret ever leaving me for someone they believed was prettier than me. I distanced myself from people who I thought were my friends when they found it funny to make statements about me always being alone for every holiday.

My mission to make everyone regret leaving me was failing miserably. My background investigator for Nassau County Corrections was giving me a hard time. I had failed the psychological exam for State Corrections, and I couldn't find a place to live that I could afford. I tried to keep hope alive, as Jesse Jackson would say, because I was up for New York City Police. They were accepting anyone and everyone at that time. I didn't really want to be a police officer, but I knew I had to do something to jump-start my life.

I started jogging every day to prepare for the mile-and-a-half run I had to do for NYPD. The days when Regina didn't come with me or couldn't keep up with me, I ran around that track talking to myself. I cursed every man who'd ever left me. I made promises to myself that I was sure I wasn't going to keep, but it sounded really good at that time and motivated me to make it around the track. Jogging made me forget about my problems. Whenever I got frustrated or angry, I would jog. I also lost a ton of weight. My boss at the shelter would say, "Sharon, if you lose any more weight, I am going to start thinking you are smoking something." Between the crash diet I went on after losing Eddie and preparing for NYPD, I went from a size 8 down to a size 4.

I felt great about myself, and then more bad news hit. I was disqualified from NYPD and Nassau County Corrections based on the failed psychological exam for State Corrections. Out of sheer frustration with being disqualified, I wrote a letter to Nassau County Corrections, Civil Service Commission, stating that I would have a lawyer contact them, because they had no grounds for disqualifying me. I had passed everything, including their psych exam, but they didn't choose me because I failed the State psych exam. Nothing was going right for me at all. I told a friend, who happened to be Eddie's cousin, about my failed attempts at law enforcement, and he suggested I apply for Federal Corrections because there was no test. I had nothing to lose at this point, so I sent in the application.

My twenty-eighth birthday was rolling around, and I was starting to feel depressed again. I was scared because we had lost the house, and everyone had to move out. My niece, Yvonne, had moved out, and Lorraine was on her way out, also. My friend Regina offered to let me stay with her and her family, but I didn't feel right about that. I knew I had to find a job that would pay me enough to afford my own place, and that's when I received a call from the Metropolitan Detention Center in Brooklyn. I went to the interview, and I was super-honest about everything. They didn't care about the Howler Monkey situation, or the previous disqualifications, just as long as I told the truth. I left there feeling confident but still unsure.

When I got home, my sister said she'd found an apartment in Queens for her and her family. My brother and I were the last ones left to find a place. I took my brother with me apartment hunting in Queens, but the place we saw was small and in the basement of a multifamily house, with the entrance in the backyard. I just pictured me coming home late at night and someone snatching me down into the dungeon. It was $500 a month, and, although the price was right, I was scared of that place, but it was perfect for a single guy. As my luck would have it, I went apartment hunting for myself and found my brother a place instead. To top it all off, I later found out that I didn't get the job at the Federal Bureau of Prisons, Metropolitan Detention Center.

One day, while throwing myself a pity party in the backyard, sipping on my favorite drink of Hennessy and ginger ale, smoking a Newport cigarette, Eddie stopped by. We talked for a little while, and I poured my heart out to him about my living situation. To my surprise, he said I could move in with him. Of course, I asked about Ms. Gray Eyes, and he said that it just hadn't worked out. He said he had to check with his mother first, but he was sure it would be okay. I appreciated the offer, and I wanted to make that my last resort, but I knew time was running out. I was the only person who didn't have a place to go. So, out of sheer desperation, a few weeks later, I moved into Eddie's house.

First things first: in order for me to be able to call this my home, I got down on my hands and knees and scrubbed that bathroom. I bought pots and pans, so that I could cook after I went food shopping. Although I was sharing his room and bed, he was still hanging out, as if I weren't there. He started spending the night out almost every night. I didn't question him about it until I received a phone call that he was sleeping with an associate of ours. I was painfully aware that I was not his girlfriend, so I had to suck it up, because I had no place to go. This particular girl was known for sniffing coke and was rumored to have herpes. I asked Eddie about what I'd heard, and he denied it.

I didn't want to believe it until she called me; in a disrespectful manner, she said, "You are a little girl, and Eddie wants a real woman. Eddie is my man now, and he's where he wants to be." I couldn't understand the purpose in her calling me to say that he was her man now, as if to say she'd taken him from me. We were not together, and I was positive that he told her that, just as he did with everyone. I told her she could have him, but she would not call my phone and be disrespectful to me.

Disrespect from a woman was something I had no tolerance for. So I surely drove over to her house in Freeport—and guess who was there? He came running outside, telling me to leave and go home and that he would see me later. She was yelling out the window, "Eddie, send that little girl home, and come eat your breakfast." I just looked at him and said, "You are not worth it. Stay here with that coked-out, herpes-having whore."

When he returned to his house, he apologized and said, "She's not my girlfriend—she made all that up." He had the nerve to try to have sex with me, but there was no way that was happening after hearing all the rumors about her having herpes. He really tried hard to get me to believe that he'd always used a condom when he slept with her. I didn't fall for it. All men say that when they get caught. I continued to sleep in the same bed next to him but without any sexual benefits.

Christmas was rolling around, and soon it would be the year 2000. I had just turned 29, living with a man who did not respect me or the fact that I was living with him in his home. He blatantly told me, "Just because you are living here doesn't mean we are together." In fact, he charged me $200 a month to sleep in his room. His mother said I didn't have to pay her anything, but the man I loved made me give him money monthly. In my mind, I still felt entitled to some respect. He got tired of the constant arguing over that issue, and he asked me to move out. His mother knew I didn't have a place to stay, so she gave me her daughter's room. Eddie still collected his $200 a month for me staying in his sister's room. I hated my life with a passion, and I secretly wished for death.

A few days before Christmas, I received a phone call from the Metropolitan Corrections Center, asking if I still wanted a job with the Bureau of Prisons. I said, "Sure, but I thought they had disqualified me. The lady on the phone informed me that it was two different institutions. She also made me aware of why I was not selected for the Brooklyn Jail. She actually called my old job on a three-way call and straightened out the problem. Then she asked if I wanted to come in on the second of January. I agreed because I was on vacation from the shelter, and I had time to run around. I had become very familiar with the process of applying for law-enforcement jobs and the constant back-and-forth. They make you jump through all these hoops, build your spirits up, and then let you down hard.

On Monday morning, I took the train to Manhattan, because I was scared to drive in the City. I was ready for my second interview with the feds. When I got there, I learned that it was my first day of work. I had no idea that the process for the feds would be that easy. I thought I was just going in for an interview, but instead I had to call and quit the shelter. I was excited and scared at the same time. During that same week, I had received a letter from Nassau County asking if I still wanted the position as a Corrections Officer, but I gave them my ass to kiss because they'd put me through too much, and, besides that, I had a career in law enforcement with the feds now.

The first two weeks of work were spent in Institution-Familiarization Class. I was quiet because I felt like the oldest person in that classroom. Now that I think about it, I was. They would have different people come in to teach class every day. When the union reps came in, I thought, *Wow— he is a really cute guy.* My self-esteem was shot to hell at that point, so it didn't even make sense to look twice at him. I knew he wouldn't want me anyway. Besides that, I was done looking for a man, and all I wanted was a better job. Honestly, I thought that was all I could handle at that point.

Once we started working the actual housing units, I realized there was money to be made here and an opportunity to grow. Because I was on a probationary rotation, my schedule changed every two weeks at first. They had changed my shift to evening watch, which was 4 p.m. to midnight. I would normally get home somewhere around 1 a.m.

The weather had started to break, and it was nice outside. His sister's room used to get really hot, so from time to time, I would go upstairs to Eddie's room when he wasn't home, because he had air conditioning. Eddie had a habit of leaving the television on, and he was also known for watching a lot of porn. It was no surprise when I heard sex moans as I walked up the stairs. I was busy running my mouth with my homegirl, Angie, who lived around the corner from Eddie, when I realized it wasn't the television. My eyes might have been deceiving me, but my ears weren't. I heard her say, "Fuck me—fuck me harder," as they proceeded to change positions.

My feet were stuck in place, and I couldn't speak. I couldn't formulate words that would make any sense of what my eyes were seeing in front of me. Most women always say they would throw hot water or hot grease on their man if they ever caught him with another woman. I learned firsthand that your brain shuts down, your feet don't move, and your heart stops. Angie was on the phone yelling my name, because I wasn't answering her. The girl opened her eyes and saw me standing there. She screamed, "Oh, shit!" Eddie looked up at me and said in the calmest voice, "Can you please excuse us?"

Angie was screaming into the phone, "Shotz, do you want me to come over there?" I couldn't focus on her words. I turned and went back downstairs to change out of my uniform. I could not believe what I had just seen, and I knew I'd had enough of this disrespectful bastard. I told Angie I would call her back as I changed into my sneakers and sweatpants. I went back upstairs and looked at him with disbelief in my eyes. He said, "Sharon, go downstairs. I will come down and talk to you in a minute. Just let her get dressed." I really didn't smoke, but when I took a pull on a cigarette, it gave me a head rush that calmed me down. I looked at him and said, "Just let me get a cigarette." This bitch had the nerve to open her mouth and say, "Baby, we have only one left."

I didn't realize my feet were moving toward her until Eddie stopped me dead in my tracks and yelled for her to just give it to me. I took the cigarette and went downstairs to the backyard. I started pacing up and down the long driveway. I went from the front of the house to the back of the house, taking long drags on that cigarette. I realized that his car was not parked in the driveway or in the front of the house. This told me that he was trying to be sneaky when he brought her there. I thought to myself, *That bastard was in my room just the night before trying to sleep with me, but I turned him down again.* I didn't care that I wasn't his girlfriend, in title, but after everything I had done for him, I deserved respect. What the fuck was he thinking—bringing this bitch up in here with me living in his house?

I decided I was going to whip someone's ass that night. I had had enough disrespect and disappointment from men, and Eddie and this chick were going to be on the receiving end of my wrath. I started wondering, *What the fuck is taking them so long to come downstairs?* As I went toward the back door, I heard loud banging and saw his mother on her knees, fiddling with the door leading into her apartment. She asked if I was okay, and I played it cool, saying, "Yes," and I proceeded to go upstairs. It was quiet when I got to the second floor. I went up to the attic, but they were gone. *How the hell did they get past me?* I thought.

I remembered his mother downstairs banging on her lock at 1:30 in the morning. I instantly knew what had happened—she had let them escape through her apartment. While I was in the backyard, she must have let them leave through the front door of her apartment. At that moment, I lost respect for her, too. I believe that right is right, and wrong is wrong. As a woman, she knew what her son was doing was wrong. I am not an ungrateful person, and, therefore, I will always be thankful to his mom for opening her home to me, but I was hurt and disappointed that night. I believe she should have let him face the music. I guess being a mother overruled the ability to speak up against right from wrong.

It almost seemed as if it were perfect timing, but the feds sent new officers away to training in Glynco, Georgia. I was happy to go away, even if it was for only three weeks. I went away for training, but I could not stop thinking about what had happened. During training, I was blessed to have gotten my own room. I loved the people who were in my class, but sometimes I wanted time to myself. There was this guy in class by the name of Steve. I found him to be really attractive. He had really nice eyes, brown skin, with a medium build. His walk was very similar to my father's, which made me even more attracted to him. He was closer to my age than the rest of my classmates, so we had a little more in common. We hung out sometimes after class. I realized how immature some people can be. In Glynco, if you hung out with someone of the opposite sex, everyone assumed you were sexing each other.

The day he came to my room turned into a gossip moment for my classmates. Little did they know that on the other side of that door was a therapy session—a well-deserved, deep conversation that I needed to have. He allowed me to talk about my childhood, straight through to Eddie, and held me as I cried. He was just what I needed at exactly the time I needed it. He actually lived in Georgia, and if we hadn't been so many states apart, I could have seen myself loving him for life. I was angry with the people in my class for turning that special moment into something degrading and demeaning.

By the third week of training, I felt so close to Steve that we did end up sharing an intimate moment. When we left Glynco, I did tell him that I wished I could take him with me, however, I would settle for a phone call every now and then. He was the only good thing about training, besides being away from Eddie.

Once I touched down in New York, I had to figure a way out of Eddie's house. The final straw came when I came home from work on the fourth of July. I found my pet parakeet, Ojay, dead. I'd had that bird for five years, and I loved him like he was family. I never left Ojay in the dark; I would always leave the television on or some other light source. On that day, Eddie's mother went into my room and turned off the light, and my bird died. I loved that bird so much that I laid him to rest with my father's ashes.

A few days after the death of my bird, I began a rigorous search for an apartment. Long Island was my home and all I knew, but I could not afford to live here on my own. I had landlords telling me that I couldn't have company after 10 o'clock at night. I had another telling me I could not park my car in their driveway or in front of the house. Another landlord was trying to rent me a basement apartment for which I had to share the bathroom and kitchen with their son. I had no other choice but to put Long Island behind me.

I had to go back to where it all started and the only borough I was familiar with. I contacted a local newspaper called *The Loot*. The first place I called said they had a one-bedroom apartment for $700 a month. With my new job, I was able to afford that with no problem. The realtor took me to a four-story walk-up building on Hawthorne Street in Flatbush. And, again, with my luck, the apartment was located on the fourth floor. That walk up to the fourth floor showed me that I was not in as good a shape as I thought I was.

Upon entering the apartment, I fell in love with the high ceiling and the huge bedroom. The bathroom was outdated, and the kitchen was small, but the living room was perfect for me. The realtor said they wanted one month's rent and one month's security deposit—plus the realtor's fee was equal to a month's rent. I had some money saved, but not that much. I was stressed out because I really wanted this place. I asked if I could use my credit card, and she turned me down. She suggested that maybe I could get a cash advance on my card. I knew that I could take a cash advance, but I also knew that I didn't have a large enough limit to get what I needed.

I called the credit union to see if they could raise my limit based on my new job. It took them two days to let me know that it was approved. I immediately called to see if the apartment was still available, and it was. I brought the check right over to the realtor and signed the lease, and she handed me the keys. I was free at last. I started telling people at work I needed to move, and I had no way of getting my things to Brooklyn. I had three officers at work agree to help me move. Officer Walkes and Officer Murphy came with me to Eddie's house and loaded up the vehicles. They barely knew me, and they were willing to help me. I could hardly find the words to express my gratitude to them.

When we finally got to Brooklyn and they realized I lived in a four-story walk-up, I am positive they were regretting their decision. My friend from the job, Ivy, gave up after a few flights up those steps, carrying my shoes. I didn't have anything, really. I didn't even have a bed. My friend Raquel offered a mattress and box spring from her boyfriend's mother. I had no choice but to accept it, because I didn't have much money left after the move. The other problem was getting it to my new apartment. This is where Eddie showed just how happy he was to get rid of me. He asked his friend to help me get the bed, my love seat, and the oversized chair that I had stored in his basement to Brooklyn. They, too, were upset when they found out it was a walk-up, but everyone really liked the apartment.

I think Eddie liked it too much. He worked at the phone-company building near my job, so my apartment was convenient for him. I was fifteen minutes from Manhattan. The first night I let him spend the night, he left his shoes at my place. When I saw those shoes, something in me turned upside down and inside out. I'd busted my ass to get this apartment on my own, and he thought he was going to move in there, one shoe at a time. I let him know that his moving in there was not an option. He, of course, claimed he wasn't trying to.

We didn't see much of each other from that point on. A phone call here and there was too much for me. All of the phone calls to Eddie were in regard to having my name taken off of his car and money he owed me. I actually had to take him to small claims court for the money he owed me. He thought he wouldn't have to pay me until the mediator informed him they will garnish his wages. After he paid me the money in full he claimed the car company wouldn't take my name off. Then I started getting letters from the car company saying he was not paying the bill, and with me being the co-signer, I was responsible for the past-due amount. Finally, I got tired of the bullshit and told them to repossess the vehicle. I told them where he parked the car, and they went and picked it up. He had to pay all the money owed on the vehicle before they would give it back to him. He finally paid the money and got the car back. Needless to say, I never had to worry about another late car payment again. When he finally paid the car off, I thought, *Yes—I am done with the Eddie saga, and my credit is safe.*

At work, the cute Union Rep from Institution Familiarization class started calling me on the housing unit. His name was Tank, and he had a medium build with a beige skin complexion. When I found myself looking forward to his phone calls, I thought, *Oh, I am in trouble.* While waiting for his phone call, another officer came into my unit, and, under the guise of general conversation, he commenced to giving me the rundown on the men in the building. The other guys in the building would call him a certified cock-blocker. This guy had one of the biggest heads I had ever seen on anyone. He wore his hair in an ill-shaped afro, which accentuated his extremely large head. I was new in the building, so I still listened to his gossip. He said, "A lot of guys in here are married but don't wear their wedding rings, so be careful of who you talk to."

I responded by saying, "I didn't come here for that," but in all reality, I was very open to the idea. Naturally, as soon as Tank called me, I asked him if he was seeing or dating anyone. He admitted that he'd just broken up with a really nice girl, because it just wasn't working out. I believed him, so I gave him my home number. He called later that night, and we talked for a few hours. We agreed to hang out one day after work. We also agreed to meet in a public place. He didn't mind coming out to Long Island, so I suggested Northeast Park. All of my friends hung out there including Eddie, so I got to give him a taste of his own medicine.

Tank mingled and interacted with my friends like he'd known them forever. All the girls thought he was cute, and that was a major plus for me. The other major plus was that he was not a local Long Island guy. He was a little corny at times, but I just thought that was because he was from Jersey. We hung out like this a few more times, and then he asked when I was going to come out to Jersey. It was only fair that I should make the trip to Jersey, but I put it off for as long as I could. He never let me forget that I said I would come out there. Every conversation ended with, "When are you coming to Jersey?"

I gave in, he broke me down, and there I was in New Jersey. He took me around the town, and then we went to his house. I met his dad, who was very nice. His father cooked shrimp and lamb chops for dinner, and we ate as a family. The meal was great, and I thought to myself, *I could get used to this*. After dinner, Tank took me on a tour of the house, with the last stop being his bedroom. It was very plain and ordinary: a bed, a computer desk, and a couple of nightstands. I can't remember how the sex started, but it wasn't bad, as far sex goes. He wasn't small, and he wasn't super large—it was just right. There was no kissing, just a lot of playing. Not like foreplay type of playing. He really got off on play fighting, similar to wrestling, and tickling.

On my way home, the night ended with a long conversation about him. When I actually thought about it, he spent a lot of time talking about himself. He mostly complained and whined about his arm. There had been some incident in which he'd fallen, and now one arm was longer than the other. You couldn't even notice it, until he pointed it out.

I put this annoying behavior aside, because I really wanted things to work out with us. He was different from the other guys I was used to, and I felt I needed a change. I also wanted to hold on and see where this could go, because he sought me out at a time when my self-esteem was gutter level. We kept our *thing* to ourselves when we were at work. We did a lot of talking on the phone, and he made a few visits to my apartment in Brooklyn; then it was time to go back to Jersey.

I remember that day very well. I wore a blue, floral-print mini-skirt, a white tee-shirt, a blue denim vest, and tan, open-toed sandals. When I got there, his dad appeared happier to see me than Tank was. His father prepared another meal for me, and, after we ate, he retired to his room. Tank and I went to watch television in the small den. The lights were dim, and I was sipping on my favorite drink, Hennessy and ginger ale, while watching one of my favorite movies, *Menace to Society*.

Approximately 10 minutes into the movie, there was a knock at the window, on the side of the house. Tank got up and went to the window with a nervous look on his face. As he turned to me, he said, "Damn."

I took a sip from my glass and asked, "Who is that?"

He said, "Kerry," very nonchalantly.

I asked him, "Who the hell is 'Kerry'?"

He simply said, "The girl I recently broke up with" and proceeded to ask me to keep quiet—and maybe she would go away.

As he said those words, a knock came from the front door, loud and strong. Her voice yelled out, "Tank, I know you're in there. Open the door!"

I looked at him, took another sip from my drink, and said, "Go open the door."

He said, "She's going to want to fight you."

I replied, "I have no problem with fighting her, but why am I fighting her?"

He said, "I was with her, but we are not together anymore."

I gave him a puzzled look, because that reason made no sense at all. I thought, *If you are not together anymore, then why is she here acting the fool?*

During this time, she was still yelling and banging on the front door. I told him to go handle his business. At this point, his dad was on his way down the stairs because of the banging on the door. Tank opened the door, and it was like something straight out of a cartoon. She snatched him off his feet and out the front door all in one motion. His father and I stood at the door and watched as they rolled around on the grass. It was actually comical to watch, but I displayed discretion and held back my laughter.

When it was over, Tank came inside, and all he could say was that she had popped his chain. She wasn't done yet—the banging on the door began again. This time, his father answered the door, and she said that she wanted to talk to me. His father came into the room, and I was sitting down, still sipping my drink; he asked if I wanted to talk to her. I really didn't care at this point, so I said, "Sure, why not?"

When she came into the house, she was obviously still very upset, but she sat down and calmly asked me if I knew that they were dating. I told her what I would tell any woman, "I have no loyalties to you—he does. For the sake of argument, he told me that he was not seeing anyone."

She started crying and proceeded to leave the house. I told Tank that he had nothing else to say to me, and I was ready to go home. He was trying to plead his case, as his father was telling him that he should not be lying to these women.

"Excellent advice. Tank, you should listen to your father," I said sarcastically. All I knew was that I was in Jersey and had no clue how to get home. She started calling on the phone, and Tank was busy trying to calm her down. I was over the situation, so I asked his dad if he could show me how to get home.

Tank had no clue that I had left his house. I made it all the way back to Brooklyn before he noticed I was gone.

Then he called my cell phone with the bullshit, "I am so sorry, and I didn't mean for that to happen like that. We were dating, and things weren't working out, and that's why I said I wasn't seeing anyone."

I've heard it all before, I thought. All I wanted was a drama-free relationship. What I learned from my brief encounter with Tank was that even the nerdy type comes with drama and lies. I was a little hurt, because I was really starting to like him, despite some of his annoying attributes. I was also thanking God that my heart wasn't vested in him.

The next few months were spent with him apologizing. I did notice the people at work staring at me like I was crazy. Kerry had spread the word among her friends, and they all hated me. They felt that she was prettier than me, and so they wondered why he would mess around with someone like me. I really didn't care, because I hadn't betrayed her. We were never friends, and he lied to me, just like he did her.

I really don't understand why a woman gets mad at the other woman. There are rules for that type of situation, and for every rule, there is an exception. If the entire world knows that he is your man and you are his woman, and another female comes at your man knowing full well that he is spoken for, then, by all means, she deserves whatever comes her way. However, if you choose to keep your relationship secret, then he is responsible for your feelings. It is his responsibility to forsake all other women. I believe that, if I'd really been disrespectful to her, then by all means she should feel away about me. I never disrespected her or any of her friends, so I felt slighted when they bad-mouthed me.

He and I eventually became friends after that incident. I won't lie—I did consider getting back with him at some point, but I learned that she was not the only person he was seeing, so I was done with him.

The Thirties

My 30th birthday came and went. I remember hanging out with my friends but still feeling very sorry for myself. Thirty years on Earth, and I was still feeling alone and undeserving of the opposite sex.

The New Year rang in again. It was 2001, and I was determined not to give up hope of finding a decent man, before I died. I was off probation at work, and I was graduating at the end of the month from St John's University, with my Bachelor's Degree in Criminal Justice. Tank said he would be there to show his support, but like every other guy in my life, he let me down. Only my sister and mother were there to see me graduate. Nothing would have been better than to have a man waiting with flowers and a big kiss, saying, "I love you, and I am proud of you."

Since Tank had received his third strike with me, I started hanging out after work with a few co-workers. I did whatever I could so that my life wouldn't seem so blah. It was early February, and stupid Valentine's Day was coming up. I wondered who'd put this damn day on the calendar. They had a Valentine's Day party at the church around the corner from the jail, which was nice, but it seemed like I was committing a sin.

A few of us had the same idea, so we decided to go to this little bar in Brooklyn, on the corner of Troy and Atlantic Avenue. I was enjoying myself laughing with my girl, Square, about our friend, Kane, who had a love for the ladies. Then the guy every woman was warned about when they started the job walked in. His name was "Big Saint," or just "Saint"—that's what everyone called him. He was the poster child for sex appeal. I'd noticed him when I started working at the jail, but he seemed to have a bad attitude. He came off as if the world revolved around him. His girlfriend had the same stinking attitude. I made it my business not to speak to either of them. In fact, I started calling them "Lurch" and "Lurchette," because they were both so damn tall.

Anyway, there was this group of girls checking him out as he made his way over to the bar, where we were. They had no discretion about wanting him. When one of the ladies finally got up the nerve to approach him, he turned and grabbed my arm. I had that deer-in-the-headlights look on my face when he told that lady that I was his girlfriend. She smiled at me and said, "You are one lucky girl, and you'd better hold on to him because somebody is going to snatch him up."

He whispered in my ear, "Don't leave me." I just smiled, and we started dancing. After that night in the bar, he actually started saying "Hi" at work. I thought to myself that maybe I shouldn't have judged him so fast.

After work one night, I invited him and a few co-workers to my place to play spades. When everyone finally found parking and made it upstairs, we had some drinks and were setting up to play spades when the phone rang. I told them to put in a movie and that I would be right back. I went into my bedroom to answer the phone, and it was Tank on the other end. I didn't tell him that I had company, so I devoted my time to talking with him on the phone. It was more of the same thing—him saying how sorry he was, and me saying it was over.

When I finally got off the phone, it was so late that everyone was ready to leave. I had to apologize for that night for at least a week. I think Saint came over thinking he was going to get some ass that night. He kept coming back, asking if I really wanted everyone to leave. I played stupid, but I knew what he was asking. Did he think that, just because he was very handsome, it would be that easy? Besides that, I knew he had a girlfriend, and I was not going down that road.

We all decided to hang out again, but this time at Saint's house on the other side of Brooklyn, in a town called Bushwick. He had a room in the basement, and, like a typical man, it wasn't properly furnished. He had a California King-size bed and a fish tank with more algae than fish. We needed drinks, so Square and another officer I'd given the nickname "No Neck" went to the liquor store. Saint took that moment as an opportunity to bring up that night at my house. I felt I had nothing to hide because I thought it was all over the jail anyway, so I told him the truth about who I was actually talking to.

I used the moment to ask about him and Lurchette. He responded with those magic words, "We are not working out." He further stated that she had children and that he just couldn't raise some other man's child. I could relate because I felt the same way after dealing with Dave and his daughters. I was still a little confused, because she had her children when they met, so I asked, "Why have you let it go on for so many years?" He said he wanted to try to make it work, but he just didn't care for her children in that way. We laughed it off, because I could relate to that as well. Then Square and No Neck returned from the liquor store.

I don't remember who won the card game, but it was getting late and time to go home. Saint hugged me goodnight and whispered in my ear, "Come back." I didn't know my way around Brooklyn very well, so I had no clue how to get back to his house. I think deep down I knew what would happen if I went back, and I just didn't want to take it there. We had exchanged phone numbers, and he called me while I was on my way home. He was still trying to convince me to come back to his house, saying he would give me directions. I made up some excuse about being almost home and very tired.

The next time we all hung out was February 27, 2001. I remember that date, because that was the day he convinced to come back after everyone left. I had to park my car on the side street because No Neck lived right up the block. It started out with us talking, and then he kissed me. I just kept thinking, *Is this real? Is he really kissing me? Does he not see my crooked teeth? Why is he doing this?*

All my guards were down. He had me right where he wanted me. I was under his spell from that moment on. I don't even remember my clothes coming off. I only remember being on top of what seemed like Mount Fuji and a volcano starting to erupt inside of me. He could tell something was happening to me that I'd never experienced before, and he whispered, "Just let it happen." I was so scared. I thought something was wrong with me. When I climbed down off the mountain, all I wanted to do was leave. I jumped up and said, "I have to go!"

He held me close and said, "You don't have to leave." I don't know why, but I felt embarrassed. So I got dressed and left. He called me on my way home to ask if I was okay, so I broke down and told him the truth, which was that I had never experienced that feeling before like that. He was so understanding and thoughtful about my revelation. He managed to gain my trust a little more in that moment. At work we maintained our co-worker-based friendship, and, at night, I allowed him to keep attempting to give me that thrill.

Approximately two months into our arrangement, he said he was going on vacation to visit his brother in Florida. I took him to the airport, and we kissed like we were never going to see each other again. He called me constantly while he was there, which made me feel special. Back at work, while listening to some of Lurchette's friends talk about her and her kids on vacation in Florida, I realized Saint had lied to me. I couldn't wait for him to call me, and, so, I called him, but he didn't answer the phone. I tried calling back to back, but he still was not answering the phone.

I couldn't sleep that night until I spoke to him. Then finally he called. He asked if something had happened, because I was calling so much. I gave him my speech: "Listen, you don't have to lie to me, and if she is what you want, then we can just be friends." I could tell he didn't even flinch when I caught him in his lie, and he said, "I am sorry I lied to you, but I didn't think you would understand. She'd booked this trip a while ago because she wanted me to spend more time with her kids to see if I would change my mind." I literally just sat on the phone listening to him complain about his trip. I'd forgotten that he'd lied to me, until he asked me to pick him up from the airport. Then it hit me—*he is using me for a ride.* So I said, "No."

A few days later, he showed up at my apartment with flowers and a gift-wrapped box. (I forgot to mention that this man had me so open, in this short period of time, that I had already given him a key to my apartment. I didn't speak to him until I walked into my apartment and found the one dozen peach-colored roses and a multi-colored shade of blue Gucci knit dress. I was in awe over the gesture. I had never had anyone do something so nice for me.

I forgave his lie and invited him over for a home-cooked meal. The dinner I made that night escapes me at the moment, but I remember him saying, "Wow, you can really cook." He compared my food to his mother's cooking, and he thought his mother was the best cook ever. My apartment became our little secret hideaway. Like I said before, parking was difficult on my block, but Saint would park his car almost two blocks away. *Who is he hiding from over here?* I always wondered.

That following weekend arrived, and he called, saying he was going to Woodbury Commons Outlet Mall, and asked if I wanted to go. Of course, I said, "Yes." On the car ride up there, we talked and got to know each other a little better. We talked about our college days and people we'd dated. I wanted to gain his trust, so I opened up about myself a little more. I wanted him to be my confidant, so I told him about the number of abortions I'd had and the number of men I'd had sexual encounters with. I say "encounters," because I didn't have sexual intercourse with everyone, but there was something about me that made men want to *taste* my love. I hoped he would see it as honest and trustworthy, because I could have been like several other women and lied about the infamous number. It was a very enlightening conversation.

Once we arrived at the Outlet, his words became icing on the cake for our secret affair. He said, "Get whatever you want." I'd never had someone take me shopping, and it felt really good. I knew I was dating a different caliber of man than I was used to. I was finally being treated the way I'd always wanted to be treated. He sat there and watched me try on clothes, gave his opinion, and purchased everything. I can't forget that he complimented me on my shape with almost every outfit. That was a big deal for me, because my self-esteem was as low as a run-down shoe heel.

I wasn't greedy about the shopping spree, but I did get a lot of stuff, and I couldn't stop thanking him. I told him that no one had ever done anything like that for me before. He felt good about making me so happy. I was falling hard for him, and I was scared to let myself go down that road again. I tried with everything I had not to fall in love quickly, so, as a distraction, I decided to have a ladies' night at my place.

My idea of ladies' night was to have all my female friends over and invite a few guys over to cook dinner for the girls. I enlisted the assistance of a male co-worker to round up a few guys. The night was going extremely well. None of the guys were in the same league as Saint, but if nothing else, I made new friends.

Saint was at work, and he kept calling to see who was at my apartment. The next call I received said he'd been brought to the hospital with chest pains. I grabbed my bag and car keys, and ran out the door, totally forgetting that I had company in my house. By this time, my niece Yvonne and I had forgiven each other, and she also lived in Brooklyn, not too far from me, so I called her to ask her to lock up my apartment when everyone left.

When I got to the hospital, the jail's gossip king was there with him. So, I played it cool and acted like a concerned co-worker. Saint was shocked to see me there. The first thing he said was, "I can't believe you left your party. You didn't have to come all the way down here. I'm okay." They are running some tests, but I should be fine." He ran everything down in one breath. I drew the curtain and kissed him for dear life.

I stayed at the hospital until they released him, sometime during the middle of the night. In the back of my mind, I was wondering, *Where is Lurchette?* I took it as a good sign that he was telling the truth about their situation. I think he saw me in a different light after that night in the hospital. At least, I hoped he did.

I had to put him through my personal test, so I invited him to my niece Marie's housewarming party, to meet my family. For me, this was a major test. I wanted to see if he would react to seeing the prettier women in my family. After the situation with Yvonne and Javon, I no longer trusted any man around my family members. Saint didn't seem to notice, or at least he pretended very well not to notice any of them. Whatever the case, I was impressed. He was scoring major points with me all across the board.

We continued to hang out in groups with our co-workers and then meet up afterwards at my place or his. We sparked suspicion with our diversionary third wheel, Officer Dee. He and I had become good friends, but he and Saint were inseparable. There was a new club in Brooklyn, on Tilliary Street, right over the Manhattan Bridge, and we all decided to go clubbing one night. I tried my best not to show any reaction to Saint's behavior, but all my life, my face has shown whatever I was thinking. Some people wear that heart on their sleeve, but I wear my feelings on my face. Someone would know what I was thinking before I ever opened my mouth.

Walking through the club, I saw Saint and his best friend, Guiliani, chatting it up with these females, and that gut feeling hit hard that something was not right with that picture. As I walked over, he had that "Oh, shit!" look on his face. He tried to play it off as if they were talking to Guiliani and hustled me to the bar to buy a drink as a distraction. The moment he brought the drinks, he disappeared again.

I found Officer Dee and stayed next to him the rest of the night. Officer Dee noticed that I was watching Saint's every move from the corner of my eye the entire night. Being the person that he is, he didn't say anything then. Officer Dee and I decided to go take a picture together. In the line, some guy kept bumping into Officer Dee, and he took it the first time, but the guy did it a second time and didn't apologize, so things got a little heated. As I was talking Officer Dee down of the ledge from whooping this guy's ass, his girlfriend approached, and things went from bad to worse. Officer Dee ended up having to stop me from fighting this chick. I knew that I was really mad at Saint, but at that point, I just needed to vent, and she was there with her bullshit, so she was going to feel the wrath.

We both walked away from that situation, but then another fight broke out in the club. Officer Dee and I were searching the club for Saint, to make sure he was not involved. Saint was known to fight in the clubs. He could not be found, and I was worried that he may have been involved in the fight and thrown out of the club, or hurt. As we were all lined up to exit the club, this guy pushed past me to get out of the club. I was still very upset at that point, and I was not having it, so I snatched him back, and we started arguing. People started looking around, and then Officer Dee stepped up to intervene.

As I looked up toward the door, I saw Saint and Guiliani with those same chicks looking back at me and Officer Dee arguing with this guy. I forgot all about that guy temporarily, because all I wanted to do was get up those steps and snatch one of those chicks. Now, I know what I said before about women taking their anger out on the other woman, but this man made me eat my words. We made it out of the club, and I didn't see where or which way Saint had gone. I said goodbye to Officer Dee and went home alone, feeling totally disgusted. I called him several times, and he didn't answer the phone.

The next day at work, I was sitting with Officer Dee, and, out of nowhere he said, "It wouldn't be in your best interest to get involved with Saint."

I denied it, of course, and said he and I were just friends.

Officer Dee said, "I saw how you watched him last night."

Again, I said, "If I was watching him, it's because I know how he gets when he drinks, and I just wanted to make sure he was okay."

He said, "I am your friend, and I don't want to see you hurt. I know that man, and I see how he is with women."

Saint was scheduled to work at 4 p.m., as I was getting off duty. We walked past each other like strangers, not even a head nod between us. Saint knew I was mad, and I really had nothing to say to him. With all I had been through, I just thought, *Oh, well—easy come, easy go.* About 12:30 a.m., there was a knock at my door, and it was Saint, with the most beautiful peach-colored roses. I let him in, and he began to tell me that it wasn't what it looked like with those girls. One of the girls was someone he and Guiliani had gone to college with, and they hadn't seen each other since college. He said they went to Junior's Restaruant, which was up the street from the club, to get something to eat, and then he went home.

Of course, I didn't believe that bullshit, but then he called Guiliani, and he vouched for Saint's story. Call me a fool, but I went for it.

Another night in the club, everyone was having a good time. There was a girl by the name of Jazz, who worked as an outside contractor in the jail, who came with us this particular night. She was a cute girl, with a really big, borderline-sloppy ass, in my opinion. Anyway, she had a little too much to drink that night, and we all agreed that our co-worker, Kane, was going to take her home. We helped her get into Kane's car, and everyone went home. Saint was supposed to meet me at my house, but he didn't. I kept calling him that entire night, because he was also drunk, and I was worried that something may have happened to him.

I called Kane to find out if he'd heard from Saint, and that's when I found out that Saint had taken Jazz home. "How the hell did she end up in his car, when I watched you pull off with her in your car?" I asked.

Kane said, "I had to pull over because Jazz had to throw up, and Saint pulled up and said he would take her home."

I said goodbye to Kane, because I didn't want to raise suspicions about my affair with Saint. When I spoke to Saint the next day, he said he took her home, and then he went home. At that time, there were several rumors going around the jail about Jazz; she was married, she was sleeping with inmates, and she was sleeping with several other staff members. Saint took the attention off himself and placed it on Officer Dee when I questioned, "Why didn't you just let Kane take her home?" He said Officer Dee was sleeping with her and that he wouldn't do that to Officer Dee. I believed him once he said that, so I let it go.

A few weeks later, I found out that several people had gone out after work, and Saint was one of them. I also found out that he'd left the club with Jazz. I confronted him in a very calm manner, by telling him one of the lessons I learned while dealing with Dave, which was, "If there is something out there that may hurt me, I should hear it from you first. If you care about me, then you would never let someone have the satisfaction of thinking they can hurt me by telling me something about you. Bottom line, Saint, let the truth come from you. No one respects a liar," I told him.

Saint said, "I am going to tell you the truth. I did sleep with Jazz, twice."

I remember sitting there thinking, *Why do I always end up here?*

He continued to say that he'd had only anal sex with her, because she wouldn't let him have vaginal sex, because that was reserved for her husband, as if that made any difference to me. I wanted to hate her, because we were becoming cool. But at the same time, I really couldn't blame her, because no one knew about me and Saint. I had to revert back to the exception to the rule of taking my anger out on the other woman. Still, I never spoke to her again for several reasons. I found out that she was sleeping with two of my other male friends at the job and a former inmate who was Eddie's cousin, all at the same time. I had no respect for her, because she had no discretion about herself as a married woman. I hate a pretty woman who can have any man she wants but who carries herself like a slut, for no reason.

Being typical Sharon, I forgave Saint for this indiscretion and put the situation behind me for the time being. Saint was shocked that he was able to tell me the truth about his fling with another woman, and after a brief discussion, everything was right back on track between us. In my mind, I believed I scored some points in his heart that day. There were a few more job-related parties, which we attended under the guise of co-workers, and it really killed me to sit back and watch as Saint let people believe he was with Lurchette. Even worse, if she wasn't in attendance, I had to watch him dance with other women to avoid any suspicion of our dealings. He had a bad habit of always picking women up high in the air whenever he would dance with them. It was always a show on the dance floor with him. I really think he did that when the girl would be out-dancing him. The ladies would swoon over his prowess. I really can't say why I agreed to be his secret lover. On some level, I felt good inside because I knew he was secretly coming to my home later.

At another party with MDC Brooklyn staff, there was almost another fight. I have a problem with people talking to me and pointing their finger in the direction of my face. Once again, Officer Dee was there to step in and quash the issue. Saint, on the other hand, looked at the scene and went back inside the dance hall, as if it hadn't been his lover out there about to fight some big amazon chick from Brooklyn. That was an eye-opening moment for me. I decided I shouldn't go out with him anymore. It was rude and disrespectful, regardless of our secret relationship. He should have just checked to make sure I was okay. Instead, when the verbal altercation was over, and I walked into the dance hall, I saw that he had some chick in the air, holding her by the crotch.

All I could do was leave the party, because I know that I can't fight everyone. My every thought was to kick that bitch's ass. I'm glad I was smart enough to know better, and, besides, it wasn't her fault that he was a drunken jackass at times.

After that party, I pretty much became his stylist whenever he was going out. I chose to either work overtime, hang out with my friends or family, or just stay home, instead of going to every party and have my feelings hurt. With all his partying, my bank account rose to an all-time high. I became addicted to making money. Saint was addicted to spending money. One of our recurring topics of conversation was his spending habits. He literally spent $700 on one pair of shoes. This was bananas to me, because that is what I was spending each month on rent. It wasn't my money, so I let that discussion go. Because Saint was Mr. Party Guy, and no one knew about us, I always heard about what took place at each party he attended without me. There were times when the inmates would tell me about what happened at parties, including what I was wearing at a party. There were no real secrets in jail.

Besides partying, everyone was getting hooked on the Officer Next Door Program. This was a program which allowed officers, firefighters, and teachers to purchase homes in a revitalization neighborhood at a discounted rate, through a bidding process. If you had a key to the lockbox, you could walk through any house before placing the bid, just to see how much work needed to be done on the property. Most of the homes in the program were foreclosures or just in the heart of a really bad neighborhood.

One day Saint showed up to my apartment and said he wanted me to take a ride with him to Long Island. He was familiar with certain areas of Long Island, because his close friend, Gary, lived in Roosevelt. I thought that's where we were going, until he pulled up in front of this pink, gray, and white house at on Bauer Avenue, in Roosevelt. The doors and windows were all boarded up with plywood. I had a moment of déjà vu, because I knew this street *and* this house. As we walked through the house, I remembered why I knew this house. Back when I was in foster care, living with the Pruitts, her daughters lived on this block, in this house, or one of the other replicas on the block.

The houses in the cul-de-sac were cookie-cutter, with regard to interior layout. As you opened the front door of the house, the staircase leading to the only bathroom and three bedrooms was directly in front of you. To the left was the living room, and to the right was the dining room. There was a small foyer which led to a small back hallway. To the left of the hallway was the door leading to the basement, and directly in front of the basement door was a hall closet. The small hallway opened up to the eat-in kitchen on the right. Two steps down, off of the kitchen, was a den, which had a side door leading to the outside, to gain access to the backyard. The den also had an interior door, to gain access to the one-car garage from the inside of the house. The garage had a set of those pull-down staircases, leading to a storage area above the garage.

I shared my memory with Saint about the house and of playing in piles of leaves during the fall when we would visit the Pruitts' daughter.

He just looked at me and said, "Do you like the house?"

I said, "Yes. It is a nice size, and I loved the back deck."

He said, "Good, because I won it in the bid on the Officer Next Door Program."

I was extremely happy for him, and his family, because that house in Brooklyn was a complete mess, in my mind. I knew of stories where people made blind bids on homes in the program and really ended up with crap in the end, so I wondered if he had seen this house prior to bidding. When I asked the question, I was not expecting the answer that I received. He answered as if I should have known that he and Lurchette had gone house hunting together. My happiness for him turned to anger quickly, however, I didn't show it. I pretended it didn't bother me, but I think he knew my attitude had changed. He kept trying to reassure me that nothing happened between them. My only question was, "Why you would take her house hunting in Long Island, when she knows nothing about LI?"

His bullshit comeback was, "I wanted to surprise you when I got the house."

I could have gone on with the questioning, but it was pointless. He had no good reason, and I would have been setting myself up for listening to one lie after another. Once all the red tape was completed and the house was officially his to begin minor construction and updating, Saint and I became bonded. We were there knocking down walls, imagining paint colors, cleaning, and cutting grass. We had only a space heater to keep us warm at night, after we cooled down from having sex on the floor in every bedroom of the house. He invested in an air mattress after the floor started taking a toll on our backs.

I have never been one of those prissy women who are afraid to get their hands dirty. When we were carrying out the old, disgusting toilet bowl down the stairs and out to the dumpster, he said, "Lurchette would never do this. She would be complaining about her nails and sweating out her roots."

Hearing this made me feel like I was scoring more points for his heart. Buying this house changed some of his routines. He was no longer spending as much money on his wardrobe or going out partying all the time. Because of this house, my situation with Saint blossomed into something I never had or felt before. I was no longer working as much overtime, because I was there in this house, turning it into a home. Saint was so excited every time he would come home to find that something new had been completed in the house. Everything—from new carpet, the hardwood floors refinished, having the phone and utilities turned on, and cable installed—was all due to me.

One of the major changes he made was converting the first-floor hall closet into a bathroom, complete with shower stall. He was so proud of himself when he picked out the tile for the walls. His goal was to complete the house as soon as possible, to bring his mother home for the first time. At this point, I had seen his mother only once, in Brooklyn, as I was leaving their house. No formal introductions had been made at that time.

As the house was coming together, I started daydreaming about being the lady of the house. Saint had given me the keys to come and go as I saw fit, so after a night of hanging with the girls, I decided to show my friends the house. The girls were beer drinkers, and they left their Heineken bottles on the floor in the upstairs master bedroom. I didn't think anything of it at the time. Saint, on the other hand, felt I was having sex with another guy in his house. There was nothing I could say to change his mind. The fact that I'd told him about the number of sexual partners I'd had in the past, coupled with how sexually free I was with him in the bedroom, he assumed that I was loose. In Saint's mind, that equaled "whore."

He said he didn't believe me when I said that it was just my girls, because I loved dick too much. He had met my friends only briefly, and he felt they would lie for me. I suggested he ask them. I knew this wasn't fair because when he'd told me to ask Guiliani, I didn't say that to him. He took the keys back, and I was no longer trusted in his home without his presence. My feelings were truly hurt, because in my heart I knew I was not that kind of girl. In the end, it was his house and his keys, so why argue?

On my day off, the plan was to come to the house, clean, and power wash the outside of the house. I received a phone call from Saint saying that Lurchette wanted to come over and see the house, and that he would call me when she leaves. I was pissed off. Where the hell was she the entire time this house was being transformed into a home? Now that the house was damn near complete, she wanted to stop by. I just hung up the phone on him. He continued to call back leaving messages, claiming to understand why I was upset but that it wasn't what I thought it was.

I had heard that before so many times from him, that I knew that it was exactly what I thought it was in the end, when the truth was revealed. When he finally called me after she left, it was almost 9:00 p.m. He said they'd talked, and she'd started crying because she knew I had been over there helping him with the house, because she'd seen my car. She also felt he would have asked her to move in by now so that they could be a family.

I didn't want to hear any of this bullshit. I went to sleep, but like a jackass in love, I was there bright and early in the morning. He called me as I was getting closer to the house and asked me to meet him around the corner, on Konig Court. I didn't understand what the reason was for going over there. I learned quickly that he wanted me to park my car on this side street so no one would see my car parked in front of his house. I wanted to get in my car and drive back to Brooklyn. That's what I wanted to do, but I didn't. I can hear you gasping as you read that last sentence.

He went on to explain that Lurchette had been doing drive-bys at night and saw my car there several times, and that had upset her. He said he told her that he was not there with me, but I was there helping him out because I knew Long Island. At work, I was not disrespectful by flaunting my situation with Saint in her face, but off work was another story. I didn't need to jump through hoops to protect her feelings or her image on my personal time. Saint felt like he owed her that much, because she did help him find the house. I went along with it, but in the back of my mind, I was thinking, *She needs to stay her ass in Queens at night and stop doing damn drive-bys.*

The day had come to bring his mother home. We were doing some minor touch-up to the paint and other areas of the house. I remember his nephew Raymond saying, "Yo, Unc. I like her—she works." Not ten minutes after he said that, Saint's mother walked in the front door. I was in the den painting the handrails for the stairs.

She looked at me and said, "Chucky, who is that?"

Saint responded like a little boy and said, "Ma, that's my friend, Sharon."

She stood in the foyer and said it as a matter of fact: "I don't like her for you. She is not your type."

I put my head down. and tears started to form in my eyes.

His nephew looked at me and said, "Don't pay her any attention."

Saint never corrected her for being rude or disrespectful; instead he just took her and his sisters upstairs to show them the bedrooms. He returned shortly and asked me to leave, saying he would call me later. I had to walk up the street and around the corner, just to get back to my car. In those minutes it took me to get to my car, I relived all those moments in my life when I'd been called "ugly." I began to cry, and I couldn't understand why people just didn't want to get to know me for me, instead of judging me based on how they think I looked.

I stayed away from the house for a little while. When I finally went back, it was at night, and I stayed in his bedroom the entire time. When his mother would knock on the bedroom door in the morning, I would hide in the walk-in closet. I just didn't want to see her or speak to her.

I needed a break from the bullshit, so when my friend Tina asked me to go with her to Las Vegas on vacation, I jumped at the chance. It was a month or so before we actually left for Vegas, so I maintained my routine of working and parking around the corner at night, just to be with Saint.

He had settled into the house by then, and so he'd started his partying again. I used to worry about him driving home drunk because he partied in Manhattan or Brooklyn, and that was a long way to drive home under the influence. I would always call, and keep calling, until I got him on the phone to make sure he made it home safe. I recall the night that he never answered his phone, but I was at work, and there was nothing I could do. That morning on my way home, I kept calling him, but still no answer. I was traveling down Flatbush Avenue in Brooklyn, when another car hit my car from behind, which caused my car to hit the car in front of me, and that car hit the car in front of them. I was stressed out because I had no idea where Saint was, and now I'd been involved in a four-way car accident on a busy street in Brooklyn. We followed typical accident protocol, which was simple because the driver of the vehicle that hit my car took full responsibility for the entire accident. All I wanted to do was get home and find Saint.

He finally called in the afternoon, saying he'd been too drunk to make it home, so he went to Lurchette's house in Queens. He said, "Sharon you have nothing to worry about; nothing happened. I was too drunk to do anything," he said. I just let it go because I was thinking he was dead somewhere, so better at Lurchette's house than dead.

That night I went to work, and I was in such pain; I attributed it to the car accident. My co-worker suggested I go to the hospital near the jail to get checked out. The morning when I got off, I went over to Beekman Hospital—or "New York Downtown Hospital," as it is currently known. The doctor came in and asked a few general questions, one of which was, "Are you pregnant?"

I said "No," and he said, "Let's run a test to be sure; then we can send you for X-rays." Saint walked into the room, and my face lit up. At that moment, the doctor came back with the results, so Saint stepped out temporarily. The doctor began by saying, "Well, we can't do the X-ray, because the pregnancy test is positive."

I started screaming for Saint to come back into the room immediately. He threw those curtains back and entered the room as if I were being murdered. I looked at him and said, "Doctor, repeat what you just said." As the doctor uttered those words—"You are pregnant"—I saw how his face changed from a look of concern to pure joy. He came over and hugged me, and said "Congratulations."

I said, "You do know that it is yours."

He said, "Of course I do."

I asked if he was happy about it, and he said, "Yes."

I thought, *Finally, I am with someone who is worthy of me bringing forth life.*

I left the hospital and went home, feeling like I was on cloud nine. Saint went back to the jail and said he would stop by after work. I was still floating on air when Saint walked into my apartment. I looked into his eyes and sensed something was wrong. I thought something had happened at work. He said he was fine, and then he hit me with the infamous *"but."*

I knew what was coming, so I braced myself as he said, "I don't think we are ready to have a baby just yet." The proverbial bottom had just fallen out. I was crushed. The only word I was able to conjure up was, "OK."

He went on with all the excuses/reasons why this was not a good time. In my mind, all I heard was, *I don't want you to have my child.* My mind also said, *You are not worthy to have my baby.*

I started thinking of places to have the abortion, immediately. I had seen all my friends end up being someone's baby mother. I was not trying to keep a man who didn't want to be kept, by having a baby whether he wanted it or not. I refused to be one of those women.

The following day, I called my girl Deidra and told her about my situation. She gave me the address and phone number of a place in Mineola, New York. I called for the first available appointment. This was the same time period my friend Tina and I were going on vacation to Las Vegas. I didn't tell her about the pregnancy, because I didn't want to be judged. I just wanted it to be over. I had the appointment for the day before I left for Vegas. I hadn't even talked to Saint about the plans to have the abortion. The only thing he knew about was the trip to Vegas.

I was prepared to be put under anesthesia; however, I was given a pill and told it would pass on its own. He said I would experience some cramping and bleeding, much like my menstrual cycle. My menstrual cycle usually lasted only three days, very light, with no cramps at all, thank God. I agreed to take the pill and enjoy myself in Vegas. I could deal with those side effects.

I went to Vegas and had a really great time despite what was going on in my body. Tina never knew I was walking around bleeding as if I were hemorrhaging. I looked cute at all times, I never complained about cramps, but I did change clothes quite often. I took pictures in every new outfit I had, which was everything I'd packed. Tina never knew what I was going through mentally, as I was walking around literally expelling a child from my body, as if nothing was happening. I was going through maxi-pads like they were paper napkins.

Maybe it was because I was a little emotional, but Tina really got on my nerves on this trip. She kept complaining about me changing my clothes all time, and her having to take my pictures in each outfit. She was a weed smoker, and she did something that could have jeopardized both of our futures, because she had to have her weed.

After that trip our friendship was never the same. At this point in my life, I'd learned to put people in categories; friends, hang-out buddies, associates, and co-workers. Tina was now dropped to hang-out buddy. A hang-out buddy is someone you have a really good time with when you are partying but who should never be trusted enough to be a loyal friend, who will have your back no matter what.

Saint did call every now and then to see how my trip was going, but he never asked about the baby or anything pertaining to the baby. I decided to tell him about me taking the abortion pill before I left New York. He gave a generic response: "Are you okay?" There was nothing heartfelt behind the words. After hearing his tone, I felt like I'd made the right choice by not keeping the baby. My desire to have children went from having two kids, to having just one, and, now, after this experience, I wanted none. I had decided to put Saint in the category of co-worker and leave him there. I returned from Vegas mentally free of any connection to a one-time friend, a baby, and an almost baby daddy.

My plan lasted just about one month after I returned. Saint somehow swindled his way back into my world. Things were back on track, and we had fallen into a routine, except now his mother was slowly starting to get used to me being around. Saint was busy, her daughters had their own issues, and I was available, so I took her everywhere. Ms. Josephine never apologized for what she'd said, but she did say, "I do see what he sees in you. You are a hard worker, and you get things done." She started calling me "Sonya." I don't know who or where that name came from, but she was so serious about calling me by that name, I stopped correcting her. Naturally, knowing Saint, I thought it was some other chick he was messing with. He assured me he didn't even know anyone named "Sonya." I started to believe him, only after I'd heard her call his friend "Guiliani." I don't know why she made these names up for us, but they stuck. It was cute that, when Saint wanted me to do something, and he knew I would say "No," he would call me "Sonya." This reminded me of my mom, my dad, and "Gwendoline."

Things remained the same at work. Saint still pretended we were just friends, and everyone else thought he was with Lurchette. It was cool with people not knowing about us, on some level. I found out a lot, because people would talk about him in front of me, not knowing I was with him. It was nice to go home after work and have someone there who understands what you went through during the day. Our conversations were free and easy, or so I thought.

There was a new-transfer officer coming to the institution, and it turned out he knew Saint from Brooklyn. His last name was Dixon, and he'd grown up on the same block as Saint. He was a really nice-looking guy, with smooth brown skin and about 5'8" or 5'9". I must mention that he was married with a child. Saint and I were having one of our easy-breezy conversations, and the question was asked, "Who do you find attractive in the building?"

I named a few people, including Dixon. I never said I wanted to sleep with any of these people—I just thought they were attractive.

Saint couldn't differentiate between the two statements. Weeks went by, and Dixon and I became cool, as co-workers. He was assigned to work outside patrol, and I worked visitation. When there were no visitors to process, I would sometimes hang outside and talk to him. Saint was assigned to the evening-watch shift, which was 4 p.m. to midnight, so on some days, Saint would arrive at work and find me standing outside talking to Dixon. I didn't see a problem with it because Dixon was a friend of his.

Saint would walk by and give the "What's up?" head nod to Dixon but would not speak to me. This wasn't unusual, but when I tried to call him on his post, he would hang up the phone on me. This would piss me off, so I would leave my post in visitation and go to confront him in control center. All he would say was, "Sharon, not now."

I got off of work at 8 p.m., totally confused, because I could not figure out what I'd done wrong. By the time Saint got off work at midnight, I would try to call to see if he wanted me to come out to Long Island, or if he was staying at my place in Brooklyn, but he wouldn't take my call. I called several times until I fell asleep. I figured he had to talk to me the following day, because we were working in control center together. While in control center, between the hours of 3:30 p.m. and 7:00 p.m., there was an uncomfortable silence, mixed with tension and frustration. At this point, I couldn't take it anymore, so I decided to break the ice and ask, "What is wrong with you?"

He responded by saying, "What's wrong with you? Why are you always up in somebody's face?" he asked with an attitude.

I was dumbfounded. Where in the hell was this coming from? My immediate response was, "What the fuck are you talking about?" He began to explain how, every time he walked up, I was up in Dixon's face. I was baffled listening to him. He also accused me of hugging everyone. He said people were calling me a hoe, because I was always around the male officers and all up in their faces. I was taken aback by these statements.

"I grew up hanging out with mostly guys, and it was never a big deal to give a hug," I tried to explain. "Giving a hug does not equal hoe, where I come from," I said.

In the middle of defending myself, the institution telephone was ringing. It was my job to answer the institution telephone lines, so I paused the conversation to answer the call. On the phone was the wife of none other than Dixon. I contacted Dixon via radio; he responded by calling me on the other phone line. I delivered the message and disconnected the call. As I turned to continue my defense against such ignorant accusations, I was assisted up out of my seat by Saint with one hand around my throat. Before I could speak, I felt a hot flash, to the left side of my face. I couldn't believe what just happened to me. I remember being on the floor in the control room, screaming for my father. I don't know why, but that is the only person I thought of in that moment. Dave was the only guy to ever *try* hitting me, and I tried to kill us both when that happened.

I looked up and saw Saint coming toward me again with his hand extended as if to help me up from the floor. Before I could completely stand up straight, I was slapped down again. As I regained my composure, I tried to pull away and turn the key to exit the control room. I was screaming, "Let me out! Let me out!" and I could hear him saying, "Sshhhhh, shhhhh." I was sobbing with snot flowing from my nose as he said, "Sharon, stop crying, and I will pop the door so you can go upstairs and wipe your face."

I felt like a statistic. I remembered my friend Regina being struck down in the park, but at least I was there for her. I felt so alone, ashamed, and embarrassed. Here I was thinking I was falling in love with this man. How could I still feel love for a man who physically abused me? I was upstairs in the ladies' locker room, looking at my face for signs of welts forming. I believe I was still in shock at what had just happened to me. I could hear the phone ringing in the staff lounge, and I don't know why I answered it, but it was Saint asking if I was okay.

I hung up the phone and immediately called the lieutenant's office to say I was sick and needed to go home. I wished I didn't have to go back into the control center, but my car keys and handbag were still in there. I couldn't even look at him as I entered the control room. He tried to speak to me and asked if he could see my face. I grabbed my bag and proceeded to leave as he was asking, "Are you going home?" I refused to respond to any of his questions.

I knew I couldn't go home. I drove straight to Long Island, to the place where I'd scattered my father's ashes. I cried and cried, and then cried some more. My father had never prepared me for this day. I missed him on that day like I'd never missed him before. I couldn't tell anyone what had just happened to me. There was no pity party for me to throw for myself. I appeared so strong to all the women and men who knew me. How could I tell someone and not have them look at me as "less than?" I was not as pretty, or tall, or even smarter, than most women I knew, but I was stronger than any of them, or so I thought.

I sat by the water as if my father was going to reach up, put his hand on my chin, and say, "Stop crying." I wanted to hear him say, "Baby girl, I will take care of this, and you will never have to worry about anyone treating you like that again." Instead all I heard was him saying, "Anything that happens to you in your life, you allowed to happen to you."

At that point I got up, got back in my car, and drove back to Brooklyn. His words were resonating in my head over and over again. I kept thinking, *What did I do to deserve that? How did my actions lead to him to slapping me down, helping me up, and slapping me down again?*

I came to the conclusion that it was the gossip at the institution and me being friendly with everyone that had led to me being abused. The weak mindset of my co-workers thinking a man and a woman can't be friends without something sexual between them led to my physical assault. I decided I was not hugging anyone anymore, and I was cutting people out of my circle. The people at MCC New York were swimming in a simple-minded river, flowing into an ocean of ignorance, and I was not going to drown with the rest of those idiots.

I couldn't sleep that night. I kept reliving that moment in control center. Part of the reason I couldn't sleep was that Saint was banging on my door and calling my phone all night. Because I wouldn't answer the phone or the door, my neighbors were threatening to call the police if he didn't leave. When he finally gave up, I watched through the peephole as he walked away. I was finally able to get two hours of sleep, and, although my face wasn't scarred or bruised, my eyes were puffy from crying and not sleeping. I couldn't go to work looking like that and have everyone constantly asking, "What's wrong?"

I wanted to stay home and just feel sorry for myself, but Saint had other plans for me. As I lay on my love seat, balled up like a snail in its shell, watching one of my favorite movies, *Love Jones*, my phone began to ring. I just wanted to be left alone with my own thoughts and emotions, but I knew he would not leave me alone unless I spoke to him. As I answered the phone, I could hear in his voice that he was shocked that I had answered at all.

He started with, "Sharon, I am so sorry, and I just want to see you and talk."

I said, "Say what you have to say, and just leave me alone."

He asked if he could come over, and I said "Yes," reluctantly. I was thinking I had at least 40 to 45 minutes before he got there to prepare myself mentally to see the man who hurt me. Maybe ten minutes had passed, and there was a knock at my door. I felt the flutter in my stomach as I walked to the door. I took a deep breath as I unlocked the door, and there he stood, the man who had violated my trust and my body.

I couldn't look him in the face, so I stepped to the side and allowed him to pass over the threshold. As he reached out to touch my cheek, I felt my body flinch. He immediately said, "I am not going to hurt you." He handed me a beautiful bouquet of assorted-color roses, with a card that read, "*Sharon: You will never know how sorry I am. The next time you speak to him, tell your father how sorry I am. P. S., I will never hurt you like that again.*"

He sat in the single oversized chair, to the right of my love seat, where I had repositioned myself to prepare to listen to whatever he had to say. There was complete silence for about fifteen minutes, so I continued watching *Love Jones*. He stood up and said, "I'm gonna go."

I simply said, "OK."

I sensed frustration in his voice as he said, "I came here to speak to you, and you're watching television."

My smart mouth took over, and I said, "I didn't ask you to come here, and you were just sitting there not saying anything."

He calmed down and said, "Sharon, I just wanted you to know how sorry I am, but I am still going to leave," and he left. The next few days were quiet. There were no annoying phone calls, and I did not see him at work. I wasn't the same person when I returned to work. Although no one knew what had taken place in the control center, I felt as if all eyes were on me. As I was leaving work and walking toward my car in the parking lot, I looked up and saw Saint. As our eyes met, I saw sorrow in his, and I felt forgiveness showing in mine. While I was driving home, he called my cell phone and told me I looked really pretty. Then he asked if he could call me later. The words fell from my lips before I knew what had happened—"Yes."

We talked over our issues, play by play, and, although it was hard, we came to an understanding. He understood that he was lucky I didn't call the police and have him arrested. I understood that he was jealous and insecure. We both agreed, once we'd arrived at an understanding, to move on as just friends.

I believe two weeks had passed, and he called to ask if I wanted to come over just to hang out. While driving out to Long Island, he texted me to say the door would be open and to meet him in the basement. As I walked down the steps leading to the basement, I noticed the lights were off; I could see the flicker of flames from clean-linen-scented candles along the floor. When I reached the bottom of the stairs, I saw Saint to my right, standing in front of the music turntables with the headset on, tapping his feet to the beat of the KC and JoJo song, "All My life." I sat on the steps watching him for a brief moment. He looked so cute from behind dancing to the song and being in his own world with the music. Then he turned around, and, when our eyes met, my heart melted. I knew I loved him, and I wanted him back.

He said, "I fixed your favorite drink of Hennessy and ginger ale." I moved from the steps to the brown microfiber sofa, facing the old-school, floor-model, big-screen television. He stood over me, took me by the hand, and pulled me up to my feet; then he kissed me soft and long. I felt it in his kiss that he was truly sorry for what he had done. That night we had sex, or better yet, we were fucking. I couldn't call it, "making love," because it was wild, freaky, and animalistic, but it was great. It hadn't been that long, but my body missed his touch. As my body began to tense up, right before the climactic release, I felt a tear roll down my cheek. I didn't notice he was looking at me, when I felt his hand slowly wiping my tear away. He held me tight and cried with me, repeating how sorry he was. We slept in each other's arms all night long—literally. We woke up the next morning and never spoke of that incident again.

Things were back on track between us. The year was closing out—it was already November—and my birthday was fast approaching. Saint continually asked me what I wanted, but I refused to answer because he had spent enough time with me to figure it out. The day of my birthday, Saint made plans to take me to my favorite restaurant, Red Lobster. I thought he was going to give me my gift over dinner, but I was wrong. While driving back to his house, I was thinking, *My gift must be at the house.* We entered the house, and, there on the kitchen table, were a dozen tri-colored roses and a card. I did the right thing and read the card first, which was beautiful, but I was still wondering where my gift was.

He went upstairs and set the bathtub. By this time, I must admit, I was getting a little pissed. He told me to come upstairs and get into the tub. I'm a sucker for a bubble bath, so I obliged. Then he came back into the bathroom with my favorite drink in hand. I was relaxed, and I almost forgot that I hadn't gotten an official gift. When I got out of the tub and walked into the bedroom, there was a jewelry box on the bed. I felt my face light up with joy.

I rushed to the bed and opened that box so fast, the earrings popped out of the slot. They were 14K gold, diamond-cut, mini-hoops. It doesn't sound like much, but they were everything to me. He was thoughtful in that way. He paid attention to me and saw that I had only one pair of earrings that I wore with everything. I wore the new ones every day from that moment on. He said he noticed I was a little upset when I thought he hadn't gotten me anything. I played it off as if that was not the case, but deep down, I knew he was on the verge of being cut off. It sounds crazy that I would cut him off for not making my birthday special but not for hitting me. Nothing that was happening between us made any sense. We enjoyed the rest of the evening and went back to business as usual the following day.

The months were going by really quickly, and, before we knew it, it was February, and Valentine's Day was around the corner. Now I know I said I don't celebrate these holidays, however, that is meant for someone having to buy me a gift. Saint was a very tall man, who spent way too much on clothes and shoes, but he had the biggest cubic-zirconia earring in his ear. That earring annoyed the life out of me. I just felt a man of his stature shouldn't be wearing fake jewelry. I had planned to surprise him on Valentine's Day with a pair of diamond earrings, in a square-shaped setting, instead of the typical round-shape setting. I wanted his earrings to stand out from the crowd. In my head, I had planned exactly how I would deliver his gift. Once again, Saint had other plans.

I was on my way to Long Island with his $700 earrings in tow when he called saying, "Can you just go by one of your friends' house for a little while?"

When I asked what was going on, he said, "Lurchette said she hadn't seen the house in a while, and she would like to come over."

I wanted to throw the earrings out of the window and tell him to go to hell. I also wanted to believe that I meant that. He said, "I promise I will call as soon as she leaves."

I went over to Javon's house. Javon was now dating Tina's sister. She and I had become close because we both shared the same occupation. I felt a little weird, because they were a couple, and it was Valentine's Day, so I decided to leave. My other friend Angie lived three blocks away from Saint, therefore, I would be closer when he decided to call.

While I was at Angie's house, he texted me, stating, "She is staying a lot longer than I thought she would." He asked if I would give him a little more time.

I texted back, "OK, but I'm getting tired, and so is Ang." The text really didn't make any damn sense to me, because, at the end of the day, it was his house, and, if he wanted her to leave, all he had to do was ask or insist. I saw that Ang was starting to fall asleep, and I felt bad for using her like that. At some point, I showed Angie the earrings and told her I was going home but that I wanted him to have the earrings on Valentine's Day. She didn't know that the reason I was at her house was that he had another woman over there. I think I told her he'd got stuck at work, and I didn't have keys.

She was mad because I didn't have keys after almost a year of dealing with him. We came up with the idea that I would place the earrings on the porch, and he would see the box when he got home. The *real* plan was for me to leave the earrings on the porch, ring the bell, and leave. I parked my car at the end of his street, and as I walked up to the house, I could see the light glaring from the kitchen and the light from the television in his bedroom illuminating through the bedroom window. I was very nervous about leaving $700 worth of jewelry on the front porch, but I was there now, and there was no turning back. I texted him, letting him know that I was going home, and proceeded to place the box on the porch. I rang the bell and then disappeared into the darkness because the streetlights were out.

When he answered the door and saw the box, I can only assume he knew it was from me. He texted me back, trying to convince me to wait and that he would get her to leave soon. He said he loved the earrings and that he couldn't believe I would spend that much on him. I drove back to Brooklyn highly agitated but happy he loved the gift.

He called me at 12:30 a.m., asking if I would come back to Long Island. He said she wouldn't leave and that he was sorry. He said she finally got upset, because it was obvious that he wanted her to go, and she wanted to spend the night.

My response was, "Then you should've let her spend the night, because I am not coming back." I wanted to believe those words as they left my lips, but as usual, I was a fool in love, eating my words all the way back to Roosevelt. He'd left the door open for me, and when I went into his room, he was lying on the bed naked with my drink on the nightstand. He was wearing the earring, and, just as I thought, it was perfect for him. That night, sexually, he wanted to show me how much he appreciated the gift. I wanted that more than anything, but only after he changed the sheets. He stood his ground and said, 'I didn't do anything with her, although she wanted to." I stood my ground and insisted the sheets be changed, before we got down with the get down. I think I believed him, but I wanted to make him think I didn't. In the end, I finally got my way, and the sheets were changed.

Months went by, and his mother and I became really close. I took her everywhere she needed to go. We didn't want her being alone in the house all day with nothing to do, so we signed her up at the Roosevelt Senior Citizen Center, to enjoy some of the daily events. I would come over after work, and she would show me how she'd danced at the party they'd held at the center. She learned to love me despite her initial statement at our first meeting. She would say I was the only one who knew how to get things done and that I was the only one she could depend on. She didn't want her daughters or even Saint, for that matter, taking her places or doing certain things with her. Even when Saint and I were having one of our moments of disagreement, she would still ask for Sonya. "I want Sonya to take me to the doctor" is what she would tell him and, naturally, he would become upset. I would call her from work sometimes just to check on her and see if she wanted me to bring anything for her. She really appreciated me doing that for her.

Christmas time was coming up, and I knew she wanted to go shopping for gifts. While at work, I called to schedule a time that would be good for her. I knew the house number by heart, so I was taken aback when I heard a woman's voice say "Hello." I hung up and dialed the number again, because it was obvious to me that I had dialed the wrong number. When the voice answered for the second time, I thought maybe it was a relative. I asked to speak with Ms. Josephine, and the person asked, "Who is this?" So, I said, "This is Sharon, and who is this?"

The woman's voice was soft and firm, as she said, "This is Saint's girlfriend, Lexus."

I said very calmly, "May I speak to Ms. Josephine?" As Ms. Josephine got on the phone, I said, "Hi" and "How are you?"

She said, "I am good. Lexus showed up to take me Christmas shopping." I asked her who Lexus was, and she said, "Saint's girlfriend."

There was no use in any further questions for Ms. Josephine, when all the answers should come from her son. I hung up the phone and proceeded to call Saint, who was working in control center. I kindly asked, "Who is Lexus?"

He replied, "Sharon, why are you asking me about somebody named Lexus at work?"

My tone went from professional at work, to ghetto in my apartment. "Don't play no fucking games with me before I come down to control and show you why I am asking about Lexus!"

"Sharon, Sharon, would you just calm down and listen to me?" he said.

"Who the fuck is she?" I screamed into the phone. "She said she was your girlfriend," I yelled.

He said, "It's not like that. Would you just calm down?"

It was obvious that he was not going to give me the answers that I needed, so I hung up the phone on him. I got off of work at 10:00 p.m., and Saint got off at midnight, so I told him, as I passed through the control-room sally port, that I was going to Long Island to find out exactly who Lexus was. I had no intention of driving to Long Island, but I wanted him to believe that I was.

As I was on my way down Flatbush Avenue, my cell phone was ringing with a restricted call. When I answered, it was Saint, begging me not to go over there. I started yelling, "Fuck that! Where the fuck were these bitches when I was there night after night sleeping on the bare floor?" I kept yelling, "Where the fuck were they when I was painting and carrying dirty fucking toilets out of the house? Now that the house is officially a home, everyone wants to come out of the fucking woodwork to stake their claim! Fuck you and them! Ya'll can all go to fucking hell! I am going home!"

As I was preparing to disconnect the call, I heard him saying, "Sharon, please just let me take care of this. I am on my way home now to find out what is going on," he said. "I promise I will call you later." "Later" never came that night. He called me the next day to say, "I was tired when I got home, so she spent the night, and I took her home this morning."

I didn't give a damn about anything he was saying at that point. I just wanted to know who she was and where had she come from all of a sudden. He began by saying, "She is my girl." My heart sank to floor. I could not believe what I was hearing.

I asked, "When the hell did she become your girlfriend, when I have been here all along?"

One of Saint's favorite lines was, "If I could just speak uninterrupted, then you can ask anything you want after that." I agreed because I needed to hear this explanation. While he was speaking, I was doing the calculation in my head. He and Lurchette had been together on and off for four years. I had been around going on two years, so where exactly did Lexus fit in?

He started telling me the story of how they'd met in a club and that she was so very pretty. In fact, he said she was the prettiest girl he ever had. He said she was from Harlem and studying to be a nurse. My mind was spinning, because if she is the prettiest, and Lurchette was the smartest, where the fuck did I fit in? He went on and on about how he'd always thought he wanted to marry a nurse or doctor. He stated some more garbage about her mother being sick and wanting them to have a baby and get married before she died. I kept listening to this story, and my mind was fading in and out.

I interrupted the long-winded details of how they'd met and what led to their relationship by asking, "How long?"

He calmed down and said, "Almost one year now."

I remember just hanging up the phone. There was nothing else I needed to hear. How the hell had he managed three women at the same time, for all this time? Of course, he called back several times, leaving many messages that meant nothing to me. Two days later, while I was at home in Brooklyn, my phone rang showing a number unknown to me. The person asked for me by name and then stated her name was Lexus. Everything in me wanted to hang up the phone, but I told myself, "No." I needed to hear what she had to say. I listened very carefully as she said, "I am here with Saint, and he is telling me that you and he are just friends and you help him look after his mother." I heard him in the background, saying, "Sharon, just tell her that we are just friends, so she can let you get back to whatever you were doing."

She said, "I am sorry to bother you, but you are a woman, so you know how men will lie to get out of trouble. I will not let Saint get away with trying to play me."

My mind was saying, *Screw him and tell her the truth about everything,* but my mouth opened and did the opposite. Before I knew it, I had just lied and took the back seat as the other woman. I had fallen so deeply in love with this man that I just lied to protect him, instead of my own dignity. He said, "Thank you, Sharon, and sorry to bother you. I will call you later." I could not wait for that phone call. How was he going to try to justify the fact he'd given her my number and asked me to lie for him, in front of her? He kept his word this time, and, about 7:00 p.m., he was calling my phone.

I answered the phone by saying, "What?" instead of my usual, "Hey, my Saint." When he was trying to butter me up, he would call me "Pumpkin Butt." He knew I had an attitude, so he started the conversation with, "Sharon, I am so sorry. She would not stop with the questions. She kept telling me to call you in front of her, so that she could hear me say that she was my girlfriend. I just wanted it to stop, so I agreed to call."

The only thought I had was, *Why?*

He said, "Sharon, I know you are hurt; come over so we can talk."

My desperate ass wanted to know *Why her and not me?* so I went. Once I got there, I had to listen to more details about his betrayal, but, somehow, I managed to put it behind me and allowed him to have sex with me. I cried while he was inside of me. This time he didn't see my tears because I changed position so he couldn't see my face. What I thought was a growing relationship had turned into a situation.

Somehow, he managed to make me feel as if Lexus didn't exist. I was still at the house and spending time with his mother. This time, when he went out partying and didn't come home, I knew he was at Lexus's house in Harlem. I knew Lurchette wasn't a factor anymore because he would tell me that she called only every three to four months looking for sex, but he would always turn her down. Like most women who know their man's sexual appetite, you know that he is sexing someone else if he is not getting it from you.

Even though she knew it was against policy to take or give out staff members' phone numbers from control center, Lurchette had gotten my number from work and decided to call me at home to ask about my relationship with Saint.

My first question to her was, "Why are you calling me?"

She responded calmly, stating, "I am not calling to fight with you. I just want the truth."

I asked her, "The truth about what?"

She started by saying, "Saint said."

I knew then that he'd done it again. He told this girl to call me, because he trusted that I would lie for him. He knew my heart, and he was right. I told her that Saint and I were just friends.

She said, "There has to be more, because when I call the house, his mother calls me by your name. Why would she call me by your name if she has known me for four years?" she asked.

I said, "I don't know. You should have asked her that question when she said it," I replied. "I don't see the point in this phone call. If you have any other questions, ask him," I told her. "And please, don't call me again with this."

"St. John, you know I am not calling to harass you, but I have been hearing that you and Saint are not just friends, and I just want to know the truth," she said.

"Again—I told you: we are just friends, and I don't have anything else to say to you," I said. I hung up the phone and called him to let him know that Lurchette had just called me. All he was concerned with was whether I told her the truth about us. I put his mind at ease and let him know I had lied for him once again. He thanked me and then asked if I wanted to go to dinner and a movie. I accepted his offer, and believe it or not, we had a good night.

Months passed, and we were still going strong with the lies. I was playing my part as the other woman with the number one-woman privileges. God help me, but I don't know why I allowed myself to be put in this position. I think I was just trying to save face. My friends and family had met him, and he'd put up the appearance that he loved me and only me. Inside the walls of his house, I was his woman. Saint would go out to the clubs in the City and stay at Lexus's house, while I was at his house, waiting on him to come home.

He would always say, "Sharon, you don't have anything to worry about, because you know I get too drunk to do anything. I spend the night over there only to keep her from coming to Long Island." On nights when he didn't go out, and we would stay at home, he would have to go downstairs into the basement to call them, just so we could have a good night without any interruptions. I accepted anything to keep what we had going, until I was able to make him see that he should choose me in the end.

This is how we passed another year in our situation. I was at the house playing wifey, and they knew nothing about our secret relationship. Lexus got tired of all the excuses as to why she couldn't come to Long Island. She started taking the train and popping up unannounced. There were days when I would be on my way to the house and I would receive a text saying, "She popped up again, so I am taking her home. I will call you later."

Every time she would call the house, Ms. Josephine would tell her that I was coming to take her to the doctor or just out shopping. Lexus must have sensed the bond that Ms. Josephine and I were forming, and she knew Saint was a big momma's boy. She was so determined to claim her place as number one; she was trying to replace me in his mother's life. She started offering to come to Long Island and take his mother out shopping. Ms. Josephine would tell me, "I don't know how she wants to take me shopping when she doesn't have a car and she doesn't know Long Island." She would actually take the train to Long Island then take a cab to his house. She would offer to take Ms. Josephine to her doctor appointments or anything she knew we did together by cab.

When her offer was rejected, she started to accuse him of cheating again, so he told her about Lurchette. He served Lurchette up on a platter, just to satisfy Lexus. He told her she was still holding onto hope of a future with him, but he knew there was no future because of her kids. He felt he had to tell Lexus something to distract her from focusing on me. At least that's the reason he gave me for telling her about Lurchette. However, Lexus still felt insecure about me because of my role in his life, with his mother.

Lexus demanded he give her a key, to prove he loved only her. I thought I had a special bond with Ms. Josephine, until I found out that she set us up to be caught. Saint and I went out to dinner, and, after dinner, he started having chest pains, so we went to the hospital. We literally spent almost two and a half hours in the hospital, only to be sent home because they couldn't find anything. When we got home, the house was dark. His mother was in her room upstairs, sleeping. We came in and went straight for his bedroom, never turning the lights on downstairs. He wanted some tea, and he needed to start a load of laundry, so we both went back downstairs.

That's when we saw Lexus sitting in the dining room in the dark.

She stood to her feet and said, "What's going on, Saint? You said she was just around to take care of your mother. Why is she here?" she asked.

Saint was shocked to see her, and he asked, "How did you get in here?"

She replied, "While you were sleeping, I made a copy of your key."

He turned to me and said, "Sharon, thank you for tonight, but you can go now."

All the way back to Brooklyn, I just kept thinking, *I spent half my night in a hospital with this man, she pops up unannounced, and I get treated like the help.* Talking aloud in my car I said, "Fuck this shit! I deserve better than this!" As I was talking to myself, my phone rang. I knew it was him, so I didn't answer. A few minutes later, my phone beeped with a notification of a voice-mail message. As I listened to the message, he sounded so sorry for what had happened. He apologized and said he was taking her home and that he would call me on his way back home. This time, he kept his word.

I was worried about his health, because he was still feeling a stiffness in his chest. I drove all the way back to Long Island to take care of him the best way I could. Our pillow talk that night revealed to me that Ms. Josephine had told Lexus that she should show up here at night to see for herself what's going on.

Approximately two weeks after that incident, Ms. Josephine did it again. I drove out to Roosevelt and parked my car two blocks over, as I always did—or should I say, *had* to do. Saint would meet me at the parking spot, and we would drive to his house. I went straight to the bedroom and took my shoes off in preparation for bed because it was almost 1:00 a.m. Saint went to put his work bag down in the small room, when I heard a loud commotion. It sounded like he'd flopped on the bed, rolled over, and hit the floor hard.

I jumped out of bed to see what was going on, and Lurchette tried to attack me. His mother came out of her room screaming, "Saint, you have to stop this! This can't go on in here!"

He held Lurchette back and told me to leave. I grabbed my shoes and my bag and walked up the street and down two blocks, in the middle of the night. I found myself in the car talking to myself again. "How can I be so stupid?" I should have stayed and fought her just to release some pent-up stress. One thing was for sure: Ms. Josephine didn't protect her son when he was doing wrong by women like Eddie's mother did.

I didn't hear from him until the next evening around 6:00 p.m. When he finally called, he said, "She refused to leave until I answered all her questions and told her everything. By 'everything,' I mean my relationship with Lexus, our situation—and, oh, by the way, Sharon, I met this girl who works at MDC Brooklyn."

Not only did I learn that Ms. Josephine had betrayed me and her son again by letting Lurchette into the house to lie in wait but also that *another* woman had been added to the equation. This was absurd. Lurchette found out about the other girl because she'd popped up at his house while the other girl was there, similar to my encounter.

I had to be the biggest fool on the planet. I had been reduced to number 4. I sat there and listened to the story of him meeting this girl at our Annual Refresher Training that had been held at the Brooklyn Jail. She was tall, with a big ass, hazel eyes, and light skin. I knew I couldn't compete with that combination, so I just sat there feeling ashamed of the body God had given me.

He continued by saying, "She was a challenge because her man was in class with us and he thought he was all that, so I wanted to show him that I could take his girl."

My thought was, *How stupid and childish can you be?* But I kept listening to the bullshit. He was so very happy to tell me the nonsense.

I learned how to switch from girlfriend mode to homegirl mode when the situation required me to. I made him feel so comfortable talking to me about anything and everything. I showed no reaction to the heart-wrenching news, even though my feelings were being steamrolled as if with a bulldozer. This was to my benefit, because I always got the full truth when he felt most relaxed with just talking. I found that, most of the time, when you let people just talk freely, they will always tell on themselves. By playing the homegirl role, I found out that 'Ms. Christina' was married and was being abused by her husband. She used to be fat; now, she'd lost all the weight but still suffered from low self-esteem. He said he wanted to help her with her self-esteem.

I thought that was ironic, because *my* self-esteem had been shot to hell, and he'd only made things worse for me.

He continued to say she had been to the house several times over the four-month period they had been dealing, and she had met his mother. According to him, his mother wanted him to leave everyone else alone and be with Christina. After hearing that, I felt used by both him and his mother.

He said he thought that would be best, because, with Christina, there was no stress. He didn't feel chest pains when he was with her. I felt that his chest pains were karma, and well deserved. I agreed to leave him alone, if that's what he really wanted to do. I left his house and swore to myself that I would not go back there again.

Three weeks passed, and I had not spoken to Saint, except at work, usually about jail business. I re-focused my mind on making money, so I worked even more overtime than usual. I finally had an evening off, and I made it a solo dinner-and-movie night. On the way home from Red Lobster Restaurant, my phone began to ring. I saw Lexus's name light up across the screen. I inhaled slowly and deeply before I answered.

"Hello. Why are you calling my phone, Lexus?" I asked.

"Sharon, I just wanted to talk to you woman to woman. Saint told me that you and he had been messing around, but not anymore. He said that he really appreciates your friendship. I don't understand: if you were dealing with this man, why would you deny it when I asked you?"

I interrupted her by stating, "Lexus, what you fail to realize is that I don't owe you anything. My business is my business."

"Saint thinks he's a player," she replied, ignoring my previous statement. "Sharon, did you know about Christina and the other girl from your job?"

I knew she was talking about Lurchette, and I felt compelled to answer her, so I said, "Yes—I knew about all of you. Why are you calling me, Lexus?" I asked her again.

"I just wanted you to know that I am leaving him alone," she said. "He will not play me. The only way he can get me back is if he buys me a car. I want a Lexus and an engagement ring for all he has put me through."

She kept talking to me as if we were friends. I learned that she'd had foot surgery and that Saint had carried her up the stairs in her building and bathed her. I thought about when I'd had liposuction because Saint was complaining that I was too thick in the mid-section and I needed a ride home from the doctor's office. When I called him, he told me to take a cab. I took a cab back to his house to get my car to drive back to Brooklyn. When I got home, my sweatpants were ruined from the blood and fluid draining from my body. Saint never even came to check on me, and when I asked—or, should I say, *complained*—about it, he said, "You did that to yourself."

He was right to some extent, but I did it because I thought if I could fix my body, maybe he would find me more desirable than some of the other women. I also spent $5000 for Invisalign to straighten my teeth. I was willing to try anything to get this man's attention. Saint didn't even notice the changes. She just kept talking, while I was reminiscing about all these disappointments. She said he actually cooked her dinner but messed up the rice. This conversation felt like déjà vu with Damon's girlfriend.

The next thing I knew it was 3:00 a.m., and I had listened to her go on and on about their entire relationship. I finally ended the conversation by saying I was tired. Saint called two hours later, to ask me for a major favor. I couldn't imagine what that could be, since I had already lied for him twice.

He said, "Sharon, I know it's a lot to ask, but could you stay at my house with my mother while I'm on vacation in the Dominican Republic with Gary?" He said that his mother had requested that I stay with her.

I still felt betrayed by her, so I was reluctant to do it, but I gave in. He thought he was sweetening the deal by saying I could park my car in front of the house. I spent the night at his house the day before he left for his trip, so I could take him to the airport. It was more of the same crap. He had to call Lexus, Lurchette, and Christina, before we could talk uninterrupted.

That night I told him about the conversation with Lexus and her demands for a ring and a car. I told him I thought she was a gold digger. He didn't want to believe she would say that because she had professed her undying love for him. I didn't care if he believed me or not, because I knew she couldn't hide her money-grubbing ways for long. Secretly, I hoped she would go back to him—and then rob his ass blind for every dime of his father's life-insurance money. I told him I wouldn't sleep in his bed, so I slept in the small room.

I took him to the airport the next day, and he thanked me for doing this despite what he had done to me. His mother was always thankful for me being there with her. She said, "Sonya, I don't know what I would do without you." Her daughter thanked me also, and she even brought me a card that read, "Thanks for taking such good care of my mother. She relies on you more than on her own daughter."

I didn't know how to take this card: was she thankful or jealous? It was a real passive-aggressive way of letting me know she had mommy issues. I can't be bothered with a grown-ass woman with mommy issues. I had enough issues of my own. At the end of the day, her mother was happy and well taken care of by me. His mother was still going to the senior citizens center and partying like she was young. I saw where Saint got it from. We had a good time laughing about the way they had to help her up because her knees were bad when she would get low dancing. Soon, I forgot about her betrayal. She did try to talk to me about why she'd done what she'd done. She felt her son was taking advantage of all of us and that he needed to get caught, so he'd be forced to decide about who he wanted to be with. It was a noble idea, but there was a better way to handle the situation.

A few days later, I came home from work, and Ms. Josephine was sitting in the dining room with a girl I could only assume was Ms.

Christina, based on her previous description. She introduced herself and stated, "I just stopped by to check on his mother because I knew he was away and she would be by herself."

I didn't respond to that comment because it was obvious he had lied to her. Ms. Josephine stood up and said, "Well, I'm tired. I am going upstairs to take a nap. Sonya, are you going to fix something to eat?"

I answered her and said, "I will fix you a plate when it's done." I went into the kitchen to fix dinner, and Christina followed me in there and sat at the kitchen table. I ignored her presence, until she started speaking. She said, "I know you and Saint have a special bond. I also know he tells you everything. I can't compete with that," she said. "He does tell me that I have nothing to worry about, because you're not his physical type. He said you're not eye candy."

As she spoke those words, I remembered the conversation with Lexus and Lurchette, because they told me that's how he described me to them also. She, too, let me know that she was not sticking it out with Saint, because he had a problem letting go of his past relationships. I didn't believe her any more than I'd believed Lexus. If it weren't for Ms. Josephine, I would have left that night. I cried myself to sleep that night. No matter how good I thought I was as a woman and girlfriend, no one would ever see past my ugly physical appearance. I thought I had gotten past the stage of feeling ugly. I thought I had learned to accept myself as I was. Listening to all these women tell me that the man who once made me feel so pretty had been telling them that he would never be with me because I was not eye candy hurt me to the core.

We spoke that night on the phone, but I didn't mention any of the details about my conversation with Christina. I told him that I'd met her only because she just showed up, thinking his mother was alone.

He said, "Sharon, we will talk when I get back. I have a lot to tell you."

I didn't want to see him, but I had previously agreed to pick him up from the airport. I didn't know how this conversation was going to work out, but I knew that it was not going to be easy. On the way home from the airport, I drove in silence. As we approached his house, I said, "I am not coming in." I'd kept my promise to stay with his mother, and now

I just wanted to go home. He begged me to stay so we could talk. He asked me to wait in the basement until he checked in with his mother.

I waited downstairs for probably a half-hour. Then, suddenly, the lights went out. I thought, *What the hell is going on?* He said, "It's okay. I want the lights off." He sat in the chair directly across from the television, and then he asked me to turn the television off as well. We sat in the dark for about five minutes before he finally spoke a word. When he did speak, I sensed a quaver and fear in his voice. He started with his by-now-infamous line, "I just need to speak freely, uninterrupted."

He said that, while he'd been in the DR, Lexus had called him to say she had been to the doctor, because she needed to get checked after finding out that he had been with all these different women. She told him her blood work had come back positive for the virus that causes herpes. As he sat there saying these words, I heard him sniffle, as if he were crying.

He said, "Sharon, I know I have a problem. I don't know why I do what I do. While I was in the DR, I slept with some girl down there, and I don't know why I did it. I didn't even like her, but she had a fat ass, so I did it. I did wear a condom with her, but with Lexus, we never used condoms because she wanted to get pregnant. You can speak now if you want to," he said.

I was filled with questions, so I asked if he'd seen any sores on his peter. (I hated the word "dick," so I called it the "peter.")

He said, "No, but I am going to make an appointment for next week."

I knew that we used condoms most of the time, but there had been a few times when we hadn't. I asked him if he'd told Christina and Lurchette.

He said, "I know you don't believe me, but I have not touched that girl in a while. As for Christina, I am going to wait until after I hear from the doctor."

"Well, Saint, I will make my appointment as well," was all I could say. "However, since you are being honest, did you tell all those girls that I am not eye candy and that you could never be with me?"

He had an immediate reaction to my question. "Sharon, Sharon. No, no—I never said that. Lexus and Lurchette asked me how I could be with you because she thought you were just ugly. I told Christina what they'd said, and she said she didn't like the word 'ugly' and that she *had* used the phrase 'not eye candy.'"

I asked him why three different women would tell me that's what he'd said about me. It just didn't make any sense, I explained to him. He proclaimed his innocence and stood firm on that. I didn't want to keep arguing about it, but, deep in my heart, I knew that he'd said it. As I stood up to leave, he rose to his feet and hugged me tight. He thanked me once again for looking out for his mother and said how much he appreciated the fact that I didn't go off like he thought I would.

I replied, "No problem" and headed toward the stairs.

He said, "Sharon, you can stay if you want."

I declined the offer and said "Goodnight."

There I was in my car again engaging in a full-on conversation with myself. *Please don't let me have herpes, Lord. Wait a minute, Sharon,* I thought to myself. *He said that she said she had ". . .the virus that causes herpes, not actual herpes."* Either you have herpes, or you don't. Something didn't sound right. Nonetheless, I was going to my doctor to confirm. That was the longest week ever, waiting to get an appointment and even longer to wait an additional week to get the results.

Saint went to the same clinic in Manhattan that Lexus had gone to. I went with him to get his blood drawn. He was really scared straight for a while. He said he wasn't having sex with anyone until he got his results. Saint received his results before me. He was sick to his stomach when that clinic told him that he also had the virus that causes herpes.

Can you imagine? I felt jealous for a brief moment that Lexus and Saint both had this thing in common, which would forever bond them. When I finally got my results, they were negative. I was relieved that I could move on from him and this situation without permanent baggage. My doctor informed me that cold sores are a form of herpes, which would give someone prone to cold sores a positive result. I remembered that Saint would develop an ugly cold sore on his bottom lip every now and then. When I delivered the news of my results, I also told him to see his primary-care doctor and get a second opinion on that clinic's results.

I recall making a joke—that wasn't really a joke—about how he and Lexus might as well get married now, because they didn't have to worry about infecting each other.

He said, "That's not funny, but it's funny that you say that, because she did ask to get back together. She was trying to convince me to get married before her mother passed away. She tried to say that I'd given her the virus and that it was only fair that we be together now. She became more demanding of items she wanted in return for her forgiveness. I used to joke and say, 'You must think I'm Kobe Bryant.' She also told me that she wanted a Lexus as a wedding gift. I said that I would think about it."

I told him that he was an absolute fool to consider her demands. Saint didn't believe me when I said Lexus was money hungry, until after the herpes scare. He eventually took my advice and sought out a second opinion from his primary-care doctor, from whom he then received a negative result. Lexus eventually received negative results as well, once Saint told her he was negative. I assumed she felt that bond break between them once she'd gotten the negative result. She would have to work harder to get that engagement ring now.

I, on the other hand, found myself smack dab in the middle of general-contractor work once again. Ms. Josephine started complaining about the stairs bothering her knees, so I suggested converting the garage into a bedroom. She loved the idea, and the fact that we had converted the closet on the first floor into a full bathroom made the idea even more appealing. We immediately got to work on cleaning out the garage for the conversion. And just like before, when the job was done, all the pretty ladies—or, I should say *prissy ladies*—wanted to stop by so they could see the results. It seemed as if every other day I was receiving a phone call saying, "Sharon, this one or that one wanted to stop by and see the house."

I think Lurchette used the excuse of wanting to see the house when she was feeling horny. Saint would normally lie to her and make up an excuse as to why she couldn't stop by. However, she had those few pop-up moments. I would always check the sheets or if he was washing any sheets after she left. He would say, "Sharon, you don't have to do that.

I told you, I don't find her attractive like that anymore. She wanted to have sex, and she tried, but I refused."

He said she would always get mad, start crying, and then she would leave. The last time she'd used that excuse to see the house, she left saying she wasn't coming back over there again, because this time my car was parked in the driveway. At this point in my life, I felt I'd worked hard, and I deserved to treat myself to something special, so I brought my dream car, which was a silver Mercedes Benz, CLK 320. I still had my first love, which was my Acura Legend, so I parked the Benz at Saint's house.

Lurchette tried to get him to have me move my car, and because he refused, she said she would no longer come to his house. I can only assume that she was trying to continue the farce at the institution that she was in a relationship with Saint. Deep down inside, I felt bad for her. She called me "ugly," and, although I felt that way on the inside, I held my head high on the outside. I used to walk with my head down with my shoulders hunched over, and the Pruitt kids use to tease me for it. I had to learn to stand up straight and hold my head high but keep my feelings inside.

I convinced many people that I was a confident and secure woman when I was in their presence. No one would ever think that I suffered from low self-esteem. With Lurchette, I noticed she always walked with her head down, and I recognized that as a sign of diminished self-worth. We weren't friends, so I couldn't do anything to uplift her. What I did know was that we were both in love with a man who was toxic to our journey of loving or respecting ourselves.

Because everyone knew about each other at this point, I didn't have to park my car up the street and two blocks over anymore. Saint used to tell the other ladies that I just parked my car there but didn't stay there. He was lying, as usual, because at this time, I spent more time at his house than at my own apartment. Most of my clothes were in the closet, in the small room. I knew if someone was at the house, because he would hide my things. He used to think I had someone on the block watching him.

Once I started to question him about who was there, he would tell on himself. Through this method, I learned that his ex-girlfriend from college, a nurse from the hospital, and his so-called homegirl, named Athena, had all came by to see the house. Somehow, I adjusted to him going downstairs to make his phone calls, or I would stay quiet when he answered his phone in front of me. My tolerance for dealing with his disrespect oddly brought us closer together, as crazy as that sounds.

Lurchette finally gave up on the idea of them being a power couple at the job and put in her paperwork for a promotion to leave New York. I was happy that she was leaving, for several reasons: she needed to find a man who was going to like her kids, and it was one fewer woman that I had to worry about. Christina turned up pregnant by someone else, just a few months after she claimed she was leaving Saint alone for good. She, too, had received a promotion and left New York. I found it hard to believe that, one minute, she was head over heels in love with Saint and three months later was pregnant by someone else. Saint claimed that Christina was a good girl, who went to church every Sunday, and he really liked her, but they just didn't fit like a glove. That became his new phrase of the month: *No one fit like a glove.*

Secretly, I believed Saint thought the baby was his, but he wasn't sure because she always denied it. She eventually married the guy who'd fathered her child. I think she was still holding onto her feelings for Saint and secretly wanted the baby to be his. There was a time, after she'd had the baby, when she called the house phone, and I answered. She asked who I was, and I said my name. I had no clue it was Christina, because I didn't think Saint was still in contact with her—after all, she was married with a baby now.

Anyway, I asked, "Who is calling?" and she stated her name as if I needed to recognize her position. I politely took her message, which was to let Saint know she had called, and I hung up the phone. She called back, and when I answered again, she yelled, "Tell Saint he will never see his daughter, and he owes me child support!"

I remained calm and said, "I will let him know."

I'd learned a long time ago: *Never let them see you sweat.* They will never know that they got to me on an emotional level. Immediately, I called Saint at work to deliver Ms. Christina's messages. He initially got mad at me for answering the house phone, and that's when I lost my cool. I can tolerate everything, but I couldn't deal with a child born of disrespect. I cursed, yelled, and screamed about all the crap I'd had to deal with up until this point, and I was not going to take it anymore. I told him I was leaving and that he could go to hell—him, the baby, *and* Christina.

Ms. Josephine heard me upstairs cursing and called up to find out what was going on. I'd hung up the phone on her son, and I told her I had had enough. She then informed me that Christina did bring the baby to see her, and the baby did look like Saint. Hearing that solidified the fact that I needed to go away and leave this man alone. I felt there was nothing he could say after this. I left that house, and I was mentally through with it all.

I was sitting in my apartment feeling like a damn fool, when I heard the door unlock and the sound of the chain preventing it from opening all the way. I got up from the couch and saw his face through the crack of the door, saying, "Sharon, open the door."

I told him to get away from my door and to go buy his baby some Pampers.

He yelled, "That is not my baby! Open the door, so I can tell you what happened."

My stupid ass heard the next-door neighbor coming out of his apartment, and I didn't want my business out there like that, so I removed the chain from the door and let him in. He sat in the oversized chair and took a long pause before he spoke, saying, "Sharon, let me start by saying, I am sorry for what she said. I asked her why she'd said that, and she said it was because she was mad that you answered the phone."

"Who the fuck is she to say whether or not I can answer the phone!?" I yelled.

He said, "Sharon, calm down. The baby is not mine. Her husband made her take a DNA test, because he thought the baby was mine, but it proved that the little girl was his."

I relaxed my tone and said, "Saint, there are a lot of things I can put up with, but someone cheating on me and creating a life is not one of them."

He said, "Sharon, let me ask you a question: Why did you answer the house phone?"

The mere fact that he asked that question set me off again. "Saint, why the fuck does it matter?" I screamed.

"Sharon, just do me a favor, and don't answer my phone."

I responded by telling him to get the fuck out of my house, because he just didn't get it.

"I will call you later," he said, as he walked out the door.

I felt I needed a break from Saint and all his bullshit. I just wanted to get away, so I booked a trip to Jamaica. My mother had told me stories about me in Jamaica as a little girl, but I had never been there as an adult. My brother, Andrew, had been illegally deported back to Jamaica, so I thought it will be great to see him.

I eventually told Saint that I was going away by myself, and he didn't believe me. He accused me of going to fuck somebody new. As a jab and a reference to his trip to the DR, I told him, "I'm not you. I will always pride myself on being a better person than you." I can't speak for any other woman, but penis is the last thing on my mind when I am down, depressed, or upset. I didn't want to give his ignorance any life, and, therefore, I didn't focus on him and his foolishness. I couldn't wait for the month and a half to pass so I could leave.

During that time, I spent less time than usual at his house, but I did call his mother every other day to check on her. While at work, I decided to call Ms. Josephine, and a woman's voice answered the phone. I was taken aback for a minute, but instantly I recognized the voice, but I still asked, "Who is this?"

She said, "This is Saint's fiancée, Lexus."

That's when I had to let her know it was Sharon on the other end of the line, and I said it with authority.

She fired right back with, "Sharon, his mother doesn't need you coming around anymore, because I am here now. She said she doesn't want you with Saint, because you are ugly and ya'll would have ugly babies." Then she giggled. "Saint don't want you, either. That's why I am here. He came back to me with a ring, so do us a favor and stay away. Go try to find someone to claim you. Saint told me that no other man ever claimed you as their girl," she said, laughing. She called out, "Mommy," as she referred to Ms. Josephine, "tell her that you don't need her here anymore."

When I heard the sound of Ms. Josephine's voice begin to repeat those words, that was it for me. I had been betrayed by his mother for the last time. I hung up the phone and called my lieutenant, saying I was sick and needed to go home now. I called Saint in control center and told him I was going to fuck his fiancée up. As I waited in the lobby for my relief, Saint kept calling, trying to find out what had happened.

When I gave him a moment to speak, he tried to explain why he'd given her a ring. He kept saying, "It's not an engagement ring; it is a promise ring."

My mouth was quick with a response: "I promise you—I am going to fuck her up! Bye, Saint. My relief is here," and hung up the phone on him. I got into my car, and my vision became completely tunnel. All I saw was her face in my head, and I kept hearing her say I was ugly and how Saint told her nobody had ever claimed me.

I knew then he had shared my deepest secret with her, because I had never shared that with anyone but him. Saint kept calling my phone, begging me to not go to his house. He was trying to get me to pull over and calm down.

He said, "I am leaving work now. Just pull over and wait for me."

I stopped taking his calls, because I was determined that she was going to see just what an ugly girl can do. My text-message alert was going off like crazy. All the messages were from Saint, saying he told his mother not to open the door when I got there. I pulled up in front of the house, and, as I was walking toward the front door, I saw Ms. Josephine through the glass.

She said, "Sonya, what is going on? Saint said not to let you in, and I don't want no trouble here."

I didn't want to verbally disrespect her, but my eyes shot her a look that obviously let her know that I meant business. I was disgusted by her actions as well. I said, "There will be no trouble. Just tell Lexus to come outside."

I started banging on the door, and I could see Lexus at the top of the stairs, smiling. I was infuriated at this point, so I began to threaten to break the glass on the front door. As I was banging on the glass door, a car pulled up in front of the house, grill to grill with my car. I recognized the driver's face. It was Gary, the cop from Freeport, and one of Saint's close friends.

He said, "Sharon, don't do this. Think about your job."

I screamed at the top of my lungs, "Fuck that job! Beating that bitch's ass will all be worth it. I have a fucking degree—I will get another job!"

At this point, Lexus made her way downstairs to the door. Gary used his body to block my path to the doorway. As he stood in between me and the door, he ordered Ms. Josephine to open the door so that he could go in.

I saw my chance, and I took it.

As the door opened, I reached around Gary and tried to snatch Lexus out of the house. I felt someone grab me from behind and lift me off the front porch. When the person let me go, I turned to face him, and I saw it was Saint. As he slowly put me down, he said, "Sharon, please leave." Then he *yelled*, "Just leave!"

I was irate by this point. I was in the front yard yelling, "Fuck this house and everybody in it—I made this house a home."

I swore I would never let any of these bitches see me like that. But before I knew it, tears were flowing down my face, and I was purging myself of all the pent-up rage I'd felt over the years. Ms. Josephine heard what I'd said, and that made her open the door, saying, "Sonya, you said 'Fuck everybody in this house.' I live here. Are you saying, 'Fuck me'?"

As I said before, I didn't want to verbally disrespect her, but if she could read my mind, then she would have known that she was definitely included.

Saint said, "Ma, close the door and go back into the house!"

Lexus must have felt protected, because she said, "Saint, tell her you don't want to be with her."

He looked at me and said, "Sharon, I can't do this anymore." It was as if she was their puppet master. Everything she told them to say, both he and his mother would repeat the words like she'd cast had a voodoo spell on them.

Lexus said, "You heard him—so now you can leave."

I saw red, and I went straight for her. Saint and Gary grabbed me, as he yelled for Lexus to go upstairs. He said, "Sharon if you don't leave, I will call the cops."

I was shocked that he would consider doing that to me. That really stopped me in my tracks for a minute. That had never been an option for me when he'd put his hands on me. I looked him dead in his face and asked, "Would you really call the police on me?"

He just replied, "Please leave."

Call it "Ghetto," but I called out, "Fuck it! Call the police then—because I ain't going nowhere." I was pacing back and forth in front of the house. As I was walking on the grass, Saint had the nerve to say, "Sharon, get off the grass."

I thought to myself, *This nigga must be out of his damn mind, to think I give two fucks about his grass right now.* My voice went to an octave I didn't even know existed, as I shouted, "I don't give a fuck about this grass! I rake this lawn, and I picked out these pavers. I did everything in this damn house."

Before I knew it, I was telling everything that I knew about him that Lexus had never known. I looked up at the top of the stairs and saw Saint and Lexus peering down at me. Saint had a look on his face that read, *Sharon, please don't do this.*

Lexus had a look of disbelief as to what she was hearing. Gary just had a look of, *What the fuck is going on here?* Ms. Josephine was just standing there, as if to say, *Saint, I told you not to have all these women.*

I just kept talking to a point when I couldn't even hear myself anymore. When I finally heard my own voice again, I heard me ask, "Is this who you want?"

He looked down at me and said in a low tone, "Yes, I choose Lexus."

She had a smirk on her face that I wanted to wipe away with my fist, but I couldn't get to her, so I used my words. I knew she was trying hard to get pregnant with Saint's child, so I yelled up the stairs, "Your dumb ass is trying to get pregnant, and I was already pregnant with his child. I am so glad that I got rid of that baby."

I was satisfied when I saw that smirk leave her face. I turned to Ms. Josephine and said, "I have always been here for you, and you flipped on me for her. That bitch is nothing but a gold digger, and I hope she takes you for every dime you have."

As I was venting, the police showed up. They noticed we were both wearing uniforms, and Gary showed his badge. They asked what was going on, and Saint and Gary spoke to the officers, trying to explain the situation. By that time, I had calmed down, and all I wanted was my clothes and shoes out of his house.

The police officer said that, normally, they would have to take someone in, however, as a courtesy, they would let this pass. Saint went inside to gather my things, and Gary helped me place them in my car. I drove off feeling as low as any human being can get. Later that evening, I received a text from Saint asking if I was OK. I never responded to his text. I didn't go to work the next day, because I had cried so hard that my face and eyes were swollen. All I could do was drown myself in work, as I anticipated going to Jamaica after that incident.

The day was finally here. I had never been away before, let alone by myself, but this trip to Jamaica was what I needed. I had a great time all by myself. My brother came to my hotel resort, and we just laughed and enjoyed each other's company. I relaxed on the beach, I climbed Dunn's River Falls, and I went shopping in the Jamaican market. I was mentally prepared to make Saint a part of my past by the end of that week.

Upon my return to work, he made every effort to contact me. He sent me flowers to the jail with an apology note. I took the flowers because they were beautiful, but they meant nothing to me in the way of "I'm sorry."

Two weeks had passed since I had returned from my trip, and I'd managed to stay Saint-free. Free from all communication, free from any visual contact, and just plain ol' free of him. Our schedule at work was perfect for me, because there wasn't an overlap in which I would see him. Unfortunately for me, I didn't take into consideration that he might work overtime. As I was waiting in the sally port for the elevator to pick me up, I was surprised to see his face as the doors opened. I had no other choice but to get on because the other elevator was broken. As the doors closed, he tried to talk to me by asking how I was doing and how my trip was. I was anticipating the elevator doors opening on the first floor, so I could get off and get away from him.

He said, "Sharon, please don't be like that."

I broke my silence, and with a major attitude, I replied, "Act like *what*, Saint? How do you want me to act?"

"Just talk to me, Sharon," he said, trying to sound sorry.

"I don't have anything to say to you except I want the sex tapes and all of the sex pictures you have of me back."

"You don't trust me?" he asked.

"I will never trust a man who calls the police on me and tries to have me arrested."

As he began to speak, the doors opened, and I bolted out of the elevator. I contemplated going home, but I made the decision not to let anyone come between me and my money. I had given Saint so much of my love, pride, and dignity, I couldn't let him come between me and my money as well.

Every chance he got to get off the elevator, he would come down to the lobby and try to talk to me. Thank God that there were always other people around, so he couldn't discuss our personal issues because we were still a secret. The entire time I was in the lobby, he kept calling, trying to get me to hear him out. In order for me to get any peace, I allowed him to just talk, as I listened.

He claimed that he'd called the police only because he didn't know what else to do. He further claimed that he told Gary to call and check on me. He said his mother was hurt when she learned I was pregnant and had an abortion. After he finished speaking, he asked me if was I going to say anything.

My response was, "I have nothing to say, and all I want is the tapes and pictures."

"Okay, Sharon," he replied, "but I will not bring them to the jail, so you have to come get them."

"No problem, Saint. Let me know when is a good time for you," I told him. "I am also trying to find someplace to keep my car, because I don't want your fiancée to do anything to it."

"Sharon, she is not my fiancée, and you know I won't let anything happen to your car. I just want you to know how sorry I am, and I didn't want you to get arrested. I just wanted you to leave. I will call you and let you know when you can stop by," he said, before he hung up.

Because of our schedule conflict, it was almost a week before I was able to go pick up the tape and pictures. When I pulled up in front of the house, a flash flood of memories came back from the last day I was there. It was hard for me to go inside. I knew I didn't want to see his mother. I also knew she didn't like going into the basement, and I knew I wasn't going into any of the bedrooms upstairs, so to the basement I went. He came downstairs with a plate of pork chops, mashed potatoes, and broccoli. I told him all I wanted was my things, but he begged me to stay because he'd made the meal himself just for me.

As we sat and ate dinner, I noticed the ceiling in the basement had been fixed. My mind went back to the night when we'd attached a sex swing to the ceiling. He sat down first, and I climbed on top, straddling him, when the entire section of the ceiling collapsed on us. His mother came to the top of the steps and attempted to come downstairs, and we both yelled, "Don't come down here! It's okay!" Afterward, we both sat on the basement floor, laughing uncontrollably. Saint noticed that I was staring at the ceiling and he said, "You remember that night? We had fun together despite everything else." He started to tell me how sorry he was again, but I interrupted him and asked if he could go to get the tape and pictures.

"Sharon, I would never do anything with those pictures and the tape. I actually watched the video the other day, and you looked so beautiful on the tape. Plus, you know I don't know how to do any of that type of stuff on the computer," he said. "Nobody has the combination to my safe, so it's safe here with me."

After giving it some thought, I decided it he was right, so I let him keep them in his safe. He tried hard to get me to spend the night, and I did. I slept in the basement on the couch. I left the next morning after I heard his mother leave for the center. Two nights later, I found myself back in his house, unbeknownst to his mother. I would hang out only in the basement, although he tried very hard to get me upstairs. He would say,

"Sharon, you don't have to hide from my mother." He really believed that was my reason for not going upstairs. My *real* reason was twofold: I didn't want to see the woman who'd betrayed me several times, and I didn't want to sleep in the same bed as all those other chicks. I told him I wasn't ready to see his mother, and I would never go back to his bed again, unless he got a new mattress. He agreed, because he needed a new mattress anyway.

We started spending more time at my apartment and going out. Saint called me at work and asked me not to work any overtime because he wanted to take me somewhere. He would not give me a clue where we were going. This reminded me of the time he surprised me with a helicopter ride to view the lights over the City at night. We parked the car in a lot, somewhere in the City, and had to walk up some dark side street. The area looked creepy to me. I just kept saying, "Where the hell do you have me?"

There was a bouncer outside the door, and all he asked was, "Just two?" Saint answered "Yes," and he opened the door to usher us in. We walked to a window, where Saint paid some lady sitting in a booth. She explained that there was a male and female locker room located down the hall, where we would find robes. She also explained that dinner would be served buffet style, straight to the back. I still had no clue where we were and what was going on.

As we were walking down the dimly lit hall, Saint explained that this was a swinging club. My feet stopped moving immediately, and my immediate reaction was to say, "*Hell*, no!"

He said, "Sharon, you don't have to do anything with anybody—just stay." I agreed to stay because I was curious as to what the hell went on in one of these places. As I entered the locker room to strip off my clothes, my mind was racing, wondering what the hell was I doing. When I exited the locker room, Saint was standing there, staring at me. He saw that I was extremely nervous, so he said, "Let's just go get something to eat; then we can leave if you want."

As we walked toward the food, it appeared to be a normal atmosphere. They didn't serve drinks, but we met another couple who'd brought their own bottle of Hennessy, and they shared a glass with us. Saint and the boyfriend were laughing at me because I had that scared look on my face. The boyfriend was really friendly, but the girl was standoffish. I had to admit—the food was good as hell. The girl and her boyfriend left to go upstairs, and he invited us to join them, but Saint knew I wanted to leave after we ate, so he told them we were going to stay downstairs a little longer.

Saint convinced me to hang around downstairs and check out the environment. We opened a door to a room that had two mattresses on the floor. One of the patrons of the establishment said that those were semi-private rooms and we could use one if we wanted to.

I said, "No, thanks" really quick. I could see Saint that was disappointed, so I suggested we go upstairs. My mind was completely blown once I got upstairs. There were rooms filled with mattresses, with couples side by side, having sex in all positions. There was a small room in the middle that had a sex swing and something that resembled a mechanical bull. I was intrigued by that contraption. As I was standing watching other people have sex, some strange man walked up behind me and ran his finger down my back. I felt a disgusting chill go down my spine. I wanted to scream, *Don't fucking touch me!*

Instead, Saint told the guy, "No, she's not with that." I tapped Saint on the shoulder and whispered in his ear that I wanted to try that bull apparatus. He was shocked and excited at the same time. I climbed on top like a pro. It was almost like riding a motorcycle, with your body in the lowest position to block the wind. This position forces my ass upwards and accentuates the natural arch in my back. Saint entered me from behind and we got started, I no longer cared that we were in the middle of a room, with people all around watching. It felt good, and I wasn't concerned about the voyeurs.

Saint decided he wanted to go into of one of the rooms with all the mattresses. As we were walking around looking for a room with an available mattress space, some Spanish girl asked me if she could fuck my man. Saint had that look on his face as if he was with it. I shut that down, right away. In fact, that blew my entire mood. I went and stood in the doorway of another room, and just watched. There was this White guy, and I assumed the girl was his woman, however, she was getting long-dicked by some Black guy and sucking the hell out of some Spanish dude's dick, at the same time. The White guy kept asking her, "Do you like that? I know you like his dick, because it's bigger than mine. Do you like the way he's fucking that pussy?"

It was the craziest mess I had ever witnessed in my life. Saint knew I was upset, so he whispered in my ear, "Sharon, I wasn't going to do it."

I said, "Let's just go downstairs." We went and sat in this room where people were just kissing, finger fucking, and dick sucking. We saw the couple from earlier in that room. He asked me if I was enjoying myself yet. I said, "It's cool—not as bad as I thought it would be."

After watching all the dick-sucking going on, I wanted to practice my skills in private, so we went to seek out a private room. We could find only a semi-private room instead. The other couple in there were having classic sex, missionary style. We went to the other side of the room, and I began to practice my skills. Something about knowing other people are watching makes you want to give it your all. Saint wanted to put on a show of our own, so he told me to stop before I made him reach his peak. The missionary couple left the room, so now, we were alone. I heard someone open the door, but they never entered the room. Then I heard, "That girl can take some dick." That comment made me feel like I was about to win the gold medal for fucking.

When Saint was about to climax, he screamed—loudly—but thank goodness the music was louder. As we were leaving, they gave us cards and asked us to come back with friends. Saint said, "We will definitely be back."

The walk back to the car was quiet, as if we were ashamed of what had just happened. I broke the ice by asking, "Have you brought anyone else here, and how did you hear about this place?"

He said, "The guy who worked in the kitchen told me about it, and, no, I have not brought anyone else here. You know none of them would ever to come to a place like this."

"So why did you bring me here?" I asked.

"Sharon, with you, I can be myself. I know you would be down to try new things," he said. "I knew you wouldn't make a big deal about coming here, and that's why I love you." I made light of the fact that he said he loved me. I quoted a line from the rapper Snoop Dog and said, "You don't love me—you just love my doggie style."

Of course, since Saint was a typical man, I had to drive home because he wanted to sleep. He claimed he'd put in more work than me in the spot. I knew this place was going to hold special memories for both of us. I felt like I had taken the lead, or at least, a step forward among all the ladies. We never did return to that place.

Saint eventually bought the new mattress, so I kept my word, and I started going back upstairs to the bedroom. We decided to break in the mattress and made a bet that he couldn't last all day. To my surprise, he was good for three rounds.

Because I no longer was hanging out in the basement, I eventually had to speak to his mother. I kept conversation to a bare minimum. One day, Saint left me upstairs while he went to the store, and his sister came over. Yes, this is the same sister who'd given me the questionable card. While she and her mother were talking in the kitchen, I came downstairs to get a drink. She asked how I was and proceeded to tell me again that she was glad I had been there for her mother.

Ms. Josephine chimed in and said, "Yes, Sonya has been really good to me."

In my mind, I was thinking, *You should have remembered how good I have been to you on several occasions, but you sided with that bitch Lexus.*

Annie said, "I've heard a little about what has been going on, and I am surprised you're still around after that. I mean, you are not really Saint's type. He likes those yellow girls with long hair."

Every time I'd seen her, she had to remind me that she practically raised him. I was thinking, *Maybe you shouldn't be bragging about that, because he did not turn out to be something to brag about.*

She went on to say, "He used to bring all his little girlfriends home to meet me."

I felt like she was throwing jabs at her mother whenever she said something like that.

She said, "There was another dark-skinned girl, like you, named Sharon, that he used to date, and he would beat that girl up all the time." Then she looked at me with sympathetic eyes, as if waiting for a reaction. When I didn't react, they both told me Saint had some girl down in the basement who was wearing brown. I couldn't show any feelings at hearing this news. At least, I couldn't show it to them. I felt like the both of them were trying to hurt me on purpose, because I saw no reason for them to betray their son/brother like this. Then she said, "I am telling you this only because I like you, and if you ever need to talk, just come by my house."

Ms. Josephine added that Lexus had just been there two days ago. Now, I really felt like they were trying to hurt me, because Ms. Josephine had never looked out for me when it came down to the other women. They couldn't hurt me with that information, because he'd called me to say that she'd showed up, again, uninvited. Their motives were questionable, but they had planted a seed, so I said, "Thank you for telling me," and I went upstairs to pack my things.

When Saint returned and found me packing my things, he asked, "What happened now?"

I just came out and said, "Who did you have here three nights ago, down in the basement wearing brown, with a big belt around her waist?"

He had a puzzled look on his face, and I said, "Don't bother to lie because your mother and sister told me they saw her."

He denied knowing who they could be talking about. He also denied beating on his former girlfriend. He didn't have an answer as to why his mother and sister would tell me any of that. I left the situation alone because I had no proof, and I didn't completely trust the source of the information. I did take a mental note that he never went downstairs to confront his mother or sister about telling me anything like that.

That night, I tried to discuss plans for my birthday. I wanted us to go somewhere together, but he kept coming up with all types of excuses. I started looking for inexpensive trips for myself. I decided to go to Acapulco, Mexico. I kept trying to get him to commit to going with me, but he said, "Sharon, just book your trip, and I will let you know."

The next few months flew by, and I ended up in Mexico by myself. That's when I decided not to wait on him—or anyone else—when I decided to do something for me. When I got back from Mexico, I learned Lexus's mother had died. As much as I wanted to say, "That's her issue," I didn't have it in my heart. When Saint said he had to go pay his respects, I totally understood. Lexus was using the death of her mother as a noose around his neck. She began to call and spend time with his niece, Chrisy. She knew Chrisy was Saint's heart. She also latched on to his mother even tighter.

One day, I went into his mother's room to check on her and saw that she had a picture of Lexus and Saint at the Circle Line Cruise Ship by her nightstand. She said, "Lexus took the train out there earlier that day, just to be with me." She said Lexus slept in the bed with her, because that's what she did with her own mother before she died. Prior to this day, Ms. Josephine was asking me to sleep in the room with her, and now I understood why. She also told me I could call her "Mommy," but I didn't feel comfortable with that. Besides, I knew all the rest of those girls were calling her "Mommy." I knew the real reason that she'd slept in the bed with Ms. Josephine was that Saint had locked his bedroom door so no one could search his room when he wasn't home. Deep down, I don't think he trusted his mother not to let anyone into the house when he wasn't home.

Lexus would lay the guilt trip on so thick when she couldn't get her way. She would cry and tell him her mother was dead and that she didn't have any family but him and his mother. I understood her grief, but this was taking advantage—at least that's how I saw it.

One night, Saint told me to stay home and that he would come to my apartment. I sat there waiting on him thinking he was on his way, but then I received a phone call from him saying he'd been arrested. I couldn't believe what I was hearing.

He said, "Lexus had me arrested."

"What the hell are you talking about?" I asked. "Where are you?" I inquired again.

He said, "Sharon, I need you."

The sound of desperation in his voice made me know it was time to wear the homegirl hat.

"I'm at the precinct in Harlem," he said. "Please call my mother and Guiliani, if you need money, just in case they ask for bail."

"How much money do you think we will need?" I asked. I heard him call to a police officer to ask the question. I could hear the police officer say, "This is your first offense, so he may release you on your own recognizance, but I would tell them to bring at least $2500."

Saint said, "I will try to call you back."

I hung up the phone and called his mother to give her the bad news. I didn't have any details, and, so, I couldn't provide her any answers to the questions she was asking. I drove out to Long Island to pick her up and then headed back toward the city. On my way, I called Guiliani, and he said he would meet me at the precinct. By the time we got to the precinct, they had taken him over to night court. As we sat and waited to hear his name called, Guiliani arrived. He started asking more questions than I had answers for—except, of course, the fact that it was Lexus who'd had him arrested.

As the court clerk called his name, he appeared from behind a glass enclosure. I could still hear his voice.

"Saint," the clerk said, as he ran down the charges against him. "The charge is domestic battery of his fiancée. He is accused of choking and slapping her," the clerk said loudly.

Once I heard the charges, I knew it was true. I flashed back to the scene in the control center. I remembered the conversation with his sister. It all made sense that he was capable of doing this. The police officer said he would be released on his own recognizance; however, the judge did issue a restraining order stating he needed to stay away from Lexus. Call me crazy, but I was sort of glad that it happened because I knew he had to stay away from her now.

Saint walked out and hugged his mother, gave his friend a pound, looked at me, and said, "We will talk later. I just want to go home and be with my mother."

Guiliani drove them back to Long Island, and I went home to await his call. Instead, what I received was a call from Lexus. She was absolutely the last person I wanted to speak to. She asked me if I'd bailed him out of jail. I ignored her question and asked her why she was calling me.

"I just wanted to know if he ever hit you," she said. I didn't respond to her question, so she kept talking. "I couldn't believe he put his hands on me," she said. "I have scratches on my neck where he grabbed me by my throat and lifted me off the ground; then he slapped me in my face. I have his fingerprints on the left side of my face. He had the nerve to start crying when I said I was calling the police. He begged me not to call, because of his job, and I told him to get out of my house and that he should lose his job for what he'd done to my face. He refused to leave, so when the police showed up and saw what he'd done to me, they had to take him in."

I just let her talk while I listened very carefully, because all I really wanted to know was what had led to all of this. She continued to ramble, and then she finally got to the part I was waiting for. She said, "He showed up at my house, unannounced, when my friend was there, and he went off."

Now it made a little more sense to me. At the same time, I thought, *Karma is a bitch.* He'd caught Miss Beautiful possibly cheating.

"He thought I was cheating on him, but why would I bring a man here, when I know he has keys?" she asked. She asked me again if he'd ever hit me, and I denied that he had. I told her, "I have to go, but I hope you feel better."

Saint never called me that night, but he did invite me over the next morning. When I saw him, I didn't say a word, until he was ready to speak about what had happened. I really wanted to hear how he ended up going to Harlem, instead of coming to Brooklyn like he was supposed to. He said he wanted her to know how it felt when someone just shows up unannounced. Of course, he started out with what he saw when he walked into her house. He said, "I walked in and heard voices, and when I walked back toward the bedroom, I saw some dude sitting on the bed." He said that he told the dude to leave, and the guy turned to Lexus and asked her if she was going to be OK. He said, "That statement pissed me off." Then he asked Lexus who the guy was, and she said, "None of your business."

"That's when I put my hand on her neck and told her not to play with me. I didn't grab her and choke her—or whatever it is she said I did."

I asked him, "How did she get scratches on her neck?"

He said, "She tried to push my hand away, and my nail scratched her."

At that point, I didn't want to hear any more, but then he said something stupid, in my opinion. He wanted to call her and get her to drop the charges. He felt he could persuade her to stop this before it got too far. Both Ms. Josephine and I told him that that was a bad idea. We both felt he needed to secure his job.

He decided to hire one of the lawyers who represented a few of the inmates at the jail, Mr. Cardenas. Mr. Cardenas also advised Saint not to contact Lexus. The jail said there was nothing they could do until the final determination of the case. If the charges were reduced to a misdemeanor, then he was not at risk of losing his job.

Saint became a little distant and withdrawn from everyone. I assumed it was because of the situation and not knowing how this would turn out. At night he would ask me to sleep in the small room or in the basement, because he wanted to be alone. I didn't argue, because I knew he had a lot on his mind however, I did feel rejected. His depression was getting the best of him, and I just wanted to be there for him.

About two weeks later, I wanted to make him relax, so I fixed him a bubble bath and his favorite drink. While he was sitting in the tub, his house phone began to ring. I brought him the phone in the bathroom without looking at the caller ID, and I proceeded to go downstairs to fix myself a drink. As I was coming back up the steps, I yelled out to ask if he needed anything else. I had no idea he was still on the phone. As I entered the bathroom, he had an upset look on his face.

I asked, "What's wrong?"

He said, "That was Lexus, but she hung up because she heard you in the background. I had her—she was talking and possibly willing to drop the charges. I'm going to call her back, so if you don't mind, can you go downstairs in the basement, and I will come get you when I'm done."

"Saint, don't call her back," I pleaded with him. "As long as it shows that she is the one calling you, then you are clear and not in violation of the restraining order. If you call her, she can say anything at that point," I said.

"Sharon, I just need to think. Can you stay at your house tonight?" he asked.

I answered, "Sure. No problem. But Saint, don't call her," I warned.

I went home that night feeling like he was going to do the right thing. I didn't hear from him the next day, until that evening. When he finally called, he said, "Sharon, you were right. I have to turn myself in tomorrow for breaking the restraining order."

"Saint, what did you do?" I asked.

"I called her back last night, and she agreed to meet me for lunch. When I got out there, we talked for a little while, and she seemed like she was coming around to dropping the charges, but then she said she would drop the charges only if I agreed never to speak to you again."

I had a look of shock and disbelief on my face, because I'd had nothing to do with what had taken place in her apartment. He recognized that look on my face as pure bewilderment.

He said, "I know, and I tried to tell her that, but she wouldn't listen. She was upset that you were here last night. I just need you to come and drive with me and my mother tomorrow, when I turn myself in," he said. "My mother wants to go with me, but I don't know if they are going to keep me, and she will need a ride to get back home," he stated.

I asked him if he'd called Mr. Cardenas.

He said, "Cardenas is going to meet us at the courthouse. He thinks they may release me again on my own recognizance, because she was the one who contacted me first."

I felt defeated by the situation, and I just agreed to go. While at the courthouse, I sat quietly, just thinking how underappreciated I felt. He noticed that I wasn't saying much and assumed I was worried about him. He whispered to me, "Don't worry. It's going to be okay. I will not go near her again."

The judge didn't think it was okay for him to disregard the restraining order, so he set bail at $2500. We were not prepared for this, based on what his lawyer had told us. Once again, I went above and beyond for the man I loved—who'd betrayed and belittled me for the woman who'd put him in jail. His mother didn't have access to their money, and Saint had left his checkbook at home. I called my bank and increased the amount I could retrieve through the ATM machine, and then I paid his bail. I made him swear on his mother's life that he would stay away from her. I felt more secure that he would stay away from her if he owned me the bail money.

The next day, he gave me my money back.

He said he just wanted to pay me back just in case something else happened and the bail was revoked. I think he really paid me back because he didn't trust himself not to stay away from her. Two days later, I received yet another call from Ms. Lexus.

She said, "Sharon, I don't know why you are so loyal to him, when he talks about you like a dog. I know you don't believe me, but you can hear it for yourself." She pressed "Play" on a recorder, and I heard his voice telling her how much he loved her and that they could go to the Justice of the Peace and get married. I heard him say that he would cut me—and everyone else—off, for her.

Lexus said, "Sharon ain't going nowhere, Saint. You keep saying that, and then she always ends up back over there," she said.

He responded by saying, "I don't want her. She's not as pretty as you. I keep her around only for my mother."

The tape stopped, and Lexus asked, "Are you still there? Sharon, do you hear how he talks about you?"

I never answered her question, and instead, I told her I had another call and I would call her back. I didn't have another call, but I was surely going to make a call. I had to let him know what kind of woman he was disrespecting me for. He immediately knew something was wrong by the tone in my voice, when I asked, "Did you tell Lexus that you keep me around only for your mother?"

I didn't wait for him to answer. I just moved on to the next thing that came to my mind. "I know you called me 'ugly,' so I'm not going to bother to ask you if you said that."

He did what he does best—lie. That's when I had to burst his bubble. "You are a lying piece of shit!" I said. "Your precious Lexus taped your entire conversation and played it to me over the phone, stupid ass. You deserve everything you get, because you keep fuckin' with that bitch."

I slammed the phone down on the charger base. He called back several times, but I didn't answer. I let them all go straight to voice mail. When I finally listened to the messages, he said, "I said those things only to get her to drop the charges. Sharon, please call me back. I need you. You and my mother are all that I have now."

I understood his desperation over the situation, however, Mr. Cardenas had already told him that, even if Lexus dropped the charges, the DA's office could still pick them up. He knew this prior to calling her, and he was stupid enough to be recorded. Approximately two to three months later, the charges were reduced to a misdemeanor harassment charge, with mandatory anger-management class. He finally got it through his head that Lexus was not to be trusted.

He didn't trust anyone over the phone anymore, so he bought a recorder of his own. He would always ask, "Do you hear that clicking in the phone? Are you recording me, also?"

I paid his paranoid ass no attention. It did bother me that he felt he couldn't trust me, after all the crap I'd put up with—not to mention how many times I'd lied for him. I will admit that he was right not to trust me in his room; I would definitely rummage through his things. He had me doing something I said I would never do as a woman, which was searching for heartache. I had free access to every other room in his house except his bedroom, when he wasn't home.

What Saint didn't know was that I had picked his bedroom-door lock on several occasions. He was not tech savvy enough to realize, when he answered the house phone, the recorder would pick up and tape his conversations if he answered after three rings. I listened to a few more conversations he had with Lexus, after he swore he wouldn't talk to her anymore. There were other conversations with women who never referred to themselves by their names during the conversation, and he never called them by their names. I could tell these were women from his past, because there was a lot of reminiscing throughout the conversation.

I went through his drawers, the closet, and computer, looking for whatever I could find. I found cards with pictures of Christina's daughter, stating, "She should be yours, and thank you for always being there for her."

I couldn't believe what I was reading. This fool has been sending her money to help her with her daughter, and she was married. He used to hide things under the mattress, and one day I slipped up and forgot to put the sheets back exactly how they were. When he came home and asked me if I'd been in his room, I told the first lie in our entire situation.

I felt bad, but I also knew I couldn't pick his lock anymore, because he would set a trap next time.

More months went by, and things got a little better between us. I felt like I had him to myself, for at least a little while, but he still didn't fully trust me. After Lexus pulled that stunt with making a copy of his key, he took my key back as well. He put me in a position to use my friends as a place to stay until he got home, before I could go to his house. My friends would make smart comments about the fact that we had been together for so long, so why didn't I have keys already? Instead of explaining my situation to anyone, I just stopped going around them. If I was at the house with his mother, I had to hang out in the basement or the small room until he got home. I did all of this because I knew Saint would eventually get over Lexus—and anyone else—and see that I was a good girl who would stick by him. The phrase was, "Ride or Die Chick." I wanted him to see that I would stand the test of time with him, if he would just give me a fair chance.

Saint started talking about going to Jamaica and taking his mother with him. He was excited about her showing him the country, from her perspective. He wanted to see where she grew up and learn more about his family. Ms. Josephine, on the other hand, didn't want to go. She didn't feel Saint loved her anymore. She said, "He doesn't talk to me like he used to." She would say, "He always snaps at me when I try to talk to him." I think Saint was probably a little disappointed with her because she set him up to be caught several times. I think she confused those feelings of disappointment with him not loving her anymore.

He was disappointed to learn that she didn't want to go back to Jamaica. She was stubborn, and I worked hard to convince her to go, because this was something that he'd always wanted to do with her. She wanted me to go as well, but I told her it would be good for her and her son to just get away together. When she finally told him that she would go, that made him so happy. He thanked me and said, "I don't know what you said to her, but thank you."

They were booked and scheduled to leave a week before Mother's Day. This was his gift to her. April 25, 2004, I drove them to the airport, and Ms. Josephine was still hesitant to go to Jamaica, but she liked to see him happy. I gave them both a hug and told them to have a good time.

I was sitting at home watching television and waiting on him to call to let me know they'd arrived safely. When the phone rang and I saw it was him, I was happy to know they'd landed safely. When I answered the phone, he said, "Sharon, she is gone."

I said, "What are you talking about, Saint?"

"Sharon, my mother is dead."

I couldn't control my emotions, and I completely lost it. He said they thought she had a heart attack mid-flight. He kept talking, and I was hearing his words, but they weren't making any sense to me. He said, "When we landed, they rushed her to the hospital, but it was too late."

Through my tears, I asked, "What do you need me to do?"

He said, "Call Donna, and I will call you later."

I told him that I loved him and that I was so sorry for his loss. I tried to gather my composure, because I had never delivered such bad news like this to anyone. I was still fighting back tears when his niece answered the phone. The moment I heard her voice, the thought of having to repeat those unbelievable words broke me down again as I said, "Chrisy, she's gone. Your grandmother passed away on the flight to Jamaica."

Chrisy instantly started crying and screaming for her mother to come to the phone. The thought of having to say those words again was unbearable, but I told Donna as much as I knew. She said, "Thanks for telling me." She was way calmer than I would be, hearing someone tell me of the sudden death of my family member.

I cried that entire night. Ms. Josephine and I had had our ups and downs, but over the past few months, I knew she loved me more than her son; moreover, I knew I loved her, too. I started researching flights so I could go to Jamaica to be with him. When he finally called me back, he said he was at his cousin Marcia's house. He said it didn't make sense for me to come to Jamaica, because he was having his mother's body flown back to the States for her final, going-home service. He said he would be home at the end of the week. He had to make sure everything was taken care of on that end for her transport.

When he arrived back in New York, I was anxious, because I didn't know what to say to him. I didn't know how he would be once he stepped into the house, knowing she would never be there again. He took such pride in the fact he'd been able to buy a house in the suburbs and take his mother out of Brooklyn. On the ride home from the airport, he just kept saying, "I can't believe she's gone." He described in detail how she collapsed in his arms. He believed that she'd died in his arms, and that gave him some comfort.

As we entered the house, we both looked around. All of the many dolls she'd made at the senior citizen center became precious items. In true Ms. Josephine fashion, I asked, "Do you want some tea?" We both smiled for a second, because it could be morning, noon, or night, but she was always offering tea. Saint went into her room and prayed for what seemed like hours. I think he just wanted to surround himself with her things.

The next day, we got to work setting up the arrangements for her service, however, it was going to take two weeks to get her body home. Saint had always prayed every day before he left the house, for exactly 10 minutes, but with the death of his mother, it was extended to 20–25 minutes. I had to be patient, and I had to be considerate; I was willing to do all of that for him. I knew the death of his mother would bring back all of those women I thought were moving on.

Saint's cousin, Marcia, came up from Jamaica with her two boys, and her husband was catching a later flight. Marcia and Saint were cousins, but distant cousins. She was a nice-looking lady, and she was really nice to me. She also made me feel a little uncomfortable, by the way she looked at Saint. When he was still in Jamaica, and I would call her house looking for him, it never seemed as if she had to leave the room to give him the phone. I didn't want to act like the jealous girlfriend, knowing he'd just lost his mother, but it made me a little suspicious. I didn't spend the night a lot at the house, because Marcia and the kids were there.

One night, when I called the house phone at 1:00 a.m., Marcia answered, but when I asked for Saint, I could hear her roll over and tap him, to wake him up. When he got on the phone, I asked, "Why would your cousin be in bed with you at 1:00 a.m., when there are four extra bedrooms in the house?"

He claimed that they were watching television in his bed, and they'd just fallen asleep. Again, I just let it go, because that was the right thing to do, given the situation. To this day, I truly believe he had sex with his cousin. Saint would never admit to sleeping with his cousin.

The day of her service came quick. I was again in a position in which I had to downplay my role in his life. Many co-workers from the jail came to pay their respects, including Lurchette. Several people wondered why his family knew me so well. I just lied and said that, after I'd learned his mother died, I stopped by his house, and that is where I met them. After the wake in Brooklyn, everyone gathered at his Godmother's house. She lived next door to them when they lived in Brooklyn. Lurchette stopped by and got in her feelings, once again, because she had been in his life for many years, and the family didn't act like they did toward me.

Saint asked me to leave and said he would see me at the house tomorrow, before the service. I was pissed, because I was the first person he'd called when she died, and I was always his first choice to leave, when these chicks came around. I held him down, and then she comes around pretending to be the girlfriend that she knew she was not. Whose self-esteem issues were worse? This man told her that he didn't like her kids and didn't find her attractive anymore. She literally had to beg him to have sex with her, only to be told "No." I may have felt ugly, and he may have called me ugly, but he was the one who always called me back, and he always wanted to have sex with me. I just didn't understand why he treated her like she was made of glass.

When I got in my car, I started thinking about some other people who'd come to show their respects, and I realized, through all of this, that Lexus had never showed her face. I wondered if he'd told her at all. She professed so much love for this woman, but she was nowhere to be found when it was time to pay her respects. I wondered if he'd questioned any of this for himself.

When I got to the house that morning, I noticed Marcia wouldn't look me in the eyes. I took it as a sign that something had happened between them before her husband arrived. I wasn't going to call him on any of this just yet, but I knew I had a few questions once things settled down. I couldn't make it to the funeral service, because I had a doctor appointment for a biopsy of a lump they'd found in my breast. I was going to cancel the appointment, but Saint said, "Sharon, go check on your health. My mother would understand, and she would want you to go to the doctor," he said. I agreed and told him that I would meet him at the cemetery.

The cemetery was beautiful, and the number of people who came out was amazing. Saint said he had a surprise, and that he did. A horse-drawn carriage pulled up with his mother's casket in the back. He gave her such a beautiful going-home service. He had everyone walk behind the carriage, as they did in days of old. He hadn't thought that part out too well, because that was a long walk, but it was worth it. Ms. Josephine was finally laid to rest with her husband and her two sons.

Funny how things worked out. I had to take Marcia, her kids, and her husband back to the house because the limousine service ended at the cemetery. I will say that, finally, Saint defended me on this day when it came to Lurchette. She asked if she could come back to the house, and he told her "No," because I was going to be there.

When we got back to the house, Saint went into his room and never came out. He called me the next day to ask, "Why did you leave?" He said that I should have just stayed in the small room. He said that he was drunk and just went to sleep. I tried to give him space, because I know that's what I would need, if I had a tragedy like his. I wanted him to know that I would be there for his every need and desire. I knew he was barely keeping it together, but I knew time heals all wounds.

When he'd had time to process everything, he would see that I was there for him through the rough times. He took an additional two weeks off of work, just to get his mind right and put things in perspective. During that time, we packed his mother's belongings and donated them to my old job at the shelter and some to the Salvation Army. We turned her room into a home gym.

It was during this time that I asked about the relationship with his cousin. He denied it at first, until I presented what I considered evidence that something had happened between them. He then said, "One night, we were watching television, and, when I was getting ready to go bed, she kissed me."

I just *knew* there was a reason why she wouldn't look at me that day.

I normally don't trust my gut feeling, but my gut led me down the right path with this situation. I asked, "Did you kiss her back?"

He said, "At first, I did, but then I stopped."

I was angry, but Marcia was gone, and there was no need in acting the fool now. I also took the time to ask about Lexus and why she hadn't been there during that time. This is when he told me that Lexus had moved to California. In that moment I felt good: Lurchette was in a different state, Lexus was in a different state, and Christina was in another state as well. I finally had him to myself. The ugly girl had won. Things were going much better than they ever had before. He gave me my key back—and the alarm code. I thought, *Finally, Saint has chosen me.*

We still kept our relationship outside of the institution. Prior to the death of his mother, there were a few new staff members at the institution. I never wanted anyone to feel the way some staff had made me feel when I was new and on probation. I reached out to the new staff and tried to make them feel as comfortable as possible. There was one girl, named Gina, who appeared to be really cool. She resembled the actress Tisha Campbell but was lighter in skin complexion. She was very outspoken, which I liked, but at the time, it was borderline offensive. She would talk about her sex life and how she liked anal sex, in front of anyone. She compared us, in the sense that we were both Scorpios, supposedly known for being freaks in the bedroom.

One of my closest friends in the building at the time, apart from the people who'd started with me, was still Officer Dee. One day, while having one of our deep conversations, he said to me that he'd messed up and started dealing with someone in the building. When he announced it was Gina, I told him, as a friend, to be careful, because she seemed young, and her mouth was a little reckless. I told him of the conversation she'd had in the front lobby, in front of other people, including his best friend, Officer Harper. I thought there could be no harm in saying this to my friend—after all, he'd given me his unsolicited advice about me falling for Saint.

What I didn't expect was that urging a friend to be cautious would turn my situation upside down. It was Thanksgiving Day, and I was at Saint's house, waiting to go to work for the evening-watch shift. He called the house phone, and when I answered, he said, "You fucking, disgusting slut! Get all your shit out of my house before I get home."

"Saint, what the fuck are you talking about!?" I screamed into the phone.

"Your black ugly ass is under investigation for fucking an inmate," he screamed back. "Get the fuck out of my house, bitch, and leave my keys," he said.

I tried to ask where all this was coming from, but he cut me off mid-sentence and said, "Gina told Officer Dee that you came to her unit and spent all your time talking to some inmate named Richardson."

Immediately I said, "That bitch is lying." At this point, I was trying to explain myself, so that he would calm down and listen to reason. "She called us up to her unit to play spades. "How is it possible for me to go fuck some inmate with four other people there?" I asked. "The inmate was in the multi-purpose area and asked me about financial-aid assistance for his brother to attend college, and that is the only time I spoke to that inmate. Furthermore, Sosa was standing right there for the entire, brief conversation. Gina locked her unit down, we all played cards, and we all left together."

He said, "Well, she said you came back by yourself after everyone left and went to his cell."

"Saint, really. Think about it. How in the hell did I get in his cell, if Gina had the keys? She is lying, and I don't know why."

His final comment was, "Get out of my bed and out of my house. I believe it, because that is the same inmate Lt. Rojas said he sees you talking to all the time when you work OP #2, on morning watch."

At that point, I became defensive, and I told him to go fuck himself. "You have been with me all these years, and you won't give me the benefit of the doubt?" I questioned. "I stood by you through all your bullshit, and *you* were actually *guilty*. Saint, fuck you and your house!" and then I slammed the phone down.

On my way into work, I couldn't wait to see Gina and check her on this bullshit. As I walked up to the front of the building, I saw Officer Dee. I pulled him to the side and asked him why was Gina spreading rumors about me.

He said, "Shots, she was very upset when she told me that you were messing with that inmate."

"Why would she even bring something like that up to you, if she had no proof?" I asked.

He said, "We were just lying in bed talking, and I mentioned what you said about her being young and how I should be careful."

That's when it hit me: she was getting in her feelings because I was warning my friend about her behavior. So, I asked him as my friend, "Why wouldn't you come to me with her so-called 'concerns'?"

He looked me in the face and said, "I felt there may be some truth to it, because other people say that inmate is always around you."

I had to ask, "How could you call yourself my friend and claim you see me as a little sister but think I would do something like that? As much as we talk—and I told you about where I'd come from—do you really feel I would risk all that I have accomplished for myself to be with an inmate? Officer Dee, let me say this one time: you have nothing else to say to me, because I don't need friends like you."

I went into the building, and I felt like everyone was staring at me. As I got off the elevator on the third floor, I saw Gina coming out of the Attorney Conference room. I called her into the staff bathroom to confront her about what she has been spreading about me. I said, "Gina, I just want to know: Why are you starting rumors about me sleeping with inmates?"

She said, "First of all, St. John, I did not start that rumor. I heard from someone else that you may be messing with an inmate on 5 South, and I just said what I saw when you came onto my unit."

Now I was really pissed, so I said, "What the fuck did you see when I came onto your unit? You invited all of us up there. What could I have possibly done with all of you up there?" I let her know that Officer Dee had said that *she'd* brought this bullshit to him.

She said, "St. John, I didn't bring this to Officer Dee—he brought this to me. I just told him what I thought was odd. St. John, I give you my word as a woman, I did not say you were fucking with that dude or that you'd come back onto my unit. All I said was that you were talking to him when ya'll came upstairs onto the unit."

I heard what she said, but I was stuck on one of her statements. "What do you mean, 'He brought it to you,' and why would he bring this to you?" I asked.

She said, "He told me that Lt. Rojas said he told that inmate to stop hanging around you."

That's all I needed to hear from her, so I left the bathroom abruptly, leaving her standing there.

I was pissed and on a mission to find Lt. Rojas. I knew of only one occasion when he made rounds outside, while I was working Outside Patrol #2. All of the cadre workers were waiting in the back of the building, to go back inside the institution. Inmates Richardson and Pineda were both standing near the booth, and we were discussing college and how expensive it is. This was the conversation that led to the brief dialogue on Gina's housing unit. When I entered Lt. Rojas' office, he was there, trying to make his usual jokes. I was too upset, and I got straight to the point with my questions. He claimed he saw the inmate talking to me twice, and he was just telling Officer Dee, because he knew how close we were. He said that he told Officer Dee to tell me to watch out because it didn't look good to have that inmate around me all the time. "How does that translate into me sleeping with this inmate?" I asked him.

"St. John, I don't know where that came from," he said.

I thought to myself, *This is absolutely useless,* and I walked out of his office. After this incident, Gina, Officer Dee, and Lt. Rojas were all on my shit list. I did find out there was no investigation but just a rumor started over pillow talk. There are no secrets in prisons, and inmates know all about the drama that officers go through, because all they do is ear-hustle. If the inmates have a little bit of respect for you, nothing will go down on your shift, and no one would talk bad about you around them, knowing that they might come back and tell you. That's how I found out that Gina, herself, had been inappropriate with the inmates on 5 South. They let me know how she would walk through the unit saying, "It's OK to look at my ass, but don't stare too long."

One inmate said he picked her up by her crotch and had her up over his head in the air. I kept all of this to myself, because if I'd said anything to Officer Dee, he would think I was just doing it out of spite. Besides, I didn't care what happened to Officer Dee, and I secretly wished Gina had broken his stupid heart. I couldn't say anything to Saint, because the rumor ruined my situation with him.

I did miss him like crazy. I missed giving him facials, lotioning his body after he took a bath or shower, watching him pretend to be a male stripper or a dee-jay. I actually missed hearing him snore at night. I missed falling asleep in his arms. I missed cooking dinner for him and receiving compliments on every meal. I missed the "just-because" gifts he would get for me. We always tried to outdo each other with gifts and surprises. We had a lot of fun in between all the bullcrap.

Sometime in December, before Christmas, he decided to call so we could "talk," as he put it. During this conversation, he said that one of the inmates had come to him and told him those rumors were not true. He told him how Gina conducted herself on the unit, and if any inmate pressed the issue, they could fuck her easily. Saint also told me that Officer Dee said that *he* could have fucked me if he wanted to. All I did was listen to this nonsense, because Officer Dee wouldn't have a snowball's chance in hell of sleeping with me. But I did wonder: *What was he hoping to gain by telling Saint that?* I was still disappointed in Saint, because at the end of the day, he had called based solely on the word of an inmate. I'd told him all along that it was not true, but when it came from an inmate, that's what led him to believe me. I loved him, so I just wanted to move past this situation.

New Year's 2005 was approaching and Saint's friend Gary was having a party at his house. Saint told me to invite my friends and that we would attend the party together. I was excited because we didn't go many places in public together. We literally took separate cars just to go food shopping or to the movies. We did this just in case we ran into anyone from the job—it would look like a coincidence.

At the party, it was cool at first. He introduced me as his friend to certain people. I was with my girls, so I didn't mind that he wasn't by my side every minute for the entire party. Then my friend Tina went to the bathroom upstairs, and when she came back, she said that there was some girl all up in Saint's face.

When I went upstairs, I noticed the same thing, so I walked over to where they were, and he gave me a strange look. I interrupted them and asked if I could talk to him outside, in the backyard.

He said, "Sharon, don't start. That's Gary's cousin, Shaun."

I accepted his explanation, because I wasn't thinking he would invite me here, with my friends, and blatantly disrespect me. I went back downstairs to tell them it was just Gary's cousin. Saint had become friends with a few of my homeboys as well, so it was cool that they were able to hang out with us. My homeboy's wife was at the party with us that night, and she got so drunk that we decided to bring her back to Saint's house, because it was close to Gary's place.

Once we got her to the house, she fell up the steps leading to the porch and needed a Band-Aid. We were all outside in front of the house, still laughing about how she'd fallen. Saint escorted her into the house to get her the Band-Aid. Tina's sister needed to use the bathroom, so we all went inside. As I opened the door, at the top of the stairs, standing in the bathroom doorway, was Saint and my homeboy's wife, were face to face. It appeared as if they were kissing, but then we saw him placing the Band-Aid on her forehead, and then her elbow. I didn't trust him: in my heart, I knew that scene wasn't right.

My homeboy and Saint went back to the party, and we stayed with her for a little while until she fell asleep. We decided to go back around to the party, and as we walked up, I saw that girl, Shaun, in his face again. I walked up and asked, "What's going on?"

The girl asked, "Saint, who is she, and why does she keep coming around?"

The scene with my homeboy's wife was playing over in my head, and now this girl was trying to play me in front of my friends. I decided

I was going to show her who I was, but Saint, of course, grabbed me to prevent me from punching that girl in her face and dragging her down the street. He was begging Tina and her sister to take me back to the house. They managed to get me into the car, but I told Saint that he'd better be right behind me, or I was coming back to shut this party down. I think Saint knew I meant business, so he was home fifteen minutes after me. He thought the party would continue at his house, with my friends, but they all decided to go home.

Saint thought he would go straight to bed once they left, but I couldn't wait for them to leave, so I could find out what the hell was on his mind to embarrass me like that in front of my friends. All he could say was, "Sharon, not now." I decided he was right, because talking to a drunken fool would get me nowhere fast. I went to sleep in the small room.

In the morning, he had a hangover and claimed he didn't remember anything from last night. I was quick to remind him. He said, "I would never do anything with Gary's cousin. But, Sharon, you embarrassed me out there trying to fight that girl."

"I thought you said you couldn't remember anything from last night."

"Sharon, I think maybe you should go home, and I will call you later, because you want to fight, and I don't feel well."

I was tired of his ass at this point, so I agreed. I got dressed and went to my sister's house in Queens. My family loved this man at this point. They thought he was the best thing that had ever happened to me. All they saw were the gifts and flowers he brought me. I was private about everything that I was going through with him.

Saint never did call later. I kept calling the house and his cell phone number, like a crazy person. I figured if someone was there, I would interrupt whatever was going on with my constant phone calls. I began to leave several messages, stating that I was on my way out there. Almost one-half hour later, he called me back claiming he'd been asleep all this time. There was a time when I would have believed him, but the trust had been broken so badly, I knew he was lying. I let him know that I knew he was lying, too.

I stayed away from his house for several weeks. We spoke now and then, when he would stop by my apartment. Sexually, I started to feel a disconnect between us. I knew something was going on with him. Saint becomes distant when there is someone else around. I would always ask, "What's going on, and who is she?" He would just tell me to relax and that he was just missing his mother and wanted some time to himself.

It was Valentine's Day and, although I didn't celebrate it with buying gifts, I still wanted to see him. Instead of asking if I could come over, I just showed up at the house. I tried not to make it obvious that I was looking for signs of another woman being there, but I found it the moment I walked into his bedroom. It was a large, framed poem written by Shaun, Gary's cousin.

He tried to say she just stopped by and brought it over because she was thinking about what he was going though, having lost his mother. The poem was really nice, but I knew there was more to the story. He said he was going downstairs to work out. While he was working out, I took it upon myself to listen to the recorder, which he'd never disconnected after the Lexus situation. I heard several conversations between him and Lexus, Shaun, and Lurchette. He would normally work out for about an hour, so I wasn't expecting him to come back upstairs so quickly. He caught me listening to the recordings. In my mind, I said, *Fuck it—I'm caught.*

But I was going to make the wrong I was doing less significant in light of the wrongs he was doing. "Saint, you still want to tell me that nothing happened between you and Shaun? And since when did you start talking to Lexus again? If she sends your ass to jail again, I will not be there this time."

He just looked at me and said, "Sharon, I can't do this anymore. I'm not happy. Yes, Shaun came over a few times, and we just talked at first. I never intended to do anything with her, because she is my man's cousin, and I didn't want to mess things up if it didn't work out. It just happened, and she said that Gary will never find out from her."

I took the news like a champ. I knew someone had his ear, because of the distance I felt from him. I asked about Lurchette and what that conversation was about that I had just listened to. He said, "Both she and Lexus want me back. They both are willing to take me back, if I stop talking to you. I know I will not get back with Lurchette, but she has always been a good friend, and she made some valid points as far as me and you go."

"What the hell does she have to do with what we do!?" I screamed.

"Sharon, just calm down," he said. "I just want to talk." Tears started rolling down his face, and my heart weakened for a moment. He went on to say that Lexus was the love of his life and that he felt he could have gotten her back if it hadn't been for me.

My heart hardened instantly, and I couldn't sit there and listen to any more of this shit. My own tears started flowing, because I couldn't believe what I was hearing. "None of these bitches was ever around for the hard times, but now they get to determine if we stay together," I said while trying to dry my tears with the back of my hands.

I guess, since he was breaking up with me, he had decided to come clean about everyone. There was a nurse from the hospital we'd worked overtime, his ex-girlfriend from college, the big-booty ex-girlfriend from Brooklyn, and yes, there was some girl in brown that his mother and sister told me about. He admitted that he'd slept with a co-worker's cousin, who was now claiming him to be the father of her child. After dealing with Christina and that baby situation, this was the last straw for me. It had become too much for me to hear all of this from the man I loved and wanted to marry someday. He was not telling me all of this because he wanted to clear the slate and start new—he wanted to let me know it was over between us and that maybe I should go on and meet someone new.

I left his house confused and broken. I decided to go to Javon's house. Of course, they asked about Saint as soon as I walked in there. I hadn't seen them since the embarrassing New Year's Eve party. She decided to ask me if I would be interested in meeting one of Javon's co-workers. I couldn't understand why she would ask me something like that. She said that they were going to have a BBQ and that I should stop by to meet him.

I asked her, "Why would you try to set me up with someone when you knew I was with Saint?" I thought a real friend would say, "Sharon, I know you like him, but I think you can do better." Instead she said, "I just thought you would want to meet someone."

So, I asked her, "Do you have a problem with my relationship?" Again, I was expecting that a real friend would give it to me straight. She chose to lie, and I chose to downgrade our friendship.

I'd lost another friend because of Saint.

To top it off, I'd just been dumped by him, but they didn't need know that. I kept to myself, but I knew his birthday was rolling around, and I still wanted to get something special for him. He loved fish tanks, and I decided I wanted to surprise him, even though we were not together. I did still have a spare key that he was unaware of. I knew he had to work on his birthday, so I decided to set up the fish tank in his bedroom before he got home. I felt like an idiot doing all of this for him, after he'd told me he didn't want to be with me. My heart was telling me this was something I wanted to do for him.

I got into the house; the alarm went off, and I didn't have the new code, but I knew him well enough to know what his password might be to override the system once they called. I guessed one of two names, and I got it right. I set everything up just as I had when I bought him the flat-screen television and surround-sound system. While I was there, I listened to more messages and went through the computer. I was looking for more-recent pictures of Lexus, which would tell me that he had been in constant communication with her.

I saw birthday cards from everyone, which he'd placed on display in the small room. I was there for a purpose, and the equipment had already been bought and paid for. So, I'd done what I'd come to do and left the house the way I found it.

When he got home, he called my phone a million times, but I wouldn't answer. I didn't want him to know it was me at first. That may sound stupid, but that's what I wanted at that time. He left several messages begging me to pick up the phone or call him back. He said that he knew it was me, and he just wanted to say "Thank you."

Eventually, I did answer the phone—and just hearing his voice made me happy inside. He asked if was I OK and thanked me again for the fish tank. He said he would like to see me, but first he wanted to know why I'd made a spare key to his house. I told him, "Just in case of emergencies," but I also told him I would give it to him whenever I saw him again.

We had different days off, and I was still working overtime five days per week, so we had to just decide on a day to get together. When we finally saw each other, he gave me a really nice hug and a kiss on the forehead. Then he whispered, "I missed you, Pumpkin Butt."

He had my drink ready; he asked if I could fix something to eat, because he was missing my cooking. I threw something together really quick, and we sat and ate dinner at the kitchen table. There was an awkward silence at first, but he broke the ice when he asked about the keys. I got my purse, took the key off my key ring, and slid it across the table. He asked me if I'd made any other copies, and I assured him that I had not.

After dinner, we went upstairs so he could show me the fish he'd bought for the tank. I did take a quick peek and noticed that the birthday cards were all gone; however, the framed poem was still on display. He caught my eye as we were looking at the poem and he said, "It's just a nice poem, and it doesn't mean anything else." As I was looking at the fish tank, he came up behind me and started rubbing my lower back; then he stroked my hair, pulled my head backwards, and gave me a long, wet kiss. The sex session was amazing that night. He showed me that he missed me and how much he appreciated the fish tank.

We continued to see each other, and things felt like they were back on track for about one month. However, all of a sudden, his college friend started showing up at the house a lot. Under the guise of full disclosure, Saint admitted that he'd slept with her once, in college, to piss off her then-boyfriend. I guess she'd never gotten over that. She was a girl who had obvious self-esteem issues as well—she was heavy set and not that easy on the eyes, as he would say.

She was in the company of me, Lurchette, and Christina, on one end of the spectrum, who believed we were lucky to have had Saint at some point or another. Lexus was at the other end of that spectrum, who believed that Saint was lucky to have had her in his life. My issue with Athena was that she didn't appear to know her place as a friend. Whenever I would come to the house, she would be upstairs in the master bedroom, sitting on the bed or lying across the bed. Saint and I would argue because she wouldn't say "Hello" when I came into the house. I felt that, as a friend, she had no business in the master bedroom, period. Of course, Saint claimed that she just wanted to see the fish tank. That would explain the first time she'd been seen in the bedroom.

Any other time, when she would pop up at the house, she would be in the bedroom. Saint said that she'd she stopped by when she was having issues with her so-called boyfriend, but I knew it was more than that. Saint finally admitted that she told him that she wanted to be with him. My instincts had been right about her. This is why she didn't speak to me and why she felt it was okay for her to hang out in our bedroom. I am sure that, if her so-called boyfriend had a female friend who was always in their bedroom, she would have a problem with that.

During one of our discussions about Athena, we started talking about rating women on a scale of 1 to 10, based on looks. I thought Athena was a solid four. He said that he thought she was almost in the same category as me. Of course, me being the glutton for punishment that I am, I asked, "What do you rate me, if Athena is almost in my category?"

He said, "Probably a six or seven."

When he saw the look on my face, he could tell that I was disappointed in his answer. Prior to having this discussion, I was starting to have the baby blues. Saint would ignore my little hints of the possibility of having a baby together. He used to say things like, "Lexus and I would have had beautiful babies." He believed that his mother would have wanted him to have a child with Lexus. He also felt that he and Lurchette would've made a tall baby, and that was appealing to him. The reason that he always ignored me when I mentioned having his child was that he viewed me in the same category as Athena, and therefore, the possibility of us having an unattractive child was great.

Saint always had a way of saying too much. He said that Lurchette would be so mad if she found out I had a baby with you. My mind was saying, *What the fuck!? Why is he considering her feelings with regards to me having a baby?* He could have kept that piece of useless information to himself. I decided to let the conversation go for the moment, but it stayed in the back of my mind.

A few days later, I popped up at his house, and his fat friend, Athena, was there and in the bedroom again. She was very relaxed, lying on the monogrammed sheets that I'd purchased for him. This time, I asked her to go downstairs myself, because it was obvious Saint had not mentioned my issue with her being in the bedroom. This pitiful bitch said to me, "If my friend Saint wanted me to go downstairs, I would be downstairs. You don't live here—you can't tell me to go downstairs."

I felt my insides starting to rise in temperature. I turned to face Saint and said, "You'd better tell her to leave now, or you will have a problem in your house tonight!"

He said to her in a low-key voice, "Athena, just leave, and I will talk to you later."

She replied, "Saint, you gonna let her put me out?"

That's when I said to her, "Go someplace else looking for pity dick!"

Saint was standing behind me, calling my name, as if to say that I'd gone too far with that comment. I started yelling, "Fuck her. She is disrespectful and a fair-weather friend," I yelled. "She comes around only when she has a problem, and she needs to leave now," I continued to yell.

She got off the bed as if she wanted to fight me, so I prepared to go to war with her. Saint grabbed me, threw me into the small room, shut the door, and held onto the knob, so I couldn't get out. I could hear her talking shit as she was going down the stairs. When she left through the front door, he let me out of the room.

He started with his normal speech: "Sharon, I can't do this anymore. You don't have the right to come in here and say where I choose to entertain my friends. She has been trying to help me figure things out, as far as what I want to do. I am not happy," he said.

I screamed, "That bitch just wants to get fucked—you've probably already given her some pity dick, and that is why she feels the need to try to fight me! There is no other reason for her to act that way toward me," I said.

He yelled back, "She is my friend, and she knows that I am not happy with you! You know what, Sharon? Sometimes you act like an ignorant Black bitch."

I said, "So now I'm a Black bitch, because I don't like your so-called friend lying all over the bed and sheets that *I* bought! Saint, you are so quick to defend your friends over me," I said. "I do everything for you, and they get all the respect," I kept screaming.

All he could say was, "Sharon, I am not happy anymore, and I just think it is best if you leave—and make sure you take everything with you."

"You act like I am forcing you to be with me, Saint."

He faced me and said, "I do feel like that at times."

I was at a loss for words. All I could say was, "Oh, yeah, Saint," as I walked out the door. He yelled for me to come get my things, and I yelled back, "Fuck it all!"

I felt like I could never forgive him for some of the things he'd said to me during these last few weeks. During one of our arguments, he'd said, "That's why I could have fucked your sister." Because of my past experience with family betrayal, this always remained in the back of my mind. I even started looking at my sister differently because of it, especially because she was the one who asked about him the most.

This man had me so messed up in the head. I was so accustomed to the "break up to make up" situation we had going on, I thought this was no different. He showed me that this time was going to be different. During the months of April to September 2005, Saint and I barely spoke to each other. I would see him at work, and he wouldn't even look at me. Every time I tried to reach out, he would not respond. He was determined to have me out of his life. I couldn't understand what I'd done wrong. *When had the love he said he had for me change to hate?* I felt that, if he was not distracted by those other women, then we would have had a fighting chance.

Here are some actual email correspondences I sent to him after that situation, based on some of our conversations prior to that incident. As you will see, he responded to only one message, telling me my things were packed. Actually, reading these emails now, I see how desperate I was. I wanted him to read my words, change his mind, and come back to me. I see how I was almost begging him to pick me, choose me, and love me. At some point, it sounded as if I had my mind right, but I knew that, inside, I was weak. On one hand, I was trying to convince myself that I was strong and resilient, but on the other hand, I was feeling like I would never have what it takes to get and keep a man. Reading them now, I have to ask myself, *Was I that broken inside?*

> **From:** *xxxxxxx@xxx.xxx*
> To: *StJohn@bop.gov*
> Date: 4/24/2005 4:31:37 PM
> Subject: PRINT IT OUT, I WILL NEVER FORGIVE YOU YOUR STUFF IS PACKED AND WAITING AND I MAY HAVE FOUND WHAT I'M LOOKING FOR?!
> >>>stjohn@bop.gov>4/24/2005 1:06:34 PM >>>

> *You may think I am only a six or a seven, but someday I will find someone who doesn't care about my physical appearance. Someone who will love me for me. Respect me because I respect and love them. They will appreciate me and think of me as a ten. I won't have to worry about someone calling me a Black bitch or a whore and talking to me like I'm a piece of shit. Someday I will be loved. You have demonstrated that you don't want to love me. Your love for your friends is more important to you. Let's see if you find someone who will put up with your so-called friendships with those bitches. I bet you will die alone before someone else deals with the shit I went through with you and them. Those bitches will be the reason you will never have a child of your own or a wife. You are not doing them any favors. You lie to them every day. A friendship is not based on lies. What we have or had was real. There were no lies between us. You say you don't like to hurt people, but you've hurt me for the last time over those bitches. No threat, but you will see how your life turns out if you hurt them for the one you say you care about. I see now that I was not worth you hurting them for. It's obvious that you felt they were worth hurting me for. I hope I am the last person you do this to. I would hate to find out things got really ugly for you. I have a question for you: Did you feel that the only way you could have a baby with me is if you're going to die, because*

you wouldn't have to deal with people knowing about us? That hurt me to the core. Would it really have been that bad if people knew that we were together? It will take some time, but I will be OK. I am better by myself anyway. Your words are ringing in my head. You are the first to call me a whore and a Black bitch. But this Black bitch will never fall off—I will only get stronger. Go back to that gold digger—she is where your heart is. I am sorry I came between you and your true love.

Hi,
  I understand you don't want this anymore. It is very hard for me to come to terms with it being over. I just wanted to tell you something. We used to say our situation/relationship was based on friendship. A friendship is not based on lies. What we have or had was real. There were no lies between us. I never lied or cheated on you. When you cheated, I believed you told me the truth about it. You have broken my spirit and my heart. I truly hope I am the last person you do this to. YOU DON'T HAVE TO WORRY ABOUT ME TRYING TO CONVINCE YOU OR FORCE YOU TO STAY WITH ME ANYMORE. You have never made it more clear to me that you just want out of this situation/relationship. It is funny how things always turn out for me. My relationships/situations have always ended because I wanted more. I always end up alone. Always feeling like I didn't have what it took to keep a man. The saying goes, "If it doesn't kill you, it builds character." Thank you for building my character. Hard lesson learned but well taught. I fell like I have wasted your time these past four years. You will never be a waste of time for me. You gave me my first glance of what love should be like. I am sorry I wasted your time and caused you to lose your true love.
  I have many regrets. At points of anger I regret being with you. I don't regret demanding what a good woman deserves, which is love and respect. I know in my heart that I have always been a good woman to you and for you. Something has clouded your

judgement of me, and that is okay because you, too, will regret losing me. Of course, you may not see it now because you are angry and you have allowed hate to replace the love you said you felt for me. I know I am going to be somebody that you would have been proud to call your woman. You taught me a lot about trust, love, hate, and jealousy. They work together, and if two people belong together, they find a way to balance them out. You won't say the words I need to move on, but if I ever loved myself, I don't need to hear those words from you. I would do it because I love myself. You are right about one thing—it does get easier with every passing day. God knows that I pray that you find what you are looking for and have all your dreams come true. My biggest regret is that it wasn't me. GOODBYE.

When I finally received a phone call from him, I was excited and nervous at the same time. I thought maybe he was calling to ask me to stop sending him emails and leaving voice-mail messages.

Instead he said, "Sharon, I want you to know that I miss you, too, but I just wanted to see how my life would be without you in it for a while. I really missed your cooking, the way you clean, and having you with me to go food shopping. I know it has been hard for you, but it has been hard for me, too. I thought about some of the things you said about "Lurchette," and you're right. I know that I will never be with her—mostly because of her kids—but I feel like I owe her so much. She has helped me a lot with my Bureau career."

I interrupted him and said, "Saint, I never asked you to not speak to anyone who showed you love and support. All that I ask is that there is some level of respect. She—and all the others—need to know that I am here, in your life, and that I am not going anywhere. They need to know that it is your choice to be with me. You have them thinking that I am just some ugly girl holding onto a dream. You have them thinking that someone like you could never possibly marry or have a child with someone like me."

He said, "Sharon, I know, and you're right. I want to see you. You can come over and help me pack, if you want," he suggested. "I am trying to find some clothes to take with me to Virginia," he went on to say.

"What's in Virginia?" I asked.

"The Crabfest—I go with the guys from Brooklyn," he replied.

I knew what went on when he goes on those boys' trips. My natural trust issues run deep, but dealing with Saint pushes me over the edge. Once again, he sensed my discomfort with him going, but there was nothing I could do about it. I was just happy that he'd called.

I went over to the house to help him pack and cooked him a nice meal. I felt like we'd just sort of made up or at least come to some sort of agreement. I tried to make the sex session extra special that night, so that he would think about me while he was away.

During his time in Virginia, he sent a few text messages now and then, letting me know how things were down there. He said that I had nothing to worry about, because there were nothing but fat women down there. Hearing that made me feel a little at ease, because I knew how he was when he's drunk. He will flirt, but he can't follow through, because he would pass out sleeping before the dick could rise. I was so happy when that trip was over. I just knew that, when he came home, we would be in a better place because of the discussion we had prior to him leaving.

August 15, 2005:

One day after he'd returned from the weekend Crabfest in Virginia, I missed him so much. I was worried before he left, because I kept having bad dreams. I just knew something bad was going to happen. He had to work that Sunday night when he came back, but we were going to be together that Monday night. When I arrived at work, he was on the phone in control center, as usual. I didn't think he was talking to Lurchette, because the conversation seemed different. I honestly thought he was talking to his sister. I walked in and called him to the back of the control room, because I wanted a quick hug to get through the day. He wouldn't put the phone down for one minute to come see what I wanted. I got in my feelings, so I left.

I was scheduled to work overtime, and I would've been his relief. I would normally have relieved him early, but I said to myself, *Forget him.* I got there right on time. Later on that evening, he called me into control center to find out why I hadn't relieved him early. He also wanted to tell me that I shouldn't wear my jealousy and emotion on my sleeve. That's when he informed me that he'd been talking to Ms. Perfect, Lurchette. I told him now that I know it was her, I was definitely mad. I felt he should have put her on hold to see what I wanted.

"I should come first," I said. I hung up the phone and hoped things would calm down. I figured I would see him later and we could talk about it then. Around 9:00 p.m., I gave him a call to see if he still wanted me to come out after work. I sensed his attitude, and I made his decision for him. I was not going to drive 45 minutes so he could act like an asshole.

As I walked in my front door, he was calling my cell phone. During this time, if you had Verizon service on your cell phone, it would beep if you were on another call, alerting the incoming caller that you were on the other line. I was on a call with another co-worker, and when I switched over the line, his jealousy took over.

"I was just calling to find out if you were still coming, but you can finish talking to whomever you were talking to."

I ignored his stupid comment and informed him I was already home.

He said, "Well, since you're home and probably tired, then you shouldn't drive."

I thought, *Now he's concerned about me driving.*

I said, "OK" and got off the phone.

Two minutes later, he called back on the house phone, stating that he didn't believe I was talking to a co-worker. He also didn't believe me when I'd told him earlier that I'd had a hard time finding parking. I offered proof of the "No parking" signs that were all over the street in Brooklyn.

He demanded that I bring the sign to his house, now.

I said, "If you want to see me, just say so."

He insisted that he only wanted to see the proof. Deep down, I wanted to see him, too, so I drove 35 minutes to show him that I was not a liar or a cheat. I couldn't wait to make him eat his words. I arrived, and I put the sign right in front of him. This bastard balled it up and threw it onto the floor. I paid him no mind. I took a shower and got ready for bed. I knew I wanted to have sex, but I was going to play hard-to-get.

He turned the lights and TV off, looked at me, and said, "You know why I called you out here?"

I answered rhetorically, "Because you want to have sex? By all means, let me give you what you want," I said, trying to be a smart ass.

He said, "That's what you do."

I was shocked for a moment. I was not expecting that response.

"*That's what I do?*" I repeated.

"Sharon, not now," he said, as he lay on his back naked, waiting for me to perform oral sex on him. For a second, I envisioned me biting it right on that black mole along the shaft and spitting it in his face. Instead, I got up and went into the small bedroom. He followed, asking me, "What are you doing?"

My voice was childlike as I said, "Saint, you hurt me with your comment."

"That's what you do!" he yelled back at me.

"That's not what I do, and I would rather sleep alone than sleep with someone who thinks I'm a slut."

He said, "Well, you won't sleep here, bitch!" He grabbed my bags and began to throw my things down the stairs.

"Saint, my gun is in there—don't!"

"I don't give a fuck!" he said.

"If you break my gun, you will pay for it," I said.

"I ain't paying for shit, bitch!" he said.

I ran down the steps and took the gun out of the bag to check to see if it was broken. He came down behind me. He didn't see that I had the gun in my hand. He began to throw my bags and clothes out on the front lawn. He looked at me and said, "Get out of my house."

I said, "Fine," and, as I went to reach for my pants, he came at me. I jumped back toward the chair in the living room. He was now standing over me, and I still had the gun in my hand, pointed toward the ground. He still didn't see it in my hand.

"Saint, get back, and don't hit me!" I yelled.

He moved back. Then he looked at me and said, "Take my shirt off and get the fuck out of my house!"

I stood straight up, ready to change my clothes and leave, and that's when he saw the gun. He completely lost it. He grabbed me by my hair, yelling, "You pulling a *gun* on me, bitch?"

I still had the gun in my hand, and I felt myself release the safety latch with my right thumb. I said, "Saint, stop. Don't make me do this! Stop, please!" I screamed. "Just step back," I warned him.

He moved back, just as I was turning around to actually point it at him. I would never hurt him on purpose, but I couldn't let him hurt me, either. A weird calm came over his face. I didn't know what that look meant for me. Was he about to really snap and try to kill me, or was he facing the realization that he could have been shot dead in his home?

I looked him in the eye and told him, "I would never hurt you." I slid the safety latch back on and set the gun on the chair with my clothes. I gathered my clothes in my arms and tried to go out the front door, half-naked. He blocked the doorway. I ran through the house and tried to go out the side door. He cornered me in the den. I felt his hands around my neck and my feet leave the floor. I opened my eyes just in time to see his face and his movements. He balled his fist to punch me in my side, but he must have changed his mind, because he didn't do it.

I heard myself saying, "Saint, you're going to kill me! Just stop now!"

"It is over! Sharon, stop talking—shut up!"

That's when I felt his hand connect with the side of my face, and my body hit the floor in the den. I crawled into a ball and said, "Saint, I just want to leave. It's done, and it is over." I don't know why, but I wasn't crying. I got up, looked at my face in the mirror, and said, "It's a good thing you don't hit hard." I went to the front door, gathered my clothes, and got dressed, but I couldn't find my car keys. I had to get a flashlight to find all my belongings sprawled over his front porch and lawn. I eventually found my keys in the grass. I had everything and was ready to go.

He stopped me. "Sharon, wait—don't go," he said. He tried to hug me, but I wouldn't let him. He tried to kiss me, but I wouldn't receive his tongue. Everything in me wanted to, but I couldn't give in to him.

He was trying to start a sex session right there on the stairs, in the house, and I stopped him.

"Saint, how can you manage to get your dick hard after what you just did to me?" I asked.

He stood to his feet, opened the door, and said, "Just go. This relationship has been over for weeks now anyway, and it doesn't even matter."

That's when the tears came flowing down my face. As I was walking to my car, he called my name again. I thought he wanted to apologize and promise never to do it again, but instead, he wanted to give me a package that had been delivered there. It was a heavy box that I couldn't lift by myself. He said he wanted everything of mine out of his house. I begged him to let it stay here until I could come back for it. He refused, still trying to put it in my car. It didn't fit, so he brought it back into the house.

I left and went to the store to buy cigarettes and gas. He called several times.

"Saint, what do you want?" I asked, with my voice cracking from crying.

"Just come back, Sharon," he said.

I didn't respond to his request, so he repeated, "Sharon, where are you? Come back."

As stupid as I was, I was already on my way back. I just didn't want him to think that it was going to be that easy. I sat in the car and smoked two cigarettes, back to back. I got dizzy, and, when I looked up, I saw him at my car door. He'd come out to help me into the house. He removed my shoes and pants and placed me in his bed. He held me like a baby for a brief moment. Then he started trying to have sex with me again.

I just couldn't do it. I thought he was trying to prove that I was a slut—that a man could do whatever he wanted to me, and I would still fuck him. He got angry again, turned over, and went to sleep. It was difficult, but I finally fell asleep as well.

The next morning, I woke up to him touching my face and rubbing my head. He was already dressed for work. I looked at my face in the mirror and decided that I would go to work also. The damage was mostly to my ego. He hugged me tight and said, "I am sorry."

I lay there and let him have his way with me. I thought he was going to let me stay, so I asked if I could wash my uniform. He looked at me like I was asking the stupidest question on earth.

"Where—here?" he asked.

"I guess not," I said, as I put my pants on and grabbed my shoes. My shirt was wet with cum spatter on the front. He watched me get into my car and had the nerve to ask me, "Is there anything you want to say?" I felt like a piece of shit. *He may as well just spit in my face*, I thought. I had to state the facts as I saw them.

"You beat me up, and then you fuck me and put me out. I guess you proved your point. You got what you wanted, Saint."

As I put the car into drive, preparing to take off, I could hear him say, "Sharon, you have it all wrong. You are going too far once again, Sharon."

I pulled out without responding. He called my phone, and I tried not to answer, but I knew he would keep calling if I didn't. He made me regret answering the phone. Although, he didn't say it outright, it sounded as if he blamed me for what had happened. I thought to myself, *All those months in therapy for anger management absolutely had not worked for him*. That conversation went badly, so we got off the phone.

Tuesday night, he called me to say he was sorry, again. He wanted to tell me, as a friend, that I need to move on with someone else. He said, "I know I don't make you happy, and I don't foresee myself making the change you need or want me to make."

My response was, "Saint, all you did was change the words around, but you are saying you don't want to be with me, again."

"Oh, Sharon. I am sorry, if I did not make it clear—but no, I can't come back to you," he said. "I broke the promise I made to my mother and myself because I thought I would never do that again."

"Saint, I broke the promise I made to my father every time I took you back. I did that because you are here, and he is not. I love you, but I won't beg you to stay," I said. The conversation ended, and so did we. I thought, *Alone again, wasting time.* I started writing down all my thoughts and questions, and exploring my emotions on paper.

Why do we argue?
1. Constant denial of our relationship
2. Lurchette, Lexus, Christina, Shaun, and others
3. Disregard for my feelings
4. Co-workers

Questions
1. Are you ashamed or embarrassed by me?
2. Is your happiness determined by what your co-workers think of you?
3. Does Lurchette or Lexus determine who you love and find happiness with?

Points
1. The present situation should have brought us closer together but instead solidified the end.
2. Your friends and family may say we don't look good together or that you tell me too much, but they can never say I didn't have your best interest at heart. At the end of the day, that's what matters.
3. If sex is all we have in common, then we have nothing at all, and this should end.
4. In the end, you either love me completely or leave me alone completely.

I spent days and nights crying and wondering why. I pushed through at work, and seeing him made things that much harder for me. Still, no one knew anything about our situation, so it was easier for us to act as if we were two people who worked in the same building who didn't know each other. When I would see him, I would look for some sign that he missed me or that he was taking the breakup as hard as I was. However, there was nothing. No signs, no facial expression, just a routine day.

I guess I didn't do a bad job of hiding my emotions, either, because no one ever suspected that I was feeling like death inside. I decided to book another solo vacation. During the interim, I had constant doubts about myself as a person, as a woman, and as a human being, longing for basic human psychological needs. I wrote these words, or should I say rambled some words, while contemplating these thoughts:

Here I go again—asking myself why this had happened to me. What am I doing wrong?

My first mistake was getting involved with someone who had someone. That's not even completely my fault because I was always led to believe that the other relationship was not going well or they were about to break up. *What is a girl to do with her feelings for a man and the hope that there may be a chance—except to hang in there and see what happens?* There are so many questions left unanswered when everything was said and done: *Did he ever care about me? Did he just use me? How do you believe him when he says that he never meant to hurt you? What did he think would happen when he told me it could never be? What do you do when you want so badly for things to work out, but he continues to lie? Can you remain just his friend?*

I wondered if I would ever find love or know what it is to be loved. I asked myself, *Why am I not good enough? Why can't men love me back? What could I have done differently to make him love me more? Is this love I feel for him, or is it the feeling of not wanting to be alone?*

Then I remembered: this man has brought a joy that I had never felt in my life—the way he spoke to me, the way he held me, and the many times he told me how beautiful I was. How do you deal with knowing that this man, this beautiful person, was a fraud? How could a person who made you feel so high one day make you feel so low the next day?

Now I was left here in this sad place, a familiar place, this lonely place. Again, I had to shut down, lock my doors, and barricade my heart. Build new walls to cover the craters in my soul's foundation. You lock away all those feelings, and you're left with only the burning feeling of stupidity. *You should have known better* are the only words you have to offer yourself. *You should have seen the signs. You should have never given so much of yourself, so fast.* You ask yourself, "What kind of person falls in love—or even *thinks* they love someone—who has no idea how to love?"

You try to convince yourself that he does care. How could he *not* care for you? Maybe I was too nice? Maybe I wasn't nice enough? Maybe I wasn't pretty enough? Maybe I wasn't smart enough? Maybe I didn't have enough money? You get mad with yourself, because you let him play you and disrespect you, all in the name of love. You hate yourself. You don't want to be around people. You can't stop the tears from flowing, and then you get mad. Now you feel as if you hate him for putting you through this. All this pain from someone who said they never wanted to hurt you. What do you do? Where do you go from there? How do you face him? Is it possible to still love him? Will you ever trust him? Will you ever trust anyone?

You replay all the shared moments: good, bad, and the worst. You hold on. They say "Only the strong will survive." You try to hold on, and then you're pushed away. You fight your way back, but to no avail, because you're pushed away again. You feel yourself slipping away, and the worst part of slipping away is that no one is there trying to hold onto you, saying, "Hold on. Be strong. I am right here."

You just slip away, not even giving it a second thought. You are now a part of his past, left behind. You think about all the things you should have said and all the things you could have done. You realize, *What difference would it have made?* You let it go without a fight, hoping never to make that mistake again.

This is a copy of the daily horoscope from September 28, 2005. My Scorpio horoscope knew what I just wasn't ready to accept.

After I sent him a copy of my horoscope, he knew that I was about to give up on us. I believed in my daily horoscope as guidance for my life. All these thoughts and self-doubts were driving me crazy inside. I was beginning to shut down. I isolated myself from all friends and family—therefore, I had no one to confide in. I always hated when my friends would break up with their boyfriend over something stupid and make it seem as if they were never going back. Then, by the next week, they are back together again. I made it my business to not be that girl. I talk about a breakup only when my heart is done with the situation. I knew my heart was not done with Saint, but I tried hard to convince myself that it was.

Not long after I sent him the horoscope, he called to talk. Once again, I listened to him tell me how much he missed my friendship, more than anything else. By the end of that conversation, we agreed to be just friends. I knew that was not what I wanted, but I would have agreed to anything just to be in his life again.

During the "trial friendship," I came into some money from my father's property in Brooklyn. I received a third of my share of one of the brownstones, which netted me $145,000. When I received the check, I asked Saint to hold the check in his safe for me until I figured out what I wanted to do with the money. I noticed he started acting differently toward me. I couldn't figure it out, but there was something different.

When I asked him what the problem was, he accused me of acting like a "Black bitch with money." Those were his exact words to me. I know I hadn't changed, but I was treating him like a friend, because that's all he said he wanted from me. When I started talking to my friend and co-worker, Harper, I think he was jealous. He didn't know that Harper was helping me to find and purchase a house. When I finally found the three-family house that I was going to buy and I told Saint about it, he didn't appear happy for me at all.

After the deal was done, and I was the proud new owner of some real estate in Brooklyn, I wanted to share that moment with Saint. When he met me at the house on Herkimer Street, before he even went inside, he said, "I don't think you should have bought this house. I think you should have waited and not let Harper talk you into buying this house."

I was a little offended, because he was implying that I didn't have a mind of my own. I spent a lot of time at my new house, remodeling and getting things ready to be rented out. I converted the basement into a one-bedroom apartment for me, so I could avoid having to pay rent at my apartment on Hawthorne. When the new apartment was ready, I invited Saint to come see all the work that had been done. He was not a fan of the basement because the ceiling was not high enough for him to stand straight up.

My intentions weren't to be there that often, anyway, because I still wanted to spend my time in Long Island, with him, at his house. Once I had all three apartments in the house rented, Saint started to come around a little more. I felt his resistance to me buying the house easing up, and he even said he was proud of me. Because I was spending so much time at my house during the renovations, Saint and I didn't spend as much time together until it was over. Before I knew it, we were back with the same routine, cleaning and food shopping on the weekends.

I was back at the house—or should I say, "playing house"—but I was content with that for now. We still drove separate cars to the supermarket, but it was okay with me. I just learned to accept this as part of our situation. Everything went on like this for a while. We definitely had some disagreements during the course of the year, but we always managed to work it out.

During some of our casual conversations, he started asking me what I was going to do for my birthday. I couldn't believe it was September of 2006 already. This time last year, he was telling me he didn't want to be with me. I told him I was thinking about going back to Jamaica. He started hinting around as if he wanted to come with me. I was excited about the idea of us being away from the job, the women, and the overall bullshit. I didn't really believe he would go with me, because he was always skeptical about us being seen together. I discovered, however, that he was very serious when he booked his ticket and emailed me his confirmation. I had never been on vacation with anyone before, so I knew it would be different. Of course, I had to hear the speech about not telling anyone at the job that we were going together. Hearing this speech simply reminded me that he felt I was not worthy, but he was going, and that made me happy.

When the day arrived for us to leave for Jamaica, he arranged for his friend Gary to take us to the airport. I could tell when we were in the airport that he was uncomfortable and leery of his surroundings, just in case someone from the job was there also. He could have been reliving the moment he last visited Jamaica and the death of his mother, but he was uncomfortable.

After arriving in Jamaica, he let his guard down, and he was able to relax because there was no need to look over his shoulder for BOP staff. When the people of Jamaica referred to me as "his wife," he didn't correct them. In fact, he went along with it, and throughout the trip, he would refer to me as his wife. I had such a good time being out of the country with Saint, even when he almost cost us our lives. Yes, you read that right.

I had been on several birthday vacations alone, and, therefore, I'd experienced a lot of the water activities associated with being on vacation. Saint, on the other hand, had not had anyone to force him out of his comfort zone. I wanted to ride the jet ski, but because Saint had never been on a jet ski before, the Jamaican dude suggested we ride together. We were enjoying the ride, and he was getting used to going straight and hitting the waves with some speed. As we began to go out too far for my tastes, I told Saint to turn around. I tried to tell him to go slow when turning, but he wanted to show me that he had this and gunned it on the turn.

Before I knew it, we were in the water behind a large rock and could not see the beach from where we were in the ocean. The jet ski had flipped upside down and floated off. We were wearing life jackets, and I knew how to dog-paddle in the water to stay afloat, but Saint had no idea what to do in the water. This very large man was grabbing onto me, trying to stay afloat, but instead, he was dragging me underwater. I dog-paddled my way over to this large rock in the middle of the ocean and tried to climb up, but Saint was dragging me back, until I finally got him to relax enough to pull him toward the rock with me. Neither of us had on shoes, but we were standing on this rock as best we could.

It was slippery with sea moss, and it was hard to hold onto. It felt like we were out there alone for a long time, but then we saw the Jamaican dude, and we both were so excited. He said the only reason they came out was that they saw the jet ski floating upside down.

When we got back to the beach and stepped foot on the sand, we realized we couldn't walk because our feet were hurting so bad on the bottom. On top of being in pain, I was mad, because inside the compartment of the jet ski was my Movado watch, my camera, and my earrings. We ended up at the nursing station in the hotel, only to find out that we'd been standing on a rock covered in sea urchins. A sea urchin's defense mechanism is that they are covered in little spines. The nurse informed us that these spines can not be picked out but that they would dissolve with ammonia. It has been said that urine will dissolve the spines. There was no way on God's green Earth that Saint or anyone else was going to pee on my feet.

We bought a bottle of ammonia and hobbled back to our room. We gave new meaning to the sexual position "69." We were literally head to feet and feet to head, applying ammonia and trying to pick those spines out. We laughed that entire night and vowed to take swimming lessons as soon as we got back to the States. The pain eased up by the next day, so we were able to walk really slow and still enjoy Jamaica. Saint promised to buy me another Movado and earrings because it was his fault we'd flipped over—and he kept his promise.

Once we got back to the States, I thought he was just playing about taking swimming lessons, but he insisted that I find a place for us to take lessons together. We started taking lessons at the Freeport Recreation Center every Saturday, or at least *I* attended every Saturday. The few lessons Saint showed up for were absolutely hilarious. I thought that he should just stay on the beach and look pretty.

I thought our situation was better than it had been in a long time after that trip. It didn't last long. By January of 2007, I found out that he was still communicating with Lexus and Christina, and now he'd added a famous video vixen to the mix. I felt my position was a little stronger in his life, so I decided to put my foot down and told him I was not going through that mess with him and all these women again.

I told him that, if that's what he wanted to do, then he should bring me my stuff, and he could go about his business.

On January 29, 2007, Saint met me on Pacific Avenue in Brooklyn, with garbage bags filled with all my clothes and shoes. I didn't even realize I had that much stuff at his house. I thought it was going to be a simple exchange, but Saint had other plans. As I approached, he got out of the truck acting like he was going to help me put my things in the Acura, but instead he threw the bags in the middle of the street. As I was picking up the clothes that had fallen out of the bag and scattered in the street, I felt his hand on the back of my head, as his fingers intertwined with my hair. He dragged me back to his truck and opened the passenger door, trying to force me into the truck. I refused to get in the car, and he spun me around and slapped me in my face hard.

I started screaming and trying to fight him back this time. I knew the police station was right on the corner, but no one was around to hear me scream. He told me, "Shut up, bitch, and come get your car out of my driveway. I hate your black ass."

He got into his truck and left me there. I just gathered my things and got in my car. I sat there on the dark street for a while, just thinking, *Why?* This was all because I'd decided to stand up for myself. Needless to say, I did receive a phone call the next day telling me that I'd better come get my car now. I found myself begging and pleading with him to give me another day, so I could find a place to park my car that was safe. He insisted that I come get my car right then, or he would have it towed. I didn't want to deal with the embarrassment of calling Javon to ask him if I could park my car at their house, so I drove out to Long Island, took my car from the driveway, and parked it across the street.

I didn't make my presence known as I moved the car, so, of course, I got a phone call on my way back to Brooklyn, stating, "Bitch, your black ass think you're slick. Come back and get your car off of my street," he said.

I said, "You wanted me to get my car out of your driveway, and I did. When I get someone to come with me, I will move it then."

He said, "You'd better come get it now. Turn your black ass around, and come get your car now!" he yelled. I realized this had nothing to do with me getting my car, so I played along. I told him that I was not coming back, exited the parkway to turn around, and hung up the phone on him. Of course, he kept calling back, but I wouldn't answer. Normally, I would answer the phone every time he called, but I wanted him to know that I was serious this time. I was feeling so many emotions as I walked up to the front door. Once I rang the bell, everything in me said to run back to my car and get the hell out of there.

It was too late—he was already at the door and turning the lock. As he unlocked the door, he just turned his back and walked toward the basement. I guess that was my cue to follow him. As I walked down the stairs, I had another déjà vu moment about when he told me about sleeping with the girl in the Dominican Republic. He turned off the lights, and we sat in the dark for about five minutes in silence. I knew this was not going to be a good conversation—or, at least, anything I wanted to hear. I heard him sniffling, as if he were crying.

I was thinking to myself, *What the fuck is he crying about? I am the one with an envelope full of my hair that he pulled out. I am the one he promised he would never hit again. I am the one picking up my clothes off the street in Brooklyn.*

When he finally opened his mouth to speak, he said, "I can't keep doing this thing. I do love you, but this is not working." He apologized for what he'd done, and then he gave me the floor to speak.

I simply said, "OK. I am not here to change your mind, Saint. I just wanted you to know that I am not going to play second fiddle to anyone, anymore. Neither of those women are here with you, and I have been the one to stick by your side through everything. But if you feel like this is how it has to be, then so be it, Saint."

As I got up from the chair to walk past him and go up the stairs to leave, he reached out for my hand and stood up to embrace me. He held me tight and whispered in my ear that he was sorry for hurting me. I told him it was OK, and I walked up the stairs to leave.

I cried on the way back to Brooklyn for several reasons. One, I hated sleeping in my new basement apartment. Two, I really wanted him to finally just say it was all about me and that no other woman mattered. The fact that he was letting me go instead of fighting for me really hurt.

All the way back to Brooklyn, I was thinking, *Why do people in my life say they care about me but leave me to fend for myself?* My mother had sent me to foster care when I was eight years old. Then she came to get me back when I was turning 13, only to leave again when I was 14. I struggled with the fact that my father could have taken me instead of letting me go into the foster care system. Through no fault of his own, he had a stroke and later died. Therefore, I never got any answers to the question of why he hadn't fought for me not to go into foster care. Every relationship I tried to have, the man walked out on me for someone else. Looking back, I think it's clear that I suffered from low self-esteem, but I was sure a psychologist would diagnose me with abandonment issues.

A few days later, while I was sleeping in the basement apartment, the boiler blew up. I mean literally blew up. There was a loud *Boom!* and then the door to the boiler room flew open, and there was soot everywhere. I was scared to death. I was thanking God there'd been no fire. I did have the presence of mind to turn off the gas before I had to deal with a gas-leak issue, too. I ended up sleeping at my sister's that night, because I didn't want to stay there inhaling soot for the rest of the night. I was pissed, because during the home inspection, the inspector said the boiler was good, because it had been updated. The plumber charged me $6000 for a brand-new boiler.

I felt like my situation with Saint *and* my bank account were hemorrhaging. I didn't want to stay at my sister's for too many nights, because they would start asking questions that I just did not feel like answering. I eventually had to call Saint to ask if I could stay at his house for a few days, in the small room. He agreed to let me stay there until the boiler was fixed.

I really did sleep in the small bedroom for the first two days. While I was there, I cooked and cleaned, like I always did, and he seemed to really like having me there. By the third night, he told me I could sleep in his bed, because he was going to hang out with Penny, from work. Penny gave new meaning to the word "crazy." I didn't mind him hanging out with her because she was a proud lesbian. The fact that he let me stay in his room was a sign that things were changing, because normally he kept his room door locked. I didn't feel the need to snoop anymore, because I learned that what was done in the dark would eventually come to light. I also learned that sometimes what's done in the dark should remain there.

Even after the boiler was fixed, he still invited me to stay at his house. I didn't mind, because I truly hated staying in Brooklyn at my place. One of our fights in the past was about me being forbidden to answer the house phone. One night, he kept calling the house phone, but I wouldn't answer it, because I'd learned my lesson the first time. He then called my cell phone and scolded me for not answering his house phone. That was his way of letting me know that it was OK for me to answer the house phone now. I thought something was going on, but he just wanted me to know he was going over to Penny's after work again.

He was starting to spend a lot of time over there, and I did start to question the friendship. I knew she was a lesbian, but it wasn't that long ago that she'd taken some ding-a-ling and got pregnant. Unfortunately, the baby did not survive, but I knew her mission was to have a baby. He assured me that there was nothing going on. He acted as if he was insulted that I would even suggest something like that.

He said he had a good time hanging out with her lesbian friends, drinking, and playing cards. She had given him a key to her house, so he could feed her fish when she was away. In the back of my mind, I was wondering, *When the hell did they get so close?*

He actually said, "Sharon, for the first time, it's only you. I'm not gonna lie—I was talking to Lexus and Christina, but they don't want to be with me if you're gonna be in my life. So, I told them I didn't see my life without you in it. Things are finally going good between us, so please don't start," he said. I decided to let it go, because things *were* going pretty well between us.

Things continued to go really well for another month or so, until I was driving home—I should I say *his* house—and my car stalled. I was driving the Acura on the Southern State Parkway, and it started acting weird. I was happy I didn't have far to go, and as soon as I got off the Parkway at exit 21, my car died at the light. It was a '92 Legend, but it had always run well, so I didn't expect it to break down like that. I called Saint to tell him what had happened, and he told me to call our mechanic, whose shop was on Babylon Turnpike. The mechanic suggested I have the car towed to his shop, and that's what I did. He took me to the house, and, in that moment, I was grateful that I had two cars and that I never moved my car from his house.

The next day, the mechanic called me to say I needed a new engine because someone had put sugar in my gas tank. I asked him if was sure, and he said, "Yes, because I tasted it."

I immediately called Saint at work and told him what it was. My car was parked at his house every night, so it had to have happened there, and it could only have been someone he knew. This was a sure sign of a bitter, jealous bitch, and I wanted to know who he was fucking with now. He insisted that he wasn't messing with anyone else. I couldn't prove it, but I knew that whoever had put sugar in my tank had something to do with Saint. I noticed that Saint wasn't mentioning hanging out with Penny as much anymore, but I paid it no mind. I guess the novelty of hanging out with a lesbian had worn off for him.

About two weeks after the sugar-in-my-tank situation, I received a call from Penny. We were not friends, but we were now cordial after the incident a few years back, in control, after my car accident. She'd caught me on a bad day, right after some Chinese lady had crashed into my first Acura. She called into control center talking some mess, and I took everything out on her and tried to fight her. It was ironic, because Saint was the person who'd separated us back then. He explained to her why everything had gone down the way it had; she understood, and we both apologized to each other.

Anyway, she said she wanted to talk to me woman to woman. Anytime a female says the phrase "woman to woman," it is a sure sign it had something to do with a man. I was totally confused. *Why would she need to talk to me?* She said, "I am just gonna say it: I have been having sex with Saint for two months now, and I just want to know what is going on between you two. He tells me that you and he are just friends, and you leave your Benz at his house. I drove out to his house a few nights ago, and I saw both your cars there."

Then she asked, "Do you stay there?"

My blood pressure was rising, and I felt my heart poundingg in my chest, at what I was hearing. My mind went straight to the fact that she was probably the person who'd put sugar in my tank. I didn't mention it, because I refused to let her know that she'd affected me in any way. I simply said to her, "I don't appreciate you calling me at work with this."

She repeated that she was just calling woman to woman and wasn't trying to start anything. So, I asked her, "Aren't you gay? Why would you be calling me, trying to talk to me woman to woman, as if you are his girlfriend? I don't understand why an openly gay woman would be sleeping with a man in the first place."

She tried to explain that they started out as just friends but that one thing had led to another.

I was even more confused by that statement, so I asked, "How could one thing lead to another, if you're gay?" I never gave her the opportunity to answer that question. I felt she needed some clarification on the situation at hand. I said, "Don't call me talking to me as if you are his woman, and I am the other woman. Let's be clear about one thing: I let him hang out with you because I knew you were gay. Do you really think he would leave me for you?" I asked. "Penny, there is no way you could have possibly believed that." Again, I didn't allow her to answer. I went on to say, "I know him, and if he did sleep with you, it was because it was something to do—something to check off his bucket list."

I really don't recall every word I said to her that night, but I know I got off the phone and then left work sick, en route to Long Island. While I had tunnel vision for a moment, I snapped out of it quickly. I went home instead; all the while, he was calling my phone. I refused to answer, so I started receiving back-to-back text messages, to which I also didn't respond. About 45 minutes later, I heard the key in my lock and the sound of the door to the basement opening.

I didn't even look in his direction as he came in and sat on the bed beside me. "Sharon, I am so sorry," he said.

I felt I had lost a little bit of respect for him at that point. I was a strong believer that respect is something that is earned. However, because I'd lost respect for him, my response to him was, "You sure are sorry."

Then I went on a verbal assault on both of them. "You would put your dick in anything. What the fuck is wrong with your dick that it would get hard looking at that? You are absolutely disgusting. What the fuck were you thinking about? She is a disgusting, sloppy excuse for a woman. She looks unkempt and dirty all the time. It looks like she doesn't know how to wash her vagina properly. There is nothing attractive about her," I said.

He interrupted me by calling my name several times, trying to get me to stop ranting about her. When I finally stopped talking and allowed him to speak, he said, "She called me in tears. I don't know what you said to her, but I never heard her cry like that before. She said you have a way with words that really hurt her. She said she never had anyone talk to her like that before," he said.

I couldn't take any more. I was thinking, *I finally allow you the floor to speak, and that's the bullshit you say.* I yelled, "I don't give a fuck about her crying. Fuck her and her tears, and don't come in here telling me about that bitch's feelings."

He said, "OK, OK. I'm sorry."

I knew one thing for sure about him: when he is caught, he will tell the entire truth. He started explaining that once he'd inherited his godmother's two-family house, which was not too far from Penny's house in Brooklyn, she offered to help him by giving him the names of some contractors she used for her home. When the house was finished and ready to be rented, she wanted to see the house. They decided to go have drinks afterwards, so he went to her house to take a shower and get changed. According to him, she came into the bathroom and made a comment about his package. He claimed he made a joke and told her that she couldn't handle it, and they both laughed. Then she offered him a threesome with one of her friends. He said, "I can't lie—I was excited."

He went on to explain that, when they had the threesome and he tried to put it in, she couldn't take it, so they stopped. He said she called him back days later and said she wanted to try again. He agreed to it, but when he went to her house, the other girl wasn't there. He said she started crying because she'd really wanted to do that for him. He claimed the only reason his dick got hard was because she did have a fat ass.

I interrupted by saying, "So any ol' fat ass will do, right?"

He said, "Sharon, it wasn't like that."

"I don't want to hear all that other bullshit!" I screamed. "Did you fuck her?" I yelled.

He held his head down in shame and said, "Yes."

I asked if he'd used a condom, and he said, "No. I figured she was clean, because she wasn't getting any dick."

I screamed again, "You are so stupid! You act like vaginas don't get diseases!" I yelled. "How do you know she wasn't trying to set you up to be her next baby-daddy victim?" I asked, still screaming.

He said, "It's funny you mentioned that, because she offered to pay me if I would get her pregnant." He said that he'd really thought about it, but then he told her "No," because he would want to be a part of his child's life.

I zoned out for a brief moment, because it dawned on me that he said he'd considered having a baby with this chick over me. I re-engaged in the conversation when he said, "The pussy was good, because it was tight, but I knew I couldn't keep doing it." He had this smirk on his face as he said that, and I envisioned myself stabbing him in the throat.

When the vision was over, he said, "I stopped going over there as much when she started coming out to Long Island and leaving notes on my car, while you were there. She also started trying to keep me from pulling out, so I could get her pregnant. Sharon, I did ask her if she'd put sugar in your tank, but she denied it."

I'd had enough of this conversation by this point, and I just wanted him to leave. "Saint, please get the fuck out of my house," I said as nicely as I could. Before he left, I told him I noticed one thing about him, and that is that he was never satisfied with just one woman. He was happy only when he has two or more women at the same time. I said, "I knew something in you had changed, because you were being very nice to me—and that's probably when you added her to your lineup."

"Sharon, that's not true," he said. "You have it all wrong. Sharon, you don't know how much I truly regret dealing with her," he said, in this pathetic voice. "She will always be one of my biggest regrets in life. That situation is over, and you never have to worry about that again." I'm gonna leave now, but I hope you call me. I know you need some time, but please forgive me," he pleaded. I didn't call him for a few days, but I did miss him. Seeing both of them at work was hard, but I pushed past it, like I always did.

I eventually ended up back over there "playing house": cooking, cleaning, and food shopping. By this time, I was paying the cable bill, because he said I was the only one watching TV most of the time. We continued our normal pattern, but I noticed a slight change in his behavior over the months. Sex with him was different now. I wasn't sure if it was him or me. I knew that every time we had sex, I had to use a lubricant because my vagina would not get wet. I actually went to the gynecologist, but he said there was nothing physically wrong that he could find.

Saint would stop in the middle of the session just to spit on his fingers and insert them into my vagina for additional lubrication. I was disgusted by this action every time. Saint appeared very distant and a little cold toward me now. There were moments when I was wishing he *did* have another woman on the side. Like I said before, he was much nicer to me then. I had to let him know how I was feeling, so I wrote him a brief note for him to find on his bed when he got home. The letter read:

Dear Saint,

You don't talk to me anymore. You don't smile with me anymore. You make love to me as if I was a blow-up doll. You don't tell me I look nice anymore. I know you don't think I am pretty, but you could lie sometimes just to make me feel good. You won't even wash my car anymore on the weekends, when you wash yours. As much as I used to love to be here, I feel used when I come here now. You're not really happy to see me—you just know that you will get a home-cooked meal. So many things you've said to me stay with me always. Things like I will never have anyone claim me, because I am ugly. I looked in the mirror every day and wish I was lighter and prettier, so that you would want me. I have tried to show you that there is more to a woman than the way she looks. I have nothing left to give of myself. I am ugly, and I have to accept that, but I am a good woman with a big heart. I pray that God will open your heart and mind and make you love me better. But, if that day never happens, I pray that I won't feel ugly and unloved for the rest of my life. There is no medicine to cure my pain. I just need the love of a strong man to help me over this hill. I just want to feel real, unconditional love from a man. I pray that man will be you, someday.

I waited to hear from him, but he never called. I called the next day to find out if he'd actually read the letter. He answered the phone with an attitude.

He said, "Sharon, I don't know what I want anymore. I just know that I am not happy, and after reading your letter, I know that you are not happy, either. Maybe, I am not the man for you. Maybe you should find someone who can make you happy."

I never understood why he would tell me to find someone else, when all he had to do was change and love me for me. I guess it was safe to assume loving me was too hard for him to do. I got off the phone feeling completely rejected by him once again.

But, like so many times before when I thought we were finally over for good, two weeks later, somehow, we always ended up back together. Time really seemed to fly by with us and all of our ups and downs. Saint suggested we go away because he needed a vacation. I had never been on a cruise, and I thought that would be a good getaway. I found a seven-day cruise leaving out of Florida in July, going to Costa Maya, Cozumel, Grand Cayman, and Belize. I was excited about the cruise, until I found out that he had already gone on a cruise with Lurchette in the past.

I didn't want to go anymore, but he convinced me. This would be our second trip together, and I was looking forward to it. I remembered how close we were in Jamaica, and I hoped that this trip would spark something between us.

I was right. As soon as we landed in Florida, his entire demeanor changed. I was being called "wife" or "girlfriend," freely and openly. The public display of affection was at an all-time high. I couldn't help but wonder why it couldn't be like this all the time. When we arrived on the Carnival Cruise Ship called the *Legend*, our cabin wasn't ready. I had to have a room with a balcony because I am slightly claustrophobic. I specifically requested that when I'd booked the cruise, but they were trying to put us in a cabin the size of an inmate's cell. While they were trying to correct the mistake with our cabin, we took a tour of the ship. As we walked around the ship hand-in-hand, we accidently ended up downstairs, where the staff quarters were. The ship security officer approached us and informed us that we couldn't be down there; then he wrote our names down.

We finally made it to the room, and it was really nice. The balcony door didn't open all the way, but I was able to get fresh air and see the ocean. We christened the room immediately. I still had to use the lubrication that my doctor had prescribed, but I hoped that I would not need it by the end of the cruise. The first night out at sea was great. We met some really cool guys from New Jersey who sat at our table in the main dining hall. The second night out at sea, before we reached the first port, we decided to go to the club on the ship. It was empty at first, but once people arrived, things picked up quickly. We ran into those Jersey guys again, and the party really got started for us. I decided I'd had enough to drink and was ready to go to bed. Saint, being the party animal that he is, decided to stay and hang out with the Jersey guys a little longer.

At 4:00 a.m., the phone in the room rang, and it was the security officer. I thought something had happened to Saint. I was scared until he told me to come get Saint because he'd been found downstairs in the staff quarters again, and he was very intoxicated. My fear went away, and I was overcome with anger. I was pissed because I had to get up to go get a grown-ass man. I must admit it was funny when he saw me enter the security office. He said, "Hey, Pumpkin Butt—you came to get me," with this drunken smile on his face. I just took him by the hand as if he were a two-year old child and led him back to the cabin, where he fell asleep instantly.

In the morning, when the ship docked at Costa Maya and we were in line to exit the ship, a loud bell sounded as we scanned our wrist bands.

It sounded as if someone had pulled a fire-alarm switch. All of a sudden, the security guard from earlier this morning came and pulled us out of the line. He brought us to this room and said the ship's Captain wanted to speak with us. A few minutes later, the Captain came out to tell us that, normally, he would have put us off the ship because of whatever Saint had done the night before.

Apparently, I hadn't gotten the full story earlier that morning from the security guard, because the Captain said they'd found him coming out of the cabin of a female crew member. In that moment, I wanted to throw his ass overboard. I was under the impression that he was wandering the halls of the crew quarters. The Captain further said that the only reason he would allow us to continue on the cruise was that it was my first time being on a cruise. He also added that, for the duration of the cruise, we were banned from consuming alcohol. We couldn't even purchase anything and bring it back to our cabin. Every docking port after that when our wrist bands were scanned, leaving and reboarding the ship, the alarm went off, and security came to check our bags. It was so embarrassing. Saint had ruined this cruise experience for me.

He apologized, of course, but it was too late. He also insisted nothing had happened in the female crew member's cabin. He claimed she told him and the Jersey guys that they could continue the party in her cabin, but when he got there, it was just him and her. She told him he had to leave and called security to get him. He said he left her room and got lost and that's when security came and got him. I didn't believe anything he had to say, and any thoughts of my vagina getting wet for him went out the window.

I spent a few nights on the ship walking around and crying by myself. I thought about all the tears this man had caused me to shed over the past years. I just wanted to be liked, loved, honored, and cherished. More than anything, I really wanted to be respected by him. Saint obviously lacked respect for me if we could go on a vacation together and he still thought it was OK to go to another female's cabin. The ship security officer saw me sitting alone and crying and asked if everything was OK between me and my husband.

I told him everything was fine and allowed him to continue to believe that Saint and I were married, instead of telling him the truth. I also said that I could really use a drink right then. He smiled and shook his head as if he understood, and then he walked off. I hated the thought of being in the small cabin looking at what most would call a handsome face. I didn't see a handsome man anymore. I saw pure heartache and pain when I looked at him. The last night at sea, before we arrived back in Florida, I entered the cabin from one of my tearful walks, and Saint finally noticed that I had been crying. He sat me down on the bed and apologized for ruining this cruise experience for me. He expressed again that nothing had happened with the crew member. At this point, I couldn't care anymore about it. I'd already threw myself a pity party, shed some tears, and let it go.

We heard a knock at the cabin door, and it was security. He was there to let us know that the Captain wanted to see us again. I gave Saint the most evil look, as if to say, *What did you do now?* He read my face and responded immediately with, "I didn't do anything."

As we followed the security officer to the Captain's office, I thought, *If Saint had found another way to disrespect and embarrass me, I am cutting his ass off for good, right here and right now.* As we entered the office, the Captain must have read the look on my face as well because he said, "Don't worry. I called you here to inform you that I am willing to lift the no-alcohol ban for the duration of the cruise. I want to warn you that if there is an incident regarding your (he pointed in Saint's direction) excessive alcohol consumption, then I will have the coast guard remove you from the ship before we arrive back in Florida."

I stepped in and said, "You will have no problem with him. I will keep an eye on him myself, and thank you very much." I couldn't wait to consume an alcoholic beverage. The ship had a theatre room where they were putting on a stage play, and we decided to attend. Saint left to go get the drinks, and, when he returned, he had a small box with five drinks in it. I told him I was not playing with him and that he'd better not get us kicked off this boat. He claimed the drinks were watered down and that's why he'd gotten so many. I went along with it, because I planned on not letting him out of my sight. Even though we had drinks while sightseeing at every port, it didn't make up for the nights without libation on the ship. This last night didn't make up for the past six nights on the ship. I was so ready to be on dry land and away from Saint.

Once we got back to New York, I tried to stay as busy as possible with work instead of spending a lot of time with Saint. I learned to forgive, but never did I forget. I had to take a look at my life. I was turning 37 in November, and I felt like I hadn't accomplished anything in life. All I had going for me was that three-family house in Brooklyn. I wanted my single-family home, with a loving man, and possibly one child. In the past, I had convinced myself that I didn't want any children, but something internal was telling me that I did now. I was trying to fight that feeling from entering and consuming my every thought, but it was hard.

I started slowly hinting and picking his brain on the topic of us having a baby together again. All he would say was, "If it happens, then it happens." I took that to mean that he didn't want to willingly impregnate me, but if an accident happened, then we would have to deal with it then. This was another shot to my self-esteem. I am not sure if Saint even realized how hurtful some of his statements were. How can you tell the woman who has stuck by you through thick and thin, loves you to the moon and back, that the only way she can have your child is by accident? I never wanted to have an "Oops" baby. I think maybe that was part of the reason that I'd had so many abortions. I dreamed of having a loving man in my life who wanted me to carry his child and raise our baby together.

The more I hinted about the idea of us having a baby, he would simply say, "We'll see what happens." The more I thought about it, I realized that that's what he said about everything. I eventually stopped hinting about the two us having a baby together and just asked him outright if he would get me pregnant because I was ready to have a baby. This man looked me in my face, while sitting on my bed, in my apartment, and told me he didn't want to have a baby with me. Me, being the quick-mouthed person that I am, said sarcastically, "But you were considering having a baby with Penny, the lesbian."

As soon as I said her name, I felt his hands putting pressure on around my neck and slightly squeezing. I was still able to speak, and, at this point, I had had enough, so I told him to kill me. I kept saying, "I am ready to die, and I hope you rot in jail for killing me." I felt the grip loosen around my neck, and then I saw a flash of light as his right hand connected with the left side of my face. I fell to the floor, and before I could open my mouth or attempt to get up, he kicked me between my legs, aiming for my vagina with everything he had. I screamed out at the *thought* of the pain, but I didn't feel any pain. My mind and body were numb. I couldn't think or comprehend what was happening in that basement at that moment. All I could do was scream for him to leave. I kept saying, "OK, Saint—you win. Just get out."

He stood over me, watching me cry. He stretched his hand down toward me, and I flinched in fear that he was trying to hit me again.

He said in a calm voice, "Sharon, I am not going to hurt you, and I don't want you to be afraid of me."

I sat on the floor, emotionally drained and void of all self-respect. As the visual image of him raising his size 14 or 15 foot to kick me replayed in my head, I repeated the words, "Just leave."

"Sharon, just get up," he said. "I don't want to leave you like this. I want to make sure that you're OK."

I raised my voice several octaves and yelled, "You're not worried about me if you can kick me in my pussy just because I asked to have your baby."

He said, "Sharon, keep your voice down before your tenants hear you."

I shouted back, "I don't give a fuck, Saint! Get out of my house—just get out of my house, and leave my fucking key." I kept repeating that until he left. I got up from the floor to lock the door and make sure he'd left. I cried myself to sleep that night. I knew the countdown was on because my level of respect for him had dropped another level. I knew from my past situations that once I'd lost all respect for someone, there was no going back.

That next day, Saint kept calling my house phone and my cell phone, but I refused to answer. Then I received a call from my sister telling me that he'd called her to ask if she had spoken to me. I lied to my sister and said I'd eaten some bad Chinese food and was throwing up all morning, so I hadn't gone to work. I told her that I forgot to tell Saint that I wasn't going to work. I also lied and said that I would call him. I did send him a text message advising him not to call my family anymore.

He replied, "Sharon, please call me."

That text message fell on deaf ears, as some old-timer would say. I was more determined than ever not to deal with him again. He tried everything to get me to respond to him. I received more flowers at work, which did not move me in the least. He sent many text messages, to which I did not respond. By this time, I had one tenant move out and a new family that I got from the shelter for homeless families move in. This program paid you three months in advance by check. My mailing address was his address, therefore, my checks went to his house. He used this as his opportunity to reach out, knowing he would get a response.

I guess he decided he had the right to be mad, so he sent a text saying, "Black bitch, come get your mail from my house, and don't use my address for shit because you don't live here."

I laughed when I read that message, because I knew it was just for effect. What he didn't know was that I had already applied for a PO Box in Freeport. I was serious this time about leaving him alone. I still had all the love in the world for him in my heart, but I knew this couldn't continue. I stayed away from him for almost two months before I had to go and pick up my mail, specifically my checks. I did ask him to bring it up to the job, but he refused. I felt like I was reliving several moments in our past when I went to his house after a traumatic event in our situation.

As always, he would come to the door, unlock it, and walk away. As I entered his house, I saw a small stack of mail on the dining-room table. I picked up the stack with the first piece addressed to me and proceeded to walk out the door. He called me before I exited and said, "I put the checks in my safe," which was upstairs in his bedroom. He came toward the door with two drinks in his hand and handed me one. He never spoke a word—he just gave me the drink and proceeded to walk upstairs toward the bedroom. I followed him upstairs and sat in the chair by the computer desk that I'd purchased. We sat in silence for a moment, as usual.

During this time, I was taking inventory of this entire home, and I realized how much I'd invested into one day calling this place my home. I mentally calculated all the money I'd spent in this house, and it made me sick to think that I no longer belonged here. I no longer felt comfortable in that house. He finally spoke and broke the mental trance I was in by saying those words that meant absolutely nothing to me now: "I'm sorry."

He went on to say, "I really think you should try to go out with someone else because I don't think I am the man for you, or the man you want and need me to be."

I agreed with him and asked for my checks, so that I could leave. Before I left that house, I let it be known exactly how I felt about that house now. I told him I'd worked hard to turn this house into a home for us, and he'd turned it into a whorehouse. I explained that every time I pulled up in front of the house, I had nothing but negative memories.

He just sat and listened to me. Then he said, "I am sorry you feel that way."

As I stood up to leave, he came and gave me a hug. I accepted his apology and left his house. He did offer me to stay, but I told him I couldn't lie in that bed because only God knows who has been in there, since we had not been speaking. He tried to assure me that he had not been with anyone. I didn't believe anything he was trying to sell me, and I could see the hurt in his face. I wasn't sure if the look of hurt was because he was losing me or because I wasn't buying his lie.

On the way back to Brooklyn, I felt like I was gaining a little power back. I felt my self-esteem rising just a little. I felt like I had taken a little bit of my dignity and self-respect back. A week or so later, he called, and this time I answered.

He said, "I didn't think that you would answer, and I was prepared to leave you a message."

I said, "Well you got me, so, what's up, Saint?"

He said, "Sharon, I really miss you."

I told him that I missed him, too. However, I knew me missing him did not mean that I wanted to be back with him on his terms. He said that he admired the way that I went on vacations by myself, and he decided to try it. He had booked a trip to the Bahamas and wanted me to take him to the airport. I agreed, but then he slipped in that the flight he booked left early in the morning and that I would have to spend the night at his house. For some reason, hearing that made me nervous.

I immediately ask when was his trip, and he replied, "Next month."

I was okay with that because that gave me some time to mentally prepare. The thought of going to that house mentally drained me. Between that phone call and the beginning of the trip, Saint did invite me to come over a lot. I always counter-offered for him to come to Brooklyn, and he did. We just hung out and played a lot of Scrabble. I got him hooked on that game. He always thought he was better than me. He was good because he always did the crossword puzzles in all the newspapers. We also played the computer version of "Who Wants to Be a Millionaire?"

Hanging out as just friends became our new thing. The trip was fast approaching, and, by this time, I felt better about us and our new situation. He asked me to come over early and bring the Scrabble game so he could bust my ass real quick, before he caught his flight in the morning. That night we played a few games of Scrabble, and, somehow it led to a sex session. I refused to let him touch me without a condom, and, of course, he had some on hand. I questioned why he had condoms, because I had not been there.

All he had to offer was that he wasn't doing anything with anyone. Just the thought of that made my vagina not react, once again. Saint enjoyed himself, but my heart wasn't in it, and I just wanted him to finish so we could go to sleep.

On the way to the airport, he was trying to convince me that he was not going to mess with anyone out there like he'd done in the Dominican Republic. I listened as he told that story, but I had no faith in whatever he was saying. He did call me several times a day when he was away. He hooked up with one of the male workers at the resort, who took him to the local parties. When he got back, he said he'd had a good time but that he would never go on vacation alone again.

While he was away for that week, I was very much aware that I was probably never going to have a child, and I just wanted something to love me. I began to research dogs and which one would be a good fit for me. I expressed my thought to Saint, and he said, "I don't want a dog in my house." I was confused because I had no intention of being at his house with my dog. I eventually settled on the idea of a teacup Shih-Tzu. I decided I wanted a male dog, and I would name him "Nipsy," sight unseen. Saint thought I was just talking to hear myself talk. I wanted unconditional love, and I was willing to pay for it. I paid $1000 for a dog that hadn't even been born yet. The breeder started sending pictures of Nipsy from the day he was born, April 10, 2008. When I showed Saint the photos of Nipsy, he realized that I was serious about getting a dog and having something that loves me.

Eight weeks later, when Nipsy was able to fly, I was so nervous because I was going to be a doggy mom. I remember thinking, *What the hell have I done?* I picked him up from Kennedy Airport, and I immediately fell in love with him when I saw that little face. This must be how a mother feels when she first lays eyes on or gets to hold her baby for the first time. It all became so real in that moment. He was here, and I had to take care of him for the rest of his life.

He'd pooped and peed on himself during the flight, so he was a little stinky. I brought him to Saint's house to give him a bath and for Saint to meet him. I thought Saint was going to say, "I asked you not to bring a dog into my house," but, instead, he had the opposite reaction. He picked little Nipsy up and put him on his bed, after he'd had a bath, of course. Nipsy was so excited, he started rolling around on the bed trying to further dry himself off, and then he started to pee on the bed. Saint jumped off the bed and started yelling, "Get him, get him!"

It was hilarious, but at the same time, I knew Nipsy would not be welcome in his home again. I brought Nipsy home to Brooklyn, and he became my only concern. He was the only thing I talked about and the only thing I cared about. Saint became jealous of all the attention I paid

Nipsy whenever he came over. Because he didn't want Nipsy at his house, I spent more time in Brooklyn, because I wasn't leaving Nipsy alone to go spend time in Long Island with Saint. Nipsy filled that void in my life. When I came home from work, he met me at the door excited to see me and just wanting to give me a thousand kisses. Although it was a dog, it felt good to have something to love me that wasn't going to judge me, something that wasn't going to care what I looked like, and something that wasn't going to betray me. I would have done anything to protect him and keep him safe.

Although I owned the building, living in a basement apartment sucked ass. Whenever my tenants would flood their bathrooms, the water would end up in the basement sump-pump room, which connects to my shower wall. Black mold started to grow inside the shower stall and in the back bedroom. All of my clothes that were in the closet smelled like mildew, and most of my shoes literally grew mold inside and out. I moved everything from the back room and hung my clothes on the hot-water pipes leading upstairs. I knew black mold was dangerous if inhaled constantly, so I tried to keep it at bay by spraying with bleach solution, but it wasn't working. I asked Saint if I could stay at his house with Nipsy, because it wasn't healthy for me to be living down there with the black mold.

I don't know whether he knew how toxic black mold was, or maybe he just didn't care, but a few times he outright said "No," and other times, he made some excuse. He started telling me again that I should maybe start thinking about dating other people. This time I didn't get as upset at the prospect of seeing someone new. After all, Saint wasn't even concerned about my health.

What Saint didn't know was that I was receptive to some flirtatious comments made by another co-worker by the name of Morales. Morales was an officer who used to work at MCC then left only to return years later. He was a cute-faced Dominican, with a nice body. He, like everyone else, didn't know about me and Saint. Morales and I finally got to a point where we exchanged telephone numbers and spent several nights talking on the phone until early morning. I eventually told Morales about me and Saint. Because I prided myself on not being a cheater, I also told Saint about Morales. Saint didn't seem to care because he felt he "looked better" than Morales, as he put it. When I told Saint that Morales asked me out on a date, he told me I should go. I guess he didn't think that I would really go, so I decided I could show him better than I could tell him, and I said, "Yes."

Morales and I made plans to see a play called *Plantanos and Collard Greens* and then go to dinner at a place called One Fish Two Fish. Before the date, Saint kept laughing, joking, and teasing me about going on the date. During dinner, Saint kept texting and calling me the entire time. I think I turned Morales off because I kept answering the phone and replying to the text messages. Morales told me that I was not ready to move beyond Saint, and he didn't want to be a part of a scheme to make him jealous. I tried to assure him that I was ready to move on, but I guess he saw through me.

As soon as I dropped him off, because he had no car—Saint called and asked me to meet him and Kane at a club in Brooklyn. When I got there, he started with the jokes again, so I told him that I kind of liked Morales and that I would probably go out with him again. Morales had bought me a t-shirt from the play, and Saint tried to throw it away, but I wouldn't let him. For some reason, the fact that I didn't allow him to throw the t-shirt into the streets of Brooklyn caused him to realize that I was serious about liking Morales. He started asking me if I had kissed Mo, and I told him that I had and that I liked it very much. I guess he had to save face in front of Kane, because he acted as if he didn't care or as if I were lying to try to make him jealous.

The next day, he asked me again about Morales, and I told him that we had made plans to go to dinner again the following weekend. He told me that he didn't want me to go out with him again. I told him "No," because that would be rude, especially since I already said "Yes." He pleaded with me not to go, and I used his phrase, "We'll see what happens."

Morales and I spoke every day leading up to the next date. He kept hinting about the fact that he didn't want to hurt me, but he knew something that might hurt me. I hate when people do things like that. Why would you mention it if you are not willing to tell it?

Over dinner at Pio Pio, a Peruvian restaurant in the Bronx, I learned that he'd moved back to New York because he'd just gone through a divorce and had to move in with his mother to re-establish his credit. These were all red flags for me, but I was willing to make an exception because he had a plan to get back on track. Saint called throughout this date as well, but this time I didn't answer the phone or reply. Morales took note of this fact, and I guess it made him a little more secure with the fact that I was making an effort to actually be with him.

He finally came out and said, "I don't know what your status is with Saint, but I think he and the Dirtbag have something going on." ("The Dirtbag" was a female I'd previously had issues with but had since become cordial with. In fact, we were talking about doing business together because I had become a certified bartender, and she was good at party planning and making cards and invitations. We thought about combining our effort to make some extra money.)

Morales said he would always catch them in the staff lounge, and they would jump when he walked in, as if something were going on. He also said that she would always bring Saint breakfast in the morning when she arrived at work. None of this really added up to cheating, but he sensed something more than just friendship was going on between them. Even though I didn't put anything past Saint, I didn't think anything of this because she used to mess with Kane, and I didn't think Saint would deal with his friend's side piece. However, I was not going to be stupid and not ask about it, either.

I told Mo that I appreciated him telling me, and we didn't speak about it again for the rest of the night. I drove Morales home, and, before I could leave his block, I was on the phone with Saint trying to find out what was going on. Saint, of course, denied the allegations and said that "The Dirtbag" came outside to talk to him about her husband and the fact that she was going to work Special Housing Unit (SHU) the next quarter; she wanted some tips on how to run it. He was furious that Morales had told me anything at all, and he said he was going to confront him. I tried to convince him that made no sense, if it was all innocent.

Saint worked the overnight shift from midnight to 8:00 a.m., as the Outside Patrol Officer, and she was working Sanitation on the same shift.

Morales worked the day shift from 8:00 a.m. to 4:00 p.m. Saint waited for Morales to come into work to tell him to keep his name out of his mouth. Morales was no punk, so they had words, but I can't speak to that because I wasn't there. The following week Morales and I actually worked the same shift, from noon to 8:00 p.m., and The Dirtbag just so happened to be working overtime with us in the lobby. Saint never called me at the institution, but for some reason, that night he called to tell me to take my pocketbook upstairs with me to the visiting floor. I would normally leave it in the drawer in the lobby. When I asked "Why?" he said only, "Just please take your bag upstairs." I didn't think anything of it, so I brought the bag upstairs.

Later when our shift was over, I offered to take Morales to the subway station. Once he was in the car, we decided to go back to my place. We were just watching a movie and enjoying each other's company when I heard several loud bangs on my door. As I peeked out of the window in the door, I didn't see anyone. Then I heard Saint say, "Sharon, come outside," from the top of the steps. I told Morales to stay inside as I went to see what was going on.

Saint was pacing in front of my house, and he had this look in his eye as if he wanted to kill me. He said, "Sharon, did you leave work with that Dominican kid?"

I replied, "Yes, I gave him a ride to the subway, and then I came home. Who told you that I'd left with him?"

He replied, "Kane told me."

I knew then that Kane's loyalties lay with Saint and not with me. I loved Kane, but I knew where he stood from that moment on. Saint asked to come inside the basement and I said, "No, because you're gonna try to hit me."

He said, "I'm not going to hit you."

I told him that I didn't trust him and that I wouldn't let him inside. He didn't argue with me for too long, because he had to go to work. When I got back in the house, Morales was ready to go home, and I couldn't blame him. He'd overheard my conversation with Saint about him hitting me, and he was genuinely concerned. I told him I would be fine, but we had to wait a little while before we left the house, because I didn't believe Saint had left the area that quick.

At approximately 1:00 a.m., I felt it was safe because Saint was at work by then. I drove Morales back to the Bronx, and, on the way back, I popped in at the institution just to see for myself what was really going on. As I pulled up, The Dirtbag was inside the Outside Patrol booth with Saint. She didn't even move when I walked up to the booth.

I said, "Dirtbag, can you excuse us for a minute?" She wouldn't leave until Saint asked her to leave. This is when I knew there might actually be something to this thing that Morales had been witnessing. Saint wanted to know what I was doing up there. I told him that I didn't like the way we'd left things and I couldn't sleep. He fell for that, so I changed the subject back to The Dirtbag being in his face. He just kept telling me to leave and that we would talk about it in the morning.

He said, "Sharon, this doesn't look good with you being up here like this."

"That's your problem. You are so worried about people finding out about us, but yet you have that little bitch in your face all night," I said, as I walked out of the booth and slammed the door shut.

Morales called me in the morning when he got to work and told me that he'd caught them in the lounge again and that he believed something was definitely going on between them. When I got to work later on that day, sitting in the lobby, I overheard two female staff members gossiping about Saint and The Dirtbag being in the back by the Warden's area. This time I couldn't overlook it because it was coming from people who didn't have an interest in our situation. I called Saint to tell him what I'd overheard and what Morales had told me, but all he could say was, "People are always talking and don't know what they are talking about. As for Morales, just tell him to stop telling you things to make you upset."

"Saint, is that all you have to say?" I asked. "You just told me about how things look when I come around you, but with the perception of the Dirtbag being around you too much, it's OK?"

He yelled, "I am not messing with that girl!"

"Well, people don't know that, and I don't know if *I* believe that—especially after seeing you with her the other night," I yelled back. "Saint,

I believe what's done in the dark will come to light, just like everything else you've done. All I am going to say to you is, if I find out that you have been messing with that girl, then I'm done with you. There will be nothing that you can say to me at that point. I need you to really understand that I mean what I am saying to you, Saint."

He never responded to any of my comments. All he said was, "I have to go."

Morales and I were still talking and hanging out during this time, but I sort of lost interest. He came over on another night, and things got a little heated, and there was some touching over the clothes, and I wasn't impressed. I took him home that night, and, on the way back, I thought to myself, *What am I doing?* When we would talk on the phone, he displayed some insecurities about me being with Saint sexually and him possibly following up. He naturally assumed, like most people do, that a tall man must have a really big penis. Don't get me wrong: Saint was no slouch, but it wasn't like a horse penis or anything.

Morales followed up his insecurities with my first dick pic, via text message. Oh, how I wish he hadn't done that, because that put the nail in his coffin. He ended up in the friend zone, really quick. I feel bad for saying this, but I sent that picture to all of my girlfriends, and we couldn't stop laughing about how skinny and pink it was. I asked him if his penis was hard in the picture, and he said, "Yes." I know everyone was not going to be the same size, but there was no way that I was going to waste his time or mine, because we would never be sexually compatible.

On his third visit to my place, things went a little further, and I allowed him to taste my essence. I knew I was going to get out of having sexual intercourse with him at all costs, even if it meant using the classic line, "It's too soon, and we should stop."

I felt like I was cheating on Saint, but not really, because he was the one who'd told me to see other people.

Morales said, "I know I am not as big as Saint, but I want to show you that size wouldn't make a difference because I love you."

I had to stop him right there. I asked, "How could you love me? You don't even know me." It hadn't been even a whole month that we had been talking.

He said, "I know your heart, and you're a good person."

I felt like he was rushing things or trying to say the right thing to get me to have sex with him. In the middle of this conversation, with me half dressed and Morales standing there with his little pink pencil exposed, anticipating sexual intercourse, a sudden banging on the door scared the hell out of both of us.

I jumped up from the bed and ran to the door. I saw Saint. I told him to hold on before I opened the door. I whispered to Morales to get dressed, and I put my pants back on. At that point Saint started kicking my front door, trying to gain entrance. When I opened the door, Saint came in like a madman and told Morales to get the fuck out. Morales actually left me there, knowing full well that Saint had hit me in the past. I knew two things for sure at that moment: one, Morales and I were done, and two, I was probably going to die that night.

Saint kept his composure for once. He said, "Sharon, did you fuck that kid?"

I told him that I hadn't, but I did let him kiss it.

Saint asked, "Were you going to fuck him?"

I told him what I'd told my girlfriend, which was that Morales and I were not sexually compatible because of the size of his penis. Saint just turned and walked out of my apartment, never looking back and not saying another word. I felt so bad because I saw the hurt in his eyes.

Morales found his way to the subway and went home. I did try to call to check on him, but he didn't answer until the next day. He said he didn't want to be a part of this type of situation. I didn't really care about what he was saying, because I knew that we would never be together.

I was grateful for the one good thing that came out of me dealing with Morales for that brief period: I think Saint got to see, for the first time, what I had experienced for years with him dealing with other women. He must have had some sort of epiphany about what his life would be like without me in it. He called two days later to express that he wasn't mad at me, because he realized he'd told me to do what I did.

I wanted him to understand that, although I was done with Morales, I wasn't coming back to him on his terms. I no longer wanted to be his biggest secret. I gave him an ultimatum: I wanted to be in a regular relationship that was out in the open, for all to see. I wanted everyone to know that he'd chosen me to be his woman. He said he understood and wanted me to come over so we could talk about it some more. When I got there, he kissed me like never before—it was one of the best kisses I'd ever shared with him. I think this came from the fact that I'd told him that Morales was a really good kisser.

He told me to go upstairs and wash up. I didn't get what that was about, because I wasn't dirty, but I did it anyway. He came upstairs shortly afterwards with my favorite drink in hand. I knew what that meant—the sex session was about to begin. Normally, the sessions would always begin with me servicing him, but this time he wanted to service me. I totally get why he wanted me to wash up now, because he almost never went down on me. To be honest, he wasn't really good at it, so I never made a big deal about it. I also attributed him going down on me to the fact that I'd told him that Morales was good at that also. I think he was trying to erase any memory of Morales from my mind. I would never have thought that all I had to do was have someone else show interest in me in order for him to see the light.

I started spending a little more time at his place, and things went well for maybe another week. He was still working overnight, so we agreed to meet at my place in the morning and then go to his house afterwards. It didn't really make sense because we were driving separate cars out there, but that was the plan.

As we pulled up in front of his house, there was the Dirtbag, attempting to leave the cul-de-sac. I used my car to block her in, and then I got out of my car to ask her what she was doing there. She began to stutter, trying to come up with some lie. Before I knew it, I was trying to snatch her out of her Jeep.

Saint came and literally picked me up and carried me into the house. She had the nerve to follow us into the house talking about, "St. John, I never disrespected you, and you shouldn't have put your hands on me."

I yelled, "Bitch, get the fuck outta here before that's not all that I'll do to you!"

This little bitch had the nerve to say, "No. I'm not going anywhere." Then she started yelling, "Saint, are you going to let her talk to me like that?"

I looked at him and said, "You'd better tell her who the fuck I am and to get the hell out!"

He said, in a low tone, "Dirtbag, please just leave."

She said, "No, Saint. I want to know why she put her hands on me."

The moment she said that, I tried to get at her again, but he caught me mid-lunge.

He started yelling, "Dirtbag, please leave before I call the police."

She said, "Saint, you would really call the police on me? Call the police—because I am going to press charges on her for putting her hands on me."

I yelled, "Bitch, I don't give a fuck about no police."

Saint interrupted and demanded for her to leave his house.

This silly hoe said, "Saint, you really want me to go?"

He said, "Yes, Dirtbag, please leave."

"So, Saint—you really gonna choose her over me?" she asked

He said, "Yes, Dirtbag. Sharon is my girl."

She finally left, and Saint let me go.

I just looked at him and said, "I am done."

I started to walk out of the house and he said, "Sharon, let me explain."

"Explain what—that you are fucking that bitch? I told you that, if I found out that you were fucking around with that girl, there was nothing that you can say to me!"

He said, "Sharon, please."

My curiosity got the better of me, and I wanted to know how long, and why her, so I stayed quiet long enough for him to explain.

He said, "It started out with her just asking about SHU, and then she started talking about her husband and how they don't have sex anymore."

I interrupted his long speech because I didn't want him to take me down memory lane with a bunch of bullshit. "Saint, I don't want to hear all of that shit! How the fuck did you end up putting your dick in that nasty whore?" I screamed.

"Sharon, I am getting to that," he said. "One morning, I was home and I heard the doorbell. When I looked out the window, I saw her Jeep. I didn't even know she knew where I lived. When I opened the door, I asked her what she was doing there."

He said that she said, "Saint, can I use your bathroom, because I'm not going to make it to Suffolk County—I will pee on myself."

He said, "I didn't think anything of it, so I let her in." He said when she came out of the bathroom, she was butt-ass naked.

I interrupted again and said, "So all it takes is a big butt and a smile? A big butt is what got you in the last disgusting situation," I said.

"No, Sharon, but you got to admit she does have a fat ass and a nice little body," he said, as if we were homeboys.

I got up to leave, and he grabbed my hand to keep me from leaving. I tried to fight it, but tears came flowing down my face. I said, "I can't believe you just keep hurting me. I am sorry that I will never have a fat ass or that I will never be any of the things you desire in a woman, but I know that I have been good to you."

He said, "Sharon, you have been good to me, and I don't mean to hurt you."

"All these people keep throwing themselves at you because you constantly act like you don't have anyone," I said through tears. "You tell everyone that you're single, as if I don't exist in your world."

"That's not true, Sharon," he said. "When she asked me if I was messing with you, I told her that we were getting down."

I screamed, "After eight years, you're still saying that we are just getting down? I am leaving, and you are fucking disgusting to me!" Then I went off on my rampage of rhetorical questions. "How could you fuck a married woman? How could you fuck someone like her? She has no class about herself. The bitch doesn't even comb her hair. On top of all of that, she used to fuck Kane, and you saw all the crap she pulled with him. Why would you go there with her? You have no loyalties to anyone or anything but your dirty dick."

As I was rattling off all the ways I was disgusted by him, I saw a tear fall from his eyes. I couldn't even care at this point. I felt he'd sunk to an all-time low with this indiscretion. I knew that this was the last bit of respect I had for him. My heart knew that I loved him, but my mind had nothing left to give this man. I got up and left him there with his tears, but before I left, I had to make him feel ashamed. I told him that his mother would be so disappointed in him.

He stood at the top of the steps and said, "Sharon, please don't go."

I just closed the door and left feeling anger, heartbreak, and disappointment. I don't know why, but I called Morales to tell him that he had been right all along. He apologized that I had been hurt by them and hoped things would get better for me. Then I called Kane to tell him about his friend's betrayal. Kane did sound a little shocked by the news, and he admitted that he had heard the rumors. He said that he'd asked Saint about it but that he'd denied it.

I think I wanted Kane to hate Saint because I was feeling hate toward him. Kane's demeanor wouldn't allow him to be angry or hateful. Kane was just happy to be free of The Dirtbag and all her obsessive shenanigans.

Saint had been calling the entire time I was on the phone, but there was no way I was going to take his call. I didn't want to go home because I thought he would show up at my place, so I went to my sister's new house in New Jersey and tried to put on a brave face. It worked for a few hours, but the ride back to Brooklyn seemed long and torturous. It was more than just a cry—I felt myself bawling with tears. I almost had two accidents on the way home that night.

When I got home, my little Nipsy was there and so happy to see me as always. I held that little dog so tight, and he licked my tears—as if he knew I was in emotional anguish. As I was preparing for bed, I heard a knock at the door, and, for the first time, I was truly hoping it was one of my tenants.

No such luck—it was Saint. I don't know why I opened the door, but he came in saying he just wanted to check on me to make sure I was OK. I told him that I would be fine; I was used to him disappointing me.

He said, "Sharon, that's not fair."

"Let's not talk about 'fair,' Saint," I retorted. "You have me looking crazy at work because people think that I'm some Saint groupie. Now you have that little piece of shit feeling like she has something on me. I stopped hanging out with all my friends because they were making slick comments about my relationship with you. Maybe they all saw what I couldn't see. You are who you are, and that is a cheater, period."

He stood there for a moment before responding. "Sharon, I don't want it to be this way," he said. "I think that maybe something's wrong with me," he suggested.

Before he could finish that stupid thought, I cut him off by saying, "Saint, I know you are not about to sit here and claim that you are a sex addict."

He had a dumb look on his face when he said, "I don't know what is wrong with me. I think I need to just get away and figure things out."

"What is there to figure out, Saint? I am done."

"Sharon, don't say that," he said. "I love you, and I can't picture my life without you in it," he proclaimed. "Sharon, you said a lot of things that really hurt my feelings today. I never knew what Penny was talking about until today, when she said you had a way with words. Listen, I called my cousin Marcia and told her I needed to get away."

I questioned, "Marcia—the cousin you fucked?"

"Sharon, that's not funny or true," he said.

"I am not trying to be funny, and I know that it's true, but you would never admit that."

He shook his head in disbelief. "Anyway, Sharon, I called work and told them I needed to take some time off, so Marcia got me tickets to leave next week."

I was tired and didn't want to hear any more or talk anymore, so I just said, "Have a safe trip and goodnight, because I want to go to bed."

He asked if he could stay with me and just hold me.

I was tired, and I didn't feel like going back and forth with him, so I said, "Yes."

Before he left on his trip to Jamaica, Saint made it his business to spend all of his time with me at my place because I refused to come to his house. I was very distant emotionally from him, and he sensed it. He would say, "I know you love me and you're just hurting—and I am sorry." Saint would always ask who I loved the most, as if that made any difference. I never understood the significance of this question. Did he think that if I admitted to loving him the most that it would negate all the disrespect, hurt, and pain that he'd caused? One day he would realize that the fact that I loved him more made him the worst person I have ever been with.

I also thought the fact that he prayed every single day for 15 minutes before he left the house—then turn around and dance with the devil all day long—solidified my childhood memory of people in church being total hypocrites. I understood that God was a forgiving God, but I had to question how many breaks he would give someone who constantly caused hurt and pain. No one deserves that many chances.

I also had to question myself. Why did I keep giving him so many chances? I was not God. I did not have to keep forgiving him. It must have been my self-esteem. All those failed attempts at trying to get someone to love me even though I wasn't as pretty as the other girls they left me for were taking a toll on me. At some point I had to believe that I couldn't do any better than Saint. Maybe I believed that persistence would eventually overcome resistance. I just couldn't figure out why I couldn't break free from this man who was feeding my soul poison. He was slowly killing my confidence with every indiscretion. I had to find a way to pull myself back together. I had to give *me* another chance. I felt the shift within me with this last betrayal from Saint.

Although he took time off work before his trip, I didn't. It was so hard for me to see that little skank every day. She would make smart little comments when people were around because she knew she was safe. She would randomly say something like, "It's always the monkey-looking girl who be trying to fight other people over a man that don't even claim them. Only a pathetic gorilla would take a cum shot flick wearing a dude rag on their head."

She had a very distinctive laugh, and she would laugh loudly at her own slick comments. Then others would laugh along with her, not knowing it was me she was referring to. There were times when I would come outside, and I would see her driving past my property in Brooklyn. There was no reason for her to be over there, because it was a one-way street and not on her way home. I told Saint about her stalking me, and he said he would talk to her. I didn't even know she knew where my house was. That's when he told me that, the night he'd come to check on me, after the confrontation at his house, she'd left a note on his car.

He also told me about the day when he'd asked me to take my bag upstairs to the visiting floor—she had gone through my purse while it was downstairs. That's when it dawned on me: *this is how she knew about those photos that Saint took of me.* I was completely disgusted all over again.

"This is the type of trash that you choose to sleep with," I said in disbelief. I originally agreed to take him to the airport for his trip, but I refused to take him anywhere after hearing all of this. She kept driving by my house and kept making stupid comments at work, trying to get laughs.

He said, "Sharon, I told her to stay away from you, but she won't listen."

"Well, since you want to be a playa, then get your unruly whore to take you to the airport," I suggested.

"Sharon, that's not fair," he would say.

I apologized and said, "Excuse me—a real playa knows how to control their hoes."

I guess the man-whore bond is built to last, because he ended up getting Kane to take him to the airport.

During this time, I decided to come clean to my homeboy, Twinkles, and tell him the truth about me and Saint. I also had to tell him about the current situation with The Dirtbag. He said, "That girl is a real scumbag." One day while Twinkles was at my house, there was a knock at the door, and some guy asked, "Do you own the little CLK Benz?"

I said, "Yes, I have a Benz," with hesitation in my voice.

Then he asked, "Did you park on the corner?"

Again, I answered, "Yes."

He said, "Well, someone threw a brick through your back window."

I ran out of the house, and I couldn't believe my eyes. Twinkles was right behind me and said, "That bitch is crazy." I took a picture of the window with the brick still sitting in it. I sent the picture to Saint in Jamaica, and then I started calling him frantically. When he didn't answer his phone, I started calling his cousin Marcia. I was going to get to in touch with him one way or another, because this was all his fault.

When he finally called me back and I told him what had happened, he sounded very shocked. I was just yelling and screaming, and he was trying to tell me to calm down. The only thing I heard him say clearly was that he would pay for my window. Twinkles followed me to the shop, and they told me they would have to order the glass special and that it would cost $1200. I didn't care if he'd said "$3000," because I knew I was not paying for it.

Saint cut his trip short and came back home the next day. After the broken-window situation, I started receiving a bunch of prank calls from a restricted number. I knew it was her, but I didn't know how she'd gotten my cell-phone number, because I'd given her only my house number. I couldn't believe this girl was going this hard, and all she got was a little bit of dick. Everything that she was doing reminded me of the Buju Banton lyric, *"Over the dickie the girls a gwan bad."*

I asked Saint outright if was there anything that he had not told me, and he swore there was nothing else. I decided to take a page out of Lexus's book and asked Saint not to speak to the Dirtbag again.

He said, "When she calls me, she doesn't talk about you."

I couldn't believe my ears. Was this man sitting in my face defending this stank whore? I yelled at him, "Are you fucking kidding me!? Look at what this bitch is doing—she is driving up and down my street, prank-calling my phone, and busting out my window. And you want to *defend* her to me?"

"Sharon, you really don't have any proof that she busted out the window, and she said she didn't do it."

I wasn't sure if he was playing devil's advocate or truly just coming to her defense. All of her other actions convinced me that she'd done it. I found out her address in Suffolk County, and I contemplated revenge for many nights. I even borrowed my friend's car and drove out there to scope it out. I knew I couldn't drive my own car because I had personalized plates on both the Acura and the Benz. After seeing that she parked her car in the garage and her husband parked in the driveway, I scratched that idea. But I knew that I wasn't going to let her get away with that.

During this time, AOL had a feature called Lifestream, where you could connect with your friends and chat. Because she also had an AOL email account and she was in my contacts because of our previous almost-business arrangement, she showed up on my Lifestream timeline whenever I logged in. This is where most of our insults would fly outside of the institution, and that's where she gave herself away about busting out my car window.

I showed Saint the proof of her guilt in her own words, and all he could say was, "Just stop responding to her."

Saint had a point, but it became my way of unleashing all that I had pent up inside from the day-to-day snide remarks at work. But I couldn't or wouldn't respond because everyone would know about me and Saint. She knew we were still trying to keep our situation outside of the institution. I would find myself going home and fixing a drink to prepare for our verbal battle as soon as I logged in. I later became more strategic with my words, because I was saving everything she said to me on Lifestream. These are some of the actual messages she posted on Lifestream. The name has been changed to protect the privacy of the person involved. However, these are some of the the actual messages.

Dirtbag do you really think a nigga wants you when he done fucked another chick in your house on your bed and ate her pussy out in your car numerous times . . . inquiring minds want to know . . . really!!!!

Dirtbag worthless, no self-esteem, no dignity, mentaly frail, sexually unfulfilling, desperate, lonely, animalistic looking, unwanted, unclaimed, damaged goods, delusional . . . did I sum it up right!!!! . . . LOL

Dirtbag WE SURELY MADE YOUR "BED" ROCK . . . LMAO!!! . . . FYI tacky sheets every time I've been there, but then again the whole damn basement apartment is raggedy, but look at the owner . . . pitiful!

Dirtbag hope you slept good on the pillows & sheets I wipe my pussy that was dripping cum all over and pissed on that cheap fake suede sofa, no it wasn't those damn dogs . . . lol

Dirtbag Only if this chick knew the half . . . her head would totally explode . . . LOL

Dirtbag REALLY HOW DUMB ARE YOU? HOW LOW IS YOUR SELF WORTH?? . . . DO NOT PRETEND FOR OTHERS YOU ARE THE ONLY ONE THAT HAVE TO LIVE WITH YOURSELF THEY ALREADY KNOW YOU ARE PITIFUL BUT STILL FEEL SORRY FOR YOU . . .

Dirtbag is the "UNCLAIMED" luggage sitting alone, no one hasn't claim it? but who claims used-up, raggedy, undesirable, cheap shit anyway . . .

Dirtbag how can you lie in your bed knowing another woman was doing him better in it?! Just a thought . . .

Dirtbag WHERE IS YOUR MAN, OH I FORGOT YOU DON'T HAVE A MAN YOU HAVE A PIECE OF SOMEONE THAT IS BUSY LOVING EVERYONE ELSE!!! . . . HA, HA, HA.

Dirtbag A DUMB BITCH YES YOU ARE!!!!!!!!!!!!!!!

Dirtbag asked yourself why he constantly embarasses you?????????? why there are always countless women even up to this day??????????? why is he putting in for Butner with Lurchette????????? why is there that chick in MDC that is claiming to be his girl and know so much? why is there a girl he fucks with at mercy hospital where he does his OT? why is there a girl in indianapolis? why when every time he comes to see me??? and not to mention the chick in bushwick that lives around the corner from his house??? ask him who is Michelle? ask him why now when he comes he drives his sister's car??? ask him why every conversation you guys have or argument I know about? how come I have pics of you and texts you sent? asked him when you called Lurchette's house or phone why was he planning on getting someone to hurt you while you were coming out of your house? ask him why i know sooooo much . . . but you already know the answer. Good Luck hope your road of misery becomes a little less bumpy for you . . .

Dirtbag LOL, LOL . . . u really are funny, dumb but really funny . . . is that the best you can come up with sharon I had faith in you in really hurting my feelings . . . you talk like you know me but I guess you take all the lies he tells you as always and hold on to it for dear life . . . the ulimate mindfucking he did to you was when you got pregnant for him and he buttered you up so good in the hospital into having abortion, you let someone butcher your body, violate your insides, why because like he said to you it wasn't the right thing for u all or because he didn't want no ties like that to you . . . he said he really didn't know how to raise monkeys. LOL

Dirtbag I know your reality really hurts!!!!! but why all the hate sharon . . . LOL

Dirtbag why are you trying soooo hard for me to join your "yes I am pathetic and I am proud" club!!!!!!! LOL, LOL, LOL

Dirtbag talk about sisters why Saint said your sister man left her with those two girls and she struggling with the house and bills and sometimes you have to pay bills for her . . . is she semi worthless as you maybe not becasue he said he would fuck her if he ever got the chance . . .

Dirtbag you masked your hurt in trying to degrade everyone else but everyone else is doing so much better than you and have left your undocumented ass on the side of the road..sweetie the pain is too much I am trying to understand your kind!!!

Dirtbag I FLY ABOVE YOU AND CONSTANTLY RUN CIRCLES AROUND YOU HATER . . . ARE YOU DIZZY YET!!!!!!

Dirtbag TALKING ABOUT FAMILY AT LEAST I HAVE A MOTHER AND FATHER AND A REAL CLOSE KNIT FAMILY . . . I NEVER LIVED IN FOSTER CARE AND HAVE FAKE SISTERS AND BROTHERS, I NEVER JUMPED FROM HOME TO HOME WITH OTHER UNDESIRABLES LIKE YOURSELF, OR WAS ON WELFARE, OR SLEEPING WITH LOTS OF DUDES FOR VALIDATION OR FOR LOVE . . . NEVER HAD TO DESPERATELY FIGHT WITH MY FATHER AND OTHER SIBLINGS TO PROVE YOU ARE A LEGITIMATE PART OF THEIR FAMLY . . . YOU ARE THE ONE THAT HAS ALWAYS BEEN "UNCLAIMED" AND VIOLATED!!!!!

Dirtbag MY FAMILY DON'T EVEN LIKE SAINT, MUCH LESS THE SOME OF MY FRIENDS!!!!! MY UNCLES SAW HIM AT A BABYSHOWER THAT HE CAME TO THAT SOME was sort of relieved by that, because I didn't want to go into the house. I sat beside him and asked what was wrong.

I thought he was going to say something regarding the Dirtbag, but instead he said he'd made lieutenant. I was taken aback by the news, because he never even mentioned that he was putting in for lieutenant. On one hand, I wanted to show support for his career, but I was sad because he was leaving. I had threatened to leave him alone, but I never thought that it would really end, especially like this. Then another thought came to mind: he was going to be a couple of hours away from Lurchette. My thoughts were, *Did he put in for that institution to be closer to her?*

I asked the question, and he vehemently denied that insinuation. I had to let it go, because this was happening whether I liked it or not. A few days later, the email came out at work for all to see, and that made the Dirtbag's antics go into overdrive. She assumed exactly what I'd assumed about Saint and Lurchette, so I had to read about that the moment I logged in. I learned through him that she'd called, crying her eyes out because he was leaving.

It was going to be at least three months before he finally moved. Somehow the news of him leaving managed to bring us a little closer together than we had been in weeks. The Dirtbag kept on with her bullcrap, and finally I'd had enough, and both Saint and I called her husband to tell him to have his wife stay away from Saint. I got his number through my homeboy, who had a friend who was friends with her husband on the police force. I know Saint was doing this only to prove that he was on "Team Sharon" in that moment. It was a three-way call that I had placed, so I started the conversation with Mr. No Balls.

It was the basic, "You don't know me, but I know you" type of conversation. Of course, he wanted to know how I got his number, and I just said, "A friend of a friend." I proceeded to tell him that his wife was sleeping with my boyfriend, and then I let him know that Saint was on the line as well. Saint told him how everything had started and that he had been trying to get her to leave him alone, but she wouldn't stop. Mr. No Balls had a few questions of his own for Saint. He wanted to verify that Saint lived in Roosevelt. I couldn't see Saint's face, but I could imagine he was shocked because I sure was.

He went on to say that he'd followed her to Saint's house one night and watched her go inside. Then he sat outside the house the entire time. He said he parked in the circle of the cul-de-sac, walked to her Jeep, and let the air out of her tires. Saint did have some recollection of that night as he described it. He then asked the all-time weird question from a husband to the man sleeping with his wife, which was, "Does she give you head? Because she won't go down on me."

I wanted to drop the phone, because I could not believe what I'd just heard. Saint proudly said, "Yes—every time we were together."

He said, "Thanks for telling me, and I will make sure she leaves you alone." With that, the converstion was over.

I thought this would be the end of the Dirtbag, but I was wrong. The text messages, prank phone calls, and Lifestream posts kept coming. She actually sent me a text message from her phone, in which she forgot to block her number this time, that read, "You and Saint think that y'all was doing something by telling my husband, but I run this over here, lol."

Apparently my calling her husband had really angered her, and, to get me back, she put something in my Lactaid Milk that I kept in the refrigerator in control center. I didn't ingest it because I noticed the color was off when I poured some in the bowl. I knew it was her because she didn't work control center, and the control-room officer said she'd come in there earlier that day and was hanging out.

I wanted to kill her when she did that. This shit had gone too damn far—*playing with my food*! I saw her go upstairs to the staff lounge. I had my co-worker pop me out of control, and I followed her upstairs. I didn't know if anyone was up there, and I didn't care at that point. We started arguing, and she kept saying, "Don't put your hands on me, because I will have you arrested this time."

I didn't even know Saint was in the locker room, and he came out and got in between us. She started telling him, "Saint, you'd better get your gorilla under control." She was standing with her back toward the top of the steps, and Saint was standing in front of her with his back toward her, facing me. I knew I couldn't punch her, because he would be expecting that, but I made damn sure to kick around him so she could fall down the entire flight of stairs. She literally moved just in the nick of time, or she would have been a little nappy-headed ball at the base of those steps.

She started yelling, "I am calling the police!"

I was still trying to get to her, and Saint said, "Sharon, stop!"

"No, Saint, let her go," she said. "I will have her job today," she yelled.

I fired back, "Bitch, I don't give a fuck about this job. I have a degree, and I will get another job, slut."

Saint called her by her first name and told her to just go downstairs. She listened to him, finally. He turned to me and said, "Sharon, this has to stop."

"Don't tell me to stop when that bitch is fucking with my food!" I screamed. I told him the story about my milk, and he just apologized again. I was so sick and tired of his apologies. I went back to my post in control center, and, in that moment, it hit me that I had to get out of MCC. I decided to put in for lieutenant as well. When I submitted my paperwork, I knew that I had to watch everything I said and did inside the institution because that would ruin my chances of getting out.

It was always a good idea to let the Captain know when you put in paperwork for a promotion because they have to conduct the voucher or reference checks when the other institution calls. During my conversation with the Captain, I filled him in on the situation between me, the Dirtbag, and Saint. He forwarded the information to the Associate Warden, and he sent out an email to both me and the Dirtbag regarding the institution's core values.

That did not stop her at all. She continued to call and send messages, so I decided that I would set the stage for a possible lawsuit with the Bureau. It was obvious that the Captain and Associate Warden thought this was something for them to laugh at behind closed doors, because they never did anything else beyond that email.

I started seeing the institution psychologist in charge of the EAP program and cried my heart out to her over the situation. I now had a witness to the fact that this entire situation had been affecting me. Within the next few weeks, the Dirtbag sent me a message saying that she was pregnant, and, of course, it was supposedly Saint's baby. Inside the jail, it was her husband's baby, because she didn't want to be seen for the whore that she was. I had to question Saint about it because the timing would have been within the timeframe of their affair. He assured me that the baby wasn't his and couldn't be his because he had stopped having sex with her months earlier. She sent him all types of crazy messages, saying that the baby was his and that it was sad that his mother was not there to meet her grandchild. I thought it was disrespectful to use the memory of his deceased mother in her childish games. It had become pathetic—how low she would stoop to try to mind-fuck me or Saint. She was trying to convince him to stay in New York for the baby's sake.

It was crazy, because I really think that she had convinced herself that the baby was Saint's. As luck and God would have it, the baby transitioned back to the heavens. I had to ask God for forgiveness because I did say out loud that it was good for her. That baby, whoever the father was, deserved better than her for a mother. At this point everyone in the institution knew there was bad blood between us, but they assumed her losing the baby would have softened my heart for her situation. They didn't know that she was still sending messages and calling my phone with her nonsense, when she should have been grieving the loss of her child.

I felt nothing for her or her situation. I heard about her performance at the funeral when she realized people from the institution were in attendance. She'd done things for attention all the time. That says a lot about a person and their home life or their upbringing. No one walks around constantly professing their happiness, if they are truly happy. This is a sure sign that they are trying to cover something up or that they are trying to convince themselves the facade is real.

Saint moved to Indiana in September of 2008, and I thought that his not being in the New York area might stop all the bullshit. I was wrong again. She tried hard to convince me that he'd come back to be at the funeral, but I knew it was a lie because I was with him in Indiana on the day of the funeral.

In October, while I was visiting my sister in Jersey, my little niece, Lee, was playing with my phone, as she always did. Apparently, the Dirtbag was in one of her moods of being a neglectful mother to her living daughter and husband, and decided to send six text messages, back to back. I was livid when I heard my little niece starting to read all of her vulgar words. That was it for me. To me it had just gone too far at that moment. I really can't put my finger on why hearing my niece read her words affected me so much, because I was used to reading her vulgar rants. When she'd been sleeping with Kane, she began harassing another female Kane was sleeping with at MDC Brooklyn. That girl pressed charges against her, and, although I didn't know the outcome of that case, I decided that's the way I wanted to go.

On my way home that evening from New Jersey, I stopped by my house to pick up the printouts of the Lifestream messages and went to the precinct in Brooklyn to formally file a complaint. I showed them the amount of phone calls and text messages, and I advised them of her previous arrest for the exact same thing with another woman. I was amazed to find out that this was the same precinct and officer who'd made the arrest the last time. He said, "The girl doesn't learn," and he informed me that she'd actually had three complaints made against her. I had no idea who the other woman was or what that situation had entailed, and I was hoping he would give me details, but he didn't.

I was sitting in a room for some time, and then the officer opened the door to let me know they had picked her up and that she was in the room next door. The officer asked me if I wanted to move forward and press charges, and I said, "Yes." The officer said that the Dirtbag wanted to speak with me and apologize. There was no way on God's green Earth that I was going to listen to anything she had to say. She'd had her opportunity to put a stop to all this, and she'd chosen to continue the bullshit. She was willing to apologize only because she was in the proverbial hot water.

When the officer walked out of the room to inform her that I was not willing to listen to her, my phone started blowing up. I received calls from Saint, Kane, Harper, and Carter, all trying to get me to drop the charges. I found it funny that all of them were calling me, but none of them had done anything to stop her antics. They weren't the one being harassed on a daily basis. They weren't the one who was being stalked by her. They weren't the one who had their car vandalized by that little piece of shit. I told them all to stop calling me, because I was not dropping the charges.

The officer let me know that I should receive a notification in the mail regarding the court date. I left the precinct feeling very satisfied. I was, however, very disturbed by the fact that Saint was one of the people who called me on her behalf. He had the nerve to tell me that I was taking things too far. If I were taking things too far, then what was she doing all this time in his mind? Was he paying attention to anything this girl had done?

I didn't want to debate this over the phone with him, because I was booked to go see him that weekend anyway. The round-trip flight was $125, which wasn't a problem for either of us, so we decided to give the long-distance relationship a try. He was staying in a hotel until he closed escrow on the new house. After work, when he would get back to the hotel, he told me the Dirtbag was calling his job nonstop claiming she was his wife. She was calling him at work because I'd requested that he change his cell phone, and he did. She actually left a message with his co-worker saying he owed her child support.

When he did take her call, she would tell him that she'd lost respect for him, because he told me everything they talked about. Everything that she was doing to me, she would tell Saint that I was doing that to her. If any of that were true, she would have had grounds for a counterclaim. She would tell him, "I don't see what you see in her, and I can't believe you chose her over me. Saint, you are turning into a real bitch when it comes to her," she would say. Saint would just tell her to stop calling him and hang up the phone on her.

Now that she had been arrested, my eight-year secret "situationship" was now revealed to the institution. I kept my head held high at work, while still trying not to be so outspoken. I just wanted to do my time until I was able to get out.

I was ready for my birthday retreat, so I booked a trip to Punta Cana, Dominican Republic. I tried to have a good time, and some parts of the trip were good. With the exception of the excursion that I'd previously booked, for the most part, I stayed in my room and cried over all that I had been through. I rehashed my life with men and my choices in men. I kept asking God, *Why do I have to feel this kind of pain and heartache?*

I knew I was a good person, and I couldn't understand why bad people kept getting rewarded for being evil. I had to think maybe I was a son of a bitch in a former life, if there was such a thing. I wracked my brain trying to remember if there had been anyone in my past that I'd screwed over and for which I was now feeling the wrath of karma. Maybe the sins of my parents had fallen back on me. I wondered if God was disappointed in the way I had been living the life he had given me.

On the day Barack Obama was elected President, I woke up feeling proud to be an ugly Black American. Every other day, I woke up feeling alone and void of all self-worth. These thoughts consumed my birthday trip, but I had to pretend when I got back that I'd had a great time. The thought of going back sucked the energy from my soul. I knew I had to suck it up and get ready. I felt that, once everyone knew that I was putting in for a lieutenant's position, all the secret haters and Dirtbag supporters were going to come at me hard. I managed to dodge most of these snakebites, but the Dirtbag managed to turn some people who I thought I was cool with against me.

There was a husband-and-wife team who actually tried to file a case against me. It was more so the wife, but the husband was lying on his dick, saying that he'd slept with me, or almost slept with me. The wife was someone I really respected because she'd trained me when I was a new officer. I actually emulated her style while working a housing unit. I was one of the first persons she told when she got pregnant and when they got married. I'd also bought her a rocking chair for her baby shower. It hurt me to know that she was willing to lie for this Dirtbag, to try to get me fired or at least get me street time.

I also had to think about her other motive, because it was her cousin who had first tried to claim Saint as her baby daddy. I was able to sidestep them because I had proof it was a lie, and according to the Master Agreement, put out by the Union, I could file against someone who'd filed a false allegation against me. I sent the wife the verbiage from the Master Agreement, and the backpedaling began really quick.

Somehow, I was unable to dodge all the bullets, even when an insecure male officer filed a workplace-violence case against me. This ass clown left his post, which required him to be popped out of three doors, followed me to my car, and argued with me. On the way back toward the front of the institution, he kept following me and nagging like a little girl, so I turned to him and said, "You're acting like a real chick right now." He claimed this statement made him feel unsafe to be around me, so now I had an open case against me. I had to pull my lieutenant paperwork until the case was resolved, because the unwritten rule was that you couldn't get promoted if you had an open case. Now there was a target on my back, and it was open season for all the haters. They figured that I already had a case, so if I caught another case, I would get terminated.

This is when the Dirtbag felt it was perfect timing for her to start with the relentless garbage again, and this time, she had backup. Most of them were females who'd wanted to sleep with Saint at one time or another. The Dirtbag was feeling herself, because I never received the papers regarding the court hearing date, and the charges were subsequently dropped. I later received the court papers from my tenant because they'd sent them to my rental property instead of my P. O. Box as instructed.

My co-worker Harper said to me one day, "Shots, you have the patience of Job. How do you do it?"

I replied, "I am focused on getting out of here, and I will not give them the satisfaction of seeing me fail."

But I could play nice for only so long around all these chicks. This big-lipped broad tried to say I pushed her, and now she thought she had my job for sure. All I can say is thank God for cameras, because it clearly showed that she'd bumped into me on purpose, and I did not react. I was truly being punk'd by several people in this building, and all the while, I maintained my composure. I prayed many nights for them to do whatever they were going to do with this open case, because I didn't know how much more of this mental torture I could take. I knew my temper, and it took a lot for me to keep it at bay.

I used my trips to see Saint every weekend, sometimes every other weekend, as a mental reset from the bullshit. Saint asked me to come see him the weekend before he moved into his new house because he had a surprise for me. He asked me not to bring Nipsy with me on this trip, so I left him with my sister. Saint hadn't been present for my birthday, and he said he had a belated birthday present for me. If he knew me, then he should have known that I don't do belated birthday anything, but I went along with it.

When he picked me up from the airport, he was so excited about his gift that I thought I was going to receive a proper proposal. As I entered the hotel room, there sat the cutest little Shih Tzu puppy. Inside I was so disappointed, because I didn't want another dog. This was not a gift for me, but a gift for Nipsy. I didn't want to come off as ungrateful, so I put on a big smile and picked up my new girl puppy, little Miss Missy.

That was a long weekend of pretending to be happy. Little Miss Missy wasn't cheap, and he told me he'd spent $1200 on her. I really wished he'd spent the $1200 on something else. The moment I got back home with her, I noticed she was sick. Saint had told me that he'd gotten her from Petland, but she had something called kennel cough, which could be deadly in puppies. Missy was costing me money already, and Saint didn't chip in on any of the vet bills. When I got back to work, I put a smile on my face and told the story—in front of the Dirtbag and her audience—of how happy I was that he surprised me with a brand-new puppy.

By this time, the Dirtbag was pregnant again and trying to tell me that the new baby was Saint's also. She claimed she got pregnant when he came up for the funeral. She started dropping hints that he was calling her crying and begging her not to leave him and that he wanted to be a part of his daughter's life. I knew not to even bother myself with that lie. Her days of trying to get under my skin were over, or so I thought.

Saint started calling me and questioning my loyalties and my faithfulness. I was wondering where all of this was coming from, because I was there spending time with him as much as I could be. I thought he was just missing me, so I booked a surprise visit. I flew into the airport, rented a car, and then drove the one-hour drive to his town. I called Saint at work to let him know that I was in town, and, of course, he didn't believe me until I told him to come outside of his job and give me the keys. He seemed really shocked that I was actually there, and I did sense some hesitation. I was trying to show him that I was still willing to work on this "situationship" so that it could develop into the relationship of my dreams.

Saint was finally in his new house, and just like old times, my mission was to make this house a home. One of my favorite stores, Circuit City, was going out of business, and I bought a new surround-sound system for his living room. I also oversaw the construction of the new bathroom, including a deep soaking tub to accommodate his tall stature. During the transition from New York to Indiana, he'd left the fish tank that I'd bought him for his birthday some years back, so he had to purchase a new tank. He'd set up the tank but never bought any fish, so I tried to surprise him with some of the same fish he had in the old tank.

I was driving around his town like it was my new hometown. When Saint got home from work, he appeared grateful for all that I had done over that weekend, but he still felt the need to tell me it wasn't OK for me to just pop up. He said that the Dirtbag had called him and told him that I was still hanging out with Morales. Instead of arguing about what was an obvious lie—because Morales had once again left the Bureau for a job with Border Patrol in Texas—I decided to see if there was any truth to the fact that she had his new cell-phone number.

He started with, "Sharon, listen," and that's when I knew it was true. He said she'd told him that she had a friend who worked for Verizon who'd gotten the number for her. The truth was that she'd called his job and pretended to be a family member and another lieutenant gave her his number. So, I asked him when he was going to tell me, and I asked if he was going to change his number again. He blatantly said, "No." He didn't feel it was necessary, and he didn't want to keep changing his number. In fact, he said he didn't want to change it the first time and that he'd done it only because I'd asked him to.

"So, she has been calling you and telling you a bunch of bullshit about me, and you believe her?" I questioned.

"It's not that I believed her, but you were messing with that kid before, and now that I'm not there, who's to say what you will do?" he answered. "She was just calling as a friend looking out for me, because

I told her that I loved you." That's when I told him that Morales no longer worked for the Bureau and asked if he still wanted to call that bitch his friend.

"Sharon, I don't know these things," he said.

"I know you don't know, but instead of asking me, you accused me based on the word of this little asshole." "It's OK, Saint, don't change your number, and keep your friend," I told him.

She'd ruined what I hoped to be a good weekend with him to celebrate the New Year. I rang in 2009 still dealing with the Dirtbag and the bullcrap. My visits to see him became more infrequent, but I was still making the trip maybe once per month at this point. Saint was good at pretending in front of people who didn't know about our trials and tribulations. On a few of the visits, we would go to hang out with some of the lieutenants that he'd become cool with. In their presence, I was his girl, and I should be trying to get a job there to be closer to him. I played along for the sake of playing along, so I let them know that, if I couldn't get a position in his prison, the flights were short and inexpensive, so it could still work for us. Saint chimed in and agreed with what I was saying.

He did make a few trips back to New York, and he did stay with me when we weren't mad at each other because of something the Dirtbag had said or done. I was still receiving Lifestream messages, but she'd started erasing her messages by this time. I was able to ignore it after dealing with it for so long, but I knew that I didn't want to be bothered for another year with this mess. Whenever she would find out that he was in town—and I don't know how she ever found out that he was in town—she would go berserk with the lies on Lifestream. I just wished that she would make time for her so-called "happy family"—that way, she could focus less on me.

I didn't have time, nor did I want to make time for that ignorant little girl. I was busy taking care of two little puppies. My dog, Missy, was terrible when she was a puppy. One day I came home from work, and she had chewed my slippers, she'd chewed the sheet rock on the wall, and she'd torn up six rolls of toilet paper. I never had that issue with Nipsy.

I had to let Saint know that I was not happy with his gift at all. I sent Saint the pictures of all of her destruction. Once he received the pictures, he called my phone yelling, "Just open the door and put the dog out, then!" I would never do that—I was just venting my frustration because Nipsy and Missy were like night and day with their doggie personalities.

One weekend, Saint popped up at my house talking about how he was going to take the dog. He got dropped off at my house, because he was staying at his sister's house in Queens, so I knew he wasn't going anywhere with her. Besides, I had been taking care of her all this time, and I had spent a small fortune getting her over her sickness and getting her spayed. There was no way I was letting him take her now.

He picked her up and tried to leave the apartment, but I was willing to fight for her, and I told him just that. "You're gonna have to beat my ass before I let you take her," I said. A pushing-and-shoving match began, and then he took her outside and started walking up the street. I gave chase at first, but then I finally gave in and said, "Forget it. Take her then. I want all the money I spent on her back," I yelled up the street in his direction. I put Nipsy in the car and left, headed for my sister's house.

I drove around the block, and, when I came back, he was sitting on my front steps holding her. I got out of the car and begged him to give her to me, but he said "No." I looked at her little face, and I made peace with it, because I still had my Nipsy. When I got to my sister's place, they asked where Missy was, and I told them the truth about what had happened. While I was there, Saint called my phone to say I could come get the dog. He had taken a cab back to his sister's house, and she told him that he was wrong for taking Missy. It probably had more to do with the fact that she didn't want Missy in her house for the weekend.

I left Jersey immediately to go get my dog. Saint wasn't slick. He wanted me to come get him as well, because Donna had only one car that she didn't drive, but she wouldn't let anyone else drive it, either. He had plans with Kane to go to a party that night. I let him use the Benz, but a man that tall should never be in a little Benz like mine. We ended up having a good weekend.

As soon as he got back home, I received a message saying that he'd gone to see The Dirtbag while driving my car. I felt so disrespected by him, once again. I didn't know what was true anymore, because how would she know that he had my car? Of course, Saint had some lame-ass excuse about how she'd shown up at the party where he and Kane were and that they'd spoken outside.

"I must have 'Stupid, Dumb Bitch' written all over me for you to think that I would fall for that bullshit," I yelled into the receiver. "How the fuck did she find out that you were here, let alone that you were at this party?" I asked.

"Sharon, I don't know how she knows this stuff; she just shows up," he said, sounding really stupid.

I couldn't take listening to his blatant lies, so I just hung up the phone on him. My visits to see him were spaced out even further after this. We still spoke on the phone almost every day. He said he'd started going to church on Sundays with some of the lieutenants he worked with. I knew there was something brewing that I wasn't going to like. Sure enough, the bomb dropped. One of those lieutenants introduced him to some female in the church named "Mia." He gave the typical Saint description of her being tall, with a big butt, and very pretty, blah, blah, blah. He did ask me to come see him again, so we could talk. I made the trip, and he did everything to make me feel comfortable, but just as with the house in Roosevelt, I felt this house was tainted also.

One particular incident convinced me that this would be my last visit to see him. When I was in the kitchen preparing dinner, I looked under the cabinet and saw a can of dog food. When he came into the kitchen, I simply asked him, "Who was here?"

He said, "Sharon, please don't start. Nobody was here."

I opened the cabinet, pointed to the dog food, and asked the question again. "Who was here?"

He had the nerve to say that *I'd* left it there.

"Saint, are you fucking serious? None of my dogs have ever been in this house. My dog came here when you were living in the hotel," I reminded him.

He said, "Alright, 'Lurchette' drove down because she wanted to see the house."

"This shit is starting all over again in a new house, in a different state," I said under my breath, or so I thought. He did hear me and said, "No, it is not going to be like that here. She didn't stay when she came here."

I took a deep breath, because this man just wouldn't stop lying. "So, you want me to believe she drove two hours to look at this house and then turned around and got back on the road. Saint, would you please stop lying? Because you are no good at it," I said.

"Sharon, let's not let this ruin our night. I set the tub for us to relax and enjoy, and, before you say anything, no one has been in the tub."

I went along with the bath, but my mind was made up. With the addition of this new chick, Lurchette possibly being in the picture again, and the never-ending Dirtbag situation—all of this, coupled with the long distance—there was no way this was going to work in my favor.

I was spending more time with my sisters on the weekends and taking care of my dogs. They were my world and all that I had who truly loved me. They were my babies. I had given up on the idea of ever having children.

The psychic reader Saint and I had gone to see in the Bronx said that I would have two children: one boy and one girl, and that would be it. I guess he was really seeing my dogs and not human children. That psychic also told Saint that he would be married one day, but not to me. I wanted to believe he was wrong about that, just like he'd been wrong about me having children.

Many of my friends and family didn't understand the bond I had with my dogs. My sister Lorraine was very cold toward my dogs. To her, they were just dogs. I think she felt her human children were more important than my dogs. When I gave Nipsy his first birthday party at her house, I felt like I was being mocked. I had a doggie cake, I'd made little hamburgers, I had balloons, and they were both dressed in matching jersey shirts. I had full wardrobes for both dogs, a designer dog bag, and a dog stroller for my babies.

Lorraine would make slick remarks that I took really personally, but I let them slide. Lorraine allowed her daughters to just drop food on the floor when they didn't want to eat anymore. I would ask her to teach them to clean up after themselves because Nipsy was greedy, and he would eat whatever hit the floor. She would say things like, "It's just a dog." I knew that dogs couldn't ingest certain foods, so I was always nervous about going to my sister's house, because she didn't keep a tidy house. On one of my visits to Jersey, Nipsy ate a grape that my niece dropped on the floor. I was so upset because I knew it could have harmed him, and her response was, "He will be fine. Stop acting like that. It's just a dog." To this day, I hate to hear her say the words, "It will be fine."

In October of 2009, I had to put my baby boy down because of that grape that he swallowed on her dirty-ass floor. And even with the death of my dog, she showed no real support for my loss. I hid away from everyone after I lost Nipsy. He was the dog that I wanted, and although I still had Missy, I didn't have the same feeling for her as I did for Nipsy. It was similar to losing my father, in the sense that I watched them both deteriorate. I spent $7000 trying to save him, hoping and praying that his prognosis would change.

I took his loss really hard, and my patience for bullshit was short. I was looking for someone to push my buttons, so I would have an excuse to unleash all that had been pent up inside for so long. As God would have it, the quarter changed at work, and I didn't have to be around any of those people, listening to the remarks and giggles in the lobby. I believe the change in post at work saved the Dirtbag and her friends and, quite frankly, my job. I knew I was capable of anything during that period in my life.

I was back working in control center, and I was able to just keep a low profile. Saint was very supportive and showed genuine concern for my loss. He decided to treat me for my birthday and paid for my birthday vacation to Aruba. We had a really good time, and, as always, the dress competition was on. The night that we wore all black turned several heads as we walked down the street. We called it a tie that night. I really needed this trip, and, for a brief moment in time, he made me feel like none of the things that had happened in the past few months mattered. We literally didn't mention anything that had a negative impact on our situation.

I'd always planned to do something I had never done on each trip, and for this trip, it was horseback riding. I think I peed a little on my horse laughing, as I watched Saint mount his horse. That horse instantly turned into a Bactrian Camel. There was no horse power in that horse whatsoever.

We also did a water excursion. The name of the water sport escapes me, but you are sitting on a rubber raft, being dragged by a speedboat. I was having so much fun as we were hitting the waves and bouncing high in the air. Saint, on the other hand, looked like he was dying a slow death, and I found that to be hilarious. I don't know why I found it so soothing to watch him squirm.

In all the years we had been together, I'd never passed gas in front of Saint. Only my family knew about how lethal my gas smelled, especially after ice cream or milk. Saint and I decided to take another bath together when one little *poot* slipped out. I thought it wasn't going to be that bad, but the smell of that little monster overpowered the candle that was burning and the smell of the bubble bath. It still makes me laugh thinking about how fast Saint jumped out of the tub and said, "Sharon, don't do that again in front of me." I almost drowned in the tub laughing so hard.

We spent most of our nights laughing about our days in Aruba. It made me sad to think this had to end, because we had to go back to living separate lives in separate states. I was more at ease when going back to work because I no longer had to hide where I went on vacation and with whom. I posted some of our vacation pictures on Facebook, before learning how to make them private. I had stopped posting things on Lifestream and responding to the Dirtbag at this point.

By this time, the institution had just acquired a new Warden, and finally my case was up for review. I was entitled to view all the evidence against me with regard to the workplace-violence charge. I learned that these people here really did not like me and had been smiling in my face. That ass clown had memoranda written by people corroborating his lie, and I know for a fact none of those people were even around when I'd made the comment. It was disheartening, to say the least, because one of the ladies was supposedly a God-fearing Christian, and she blatantly lied in her memorandum.

I wrote my memorandum, documenting everything from my perspective and why I felt the charges should be dropped. I also requested the video-camera footages from that day, but, of course, the video did not exist anymore. I made note of that as well in my memorandum, because it just so happened that the officer working in the Comm Tech Room was my nemesis's close friend, who actually was standing in the front when everything went down. The new Warden took into consideration all that I had to say, and he agreed that the charges would be dropped. His specific words were, "I believe that he followed you to your car, and that you gave him what he was looking for."

This, in and of itself, frustrated the Dirtbag, because she wholeheartedly believed that I was going to get fired or possibly get street time for this case. This is when I started receiving a barrage of phone calls at work. I would hang up as soon as I would hear her voice, and she would keep calling back. My job was to answer the phone calls coming into the institution, so I had to answer the phone not knowing whether it was her or not. Saint was also calling, but now he was complaining about the fact that I'd posted the pictures on Facebook.

"Saint, my question to you is, how do you know I posted the pictures on Facebook? Because you don't have a Facebook account." This is when I found out that Little Miss Dirtbag had been stalking my page. Now, it all made sense: this was why she'd started psycho-dialing me in control like crazy. I learned really quick how to block someone from viewing my page on Facebook, and I also learned that I could block her on Lifestream. I could have saved myself a lot of drama if I'd have known how to block her sooner.

Going back to Saint, I thought we had created a new foundation, but it was obvious I was wrong. He was obviously still ashamed of me, because there would be no other reason for him to ask me to take the pictures down on Facebook. Every time Saint denied me or made me feel unworthy, it chipped away at my self-confidence.

The Forties

I had had enough by New Year's 2010. I was just tired of the constant fights with him and the stupid phone calls from her. The warnings from the Captain, the Associate Warden, and the arrest didn't work. On Monday, January 11, 2010, I decided I would place another call to her husband letting him know that she had not stopped calling Saint and me. I told him that I'd had her arrested and that she still wouldn't stop. He was shocked to learn that she'd been arrested. When I heard the astonishment in his voice, I took that as my cue to let him in on everything. I became the snitch bitch that everyone hates.

I told him about her affair with Kane, the other two arrests, and the rumor of the new guy she was supposedly dealing with on the job. He asked me to call him back with the arresting officer's name and number. I did as he requested and called him back with the information, and we stayed on the phone for about 40 minutes after that. On Wednesday, January 13, 2010, I was working overtime in the front lobby, and Penny called me to tell me that I had an outside call. To my surprise, it was her husband, and I immediately asked him how he'd gotten my last name. Up until this point I had never given him my last name, not even when we were on the three-way call with Saint. He said something stupid like he knew people who knew me.

We spoke for about 15 minutes, and he told me that he had spoken with the arresting officers and found that it was all true. Now it made sense—how he'd really gotten my name.

"I have no reason to lie to you. I just want her to stop calling me and calling my boyfriend," I said to him. On Monday, January 18, 2010, I learned that the Captain had been called at home by the Dirtbag, because her husband confronted her with everything he'd learned from me and the arresting officer.

On Tuesday, January 19, 2010, I spoke with the Captain and made him aware that I felt nothing was being done to handle this situation within the institution when I'd reported it through proper channels. I let him know that I was seeing the staff psychologist for this situation and that I'd told her I didn't feel I was being supported by the administration. I saw the look in his eyes when I said that, and I could tell he knew exactly what path I was on. He said he would talk to her, and then he advised me to bring it to him if anything else took place.

Later that day, the Dirtbag came down to the lobby, where I was working overtime, and asked me to accompany her to the bathroom in the Warden's area. I have no idea why I actually went back there, but I can only assume it was pure curiosity. "St. John, I just want you to hear something," she said. Upon entering the bathroom, she pulled out her cellphone and began to play a message left by Saint on her phone. I heard him say to her, "Please don't leave me. I love you, honey bun." His voice did sound like he was in tears as he left that message.

I stopped listening at that point, and I gave her a stern warning to stay away from me and not to say anything else to me. I left the bathroom and went back to the lobby to call the Captain to let him know that she'd just left her post to confront me in the bathroom. I told him that I was really trying not to get into anything but that she was pushing me to the limit. He said, "I just spoke to her and told her to stay away from you."

I said, "Now you see what I mean, Sir. She wants me to put my hands on her, so I can get in trouble, and I am trying my best not to let her take me there." He reassured me that he would talk to her again. My second call was to Saint to let him know that his "honey bun" had been recording his dumb ass. I told him that I listened to him tell that silly bitch that he loved her.

"Sharon, that must be an old conversation, because I have not said that in a while."

I couldn't yell because I was in the front lobby, but I said, "What the fuck are you talking about?" in a low voice, filled with anger and bitterness. "I don't give a fuck *when* you said it!" You were on the phone crying, telling this bitch that you loved her! You sound like a fucking idiot!" I screamed, as I looked around to make sure no one was close by.

He just kept calling my name, and I can only assume that was because he couldn't think of another lie. When I got off work that night, I noticed that I had a missed call from Mr. No Balls, on my cell phone. I assumed that the Dirtbag had given him my cell-phone number.

His message said, "Yo, listen. I'm happy with The Dirtbag, and I would appreciate it if you would stop calling my phone telling me the things that she is doing. As long as she's doing what she's doing, then I can do what the fuck I want to do. So stop calling my phone letting me know what she is doing. Please. Thank you."

I had to laugh when I heard that message. It confirmed that he was the sucker that I thought he was—unless he was using the information as justification for the girl he was sleeping with in Uniondale. Either way, I found it funny because he sounded as if he were reading from a piece of paper. On Wednesday, January 20, 2010, the Dirtbag came through the lobby stating, "I don't know why he is still calling me crying," on her way toward the Warden's area. It took everything in me not to reach out and snatch her by the pubic hairs on her head.

I stayed focused on my goal, and I called the Captain instead. I let him know what had just taken place and asked him again to keep her away from me. Once again, I received lip service from the Captain as he said, "I will talk to her." I was tired of the Captain at this point, so I decided to write a memorandum to his supervisor, the new Associate Warden. The memorandum summarized the chain of events and ended with me requesting permanent separation from The Dirtbag, until I was able to secure a promotion as lieutenant and leave MCC for good.

I was all set after this to just file my claim against the institution, because no one was doing anything to protect me. I sat in the lobby wishing I wasn't on overtime, because I still had to work my regular eight-hour shift in control. I knew that she would be calling on the institution phone, because that way, I couldn't prove she was still calling me. Just as sure as my name is Sharon, that lowlife called me.

She said, "St. John, don't hang up. I just want to tell you that you don't know everything. I did not make up the past two years. I have been dealing with him for two years, and he wanted me to leave my husband for him, but I wouldn't do it. My daughter calls him 'Uncle Saint,' and he has taken me to meet his sister in Queens. Saint is just a dog, and he is trying to have his cake and eat it, too."

I couldn't hear any more. I didn't want to hear any more. I knew there was a reason this bitch was going so hard. No woman acts the way she was acting for no reason at all. I still couldn't take her word for anything, because she had told so many lies over the course of the entire situation. I also couldn't help but think, *If she wasn't the bottom feeder that she was, she could have come to me woman to woman,* to say all of this back then. She projected her anger at him onto me, because she was being rejected by him, for me.

I assume she thought I was going to lose my cool or start crying, but I simply said to her, "Is that all you want to say?"

She replied, "I just wanted you to know."

I just hung up the phone on her. My stomach had the feeling of being on a roller coaster, right before you throw up. I just sat there wondering, *Where the hell have I been for the past two years that I didn't notice this relationship taking place right under my nose?* This had to have been when I started spending more time in Brooklyn instead of Long Island. I believe that she must have told the Captain all of this as well, and now it made sense why he wasn't doing anything to put a stop to it. The Captain must have had a conversation with Harper regarding the situation with me and The Dirtbag. I had never talked to Harper about my personal business before, and I was a little pissed that the Captain did.

Harper worked the front lobby during the evening-watch shift, and I would leave control just to go hang out with him sometimes. One particular night, he broke the ice and said, "Shots, the Captain came and talked to me today about you. Saint is foul for what he's doing. He's over there, and you guys are over here arguing and about to come to blows over him. She's not lying about everything, Shots. She let me listen to a lot of his calls, and he has been telling her that he wants to be with her, and that's not fair to you. She told me that she has been dealing with him for two years, and I believe her."

I considered everything he had to say, but none of that excused her behavior.

"Harper, even if she is telling the truth about the two years, why do everything that she was doing to me? Why would she bust out my car window, and not his? At that point, her beef shouldn't have been with me—it should be with him, and for that I will never, ever forgive her. Harp, she could have just been a woman about the entire situation, because at the end of the day, she was a married woman, and Saint was her other man."

"Shots, you have a point," he said. I don't know why she did any of that, but he still is a foul dude for leaving and not clearing this up."

I went upstairs to the staff lounge and called Saint to let him know that I knew everything now. He denied that it was two years, which I expected he would. He told me that she had called him but that he hadn't taken her call because he didn't trust that she wasn't going to tape him again.

"Saint, is that what you are really worried about—whether or not she records your conversation? I am sitting at work crying over you, and you only care about whether she is recording you? You know what, Saint? I am done shedding tears over you. It finally hit me that you are just a no-good ass nigga."

He interjected saying, "Sharon, I know you're hurt, but don't talk to me like that."

"Like *what*?" I said. "That's your problem Saint—you don't like to hear the truth about yourself."

He cut me off again saying, "That's not true, and you know that is not true."

"One thing is for sure, and that is that you will never change, and you will die a disloyal cheater," I told him.

He said, "Sharon, I will not keep allowing you to disrespect me."

I interrupted his sentence and said, "Why not? You disrespect yourself daily. Look at the caliber of trash you choose to stick your dick in." Learning the truth about him and The Dirtbag sent the last bit of respect that I had for him up in flames.

All he could say was, "I am hanging up so you can calm down, and I will call you later."

"Saint, you are hanging up because you have finally been caught in all your lies. Don't bother calling me, because I have nothing to say to you, Saint." I stuck to my word and I did not take any of his calls. I received several voice-mail messages, much like the one he'd left on the Dirtbag's phone. That further infuriated me, because he used his tears as a way to try to pierce my armor. He could have cried a river, and it wouldn't have meant anything to me by then.

I withdrew from everyone around me, including friends, family, and co-workers. I limited my conversations with everyone, especially at work. Because I worked so much overtime, I spent most of my time in the jail, where I felt everyone was laughing at me behind my back. My name became the constant source of gossip and giggles. As for my family, I stayed away from them as well. For two weekends in a row, I didn't call or show up in Jersey. What I learned was that no one had even tried to check on me to see if I was OK or dead in the basement.

I realized there was nothing left for me in New York. I was ready to go, and, with that thought, I resubmitted my paperwork for the lieutenant position. I gave up on the idea of filing a claim against the institution, because I didn't want to be bothered with anything that would keep me here longer. I stayed strictly to myself, and I started writing. I started thinking about betrayals and the people who'd betrayed me. My deepest betrayal was from family, starting with my niece. I started writing, and the characters developed from that situation. The interactions between the characters—and being able to visualize each persona in my mind—was freeing.

I didn't focus on Saint and my personal heartbreak. I think Saint did influence the main male character in my story. Writing became my distraction from everything going on around me.

I had some vacation time coming up, and I decided to go California. I spent that time sitting on the beach and writing, totally immersed in my characters' lives. I liked the story I'd created, so I decided to self-publish my book. I titled the book *Issues*. I created a Twitter account and an Instagram account in order to help push the sale of my book. My psycho stalker, aka, The Dirtbag, was checking my page daily. One would think that after she'd finally exposed Saint for the liar that he is, she would stop with the other nonsense. But no, I had to block her from viewing my pages on all social media outlets.

Through the publishing company, I wasn't able to see the name of the person who was buying my book, but I was able to see the city and state where the purchase had been made. I didn't have any friends in Suffolk County, but there was a book purchase made in Suffolk County. This girl was so obsessed with me that she purchased my book. I couldn't complain, because royalties were royalties. Of course, she denied making the purchase, but the facts are the facts.

What I also noticed when checking my book sales was that there had been no purchases made in Saint's state. There were also no purchases made in Bergenfield, New Jersey, where not just one, but both of my sisters lived. I was disappointed, to say the least, but that solidified the fact that I'd made the best decision to try to get out of New York.

I was sitting in the lobby, working my overtime, and I told my co-worker the dream I'd had the night before about getting selected for Beaumont, Texas. Beaumont was a town about one hour and 45 minutes outside of Houston. I initially thought this would be a good place to go because my brother lived in Houston. But once I noticed that my brother hadn't purchased my book, either, I unchecked the institution from my list of places I would consider.

Later on that day, the Warden's secretary called me in the lobby to say the Warden wanted to see me in her office, because of an incident that had taken place with an attorney and the lobby badges. She told me to bring the box with the badges, so I could explain to her how the system worked. I wasn't nervous, because I knew that I hadn't done anything wrong, so I entered her office with confidence and began to explain how the system worked.

She interrupted me and said, "Well, good. You can explain all of that as a lieutenant in Beaumont, Texas."

I was a little bewildered because I knew I'd removed that institution from my list. She sensed my hesitation, so I had to explain that I was grateful for the opportunity, but I didn't want to go to Texas anymore. She explained that the Bureau is very sensitive, and if I turned this down now, there was no telling if or when I would get selected again. She advised me to go and do the eighteen months to two years and then put in for another institution. It became a no-brainer for me in that moment, because I knew I didn't want to be in New York any longer.

When I got back to the lobby, I told my co-worker and he said, "You should play the lottery, because that is crazy how you just had that dream, and now you're leaving for Beaumont. Congratulations!"

I was excited to finally be getting out of MCC, and I could put the Dirtbag and the embarrassment of the entire Saint situation behind me. I was ready to start over someplace new. I wanted to tell my mother and sisters first, but when I called my sister Camielle, the conversation didn't go as planned. I decided I would ask her directly why she hadn't purchased my book, and her reply hit me hard. She said, "Did you write the book for us to buy it, or did you write it for yourself?"

Right then and there, I thought if I could cut these people out of my life for good, I would. I decided not to tell them anything, and I didn't go back out to New Jersey after that conversation. I didn't even get the chance to tell Saint myself, because the Dirtbag beat me to it, once they'd sent out the email notification. He called me in the lobby to congratulate me, which I appreciated, but the undertone of the conversation felt fake. I was still harboring hateful feelings toward him, and he felt the way I spoke to him was too disrespectful. I will admit my mouth would get very reckless when I just don't care anymore, and this situation with him and the Dirtbag was too much for me.

He actually said to me, "Why can't you just let it go?"

It was the proverbial straw that broke the camel's back. I realized that was the problem. I had forgiven him for every indiscretion, and it became normal for him to disrespect me in that manner and for me to just let it go. In his mind, this time was no different than any other, but I saw it from a different viewpoint. None of his other women had focused in on me the way the Dirtbag had. Maybe it was the caliber of the other women that made the difference. The Dirtbag was a true bottom-feeding roach, and I guess, in her mind, I took her man, even though she was married to another man. Maybe she was really in love with him, and I'd prevented that love from flourishing. I don't know, and I really didn't care who loved whom, but the constant harassment was uncalled for.

The next day I received the most beautiful array of white roses delivered to the jail, from Saint. I had to accept them for what they were, a congratulatory gift. All of the other roses I'd received from Saint were because he'd hurt me in some way, either physically or emotionally. To this day, roses don't mean anything to me. I left the roses in the lobby until the end of the day, because I knew she couldn't help herself but to be nosy and read the card. I purposely made a small production scene, as I picked them up to bring to my car. When all the ooos and awws over the flowers were coming my way, I made sure to let everyone know they were from Saint.

In May of 2010, I was preparing for my transition out of New York to Texas. My girls from the job, Sosa and Square, organized my going-away party. I wanted to have a bowling party and not the typical go-to-a-bar, stand-around type of party. My girl Square took point on finding the bowling alley and securing the venue. The night before the party, Square called the venue to go over the details and to ensure everything was good to go. The lady on the phone was confused, because she said someone had called to cancel the party already. We all knew immediately who it was. That little Dirtbag would stop at nothing to try to block my happiness.

I had to ask myself, *How does someone with two young kids and a husband still find time to stalk my life?*

Square informed the lady not to speak to anyone but her regarding the party arrangements. When I arrived at my party, I couldn't believe how many people had come out for me that night. Saint even flew in, to be there for me. I know everyone was watching him and giving him the side eye, because this was the first time anyone had seen him since everything had been made public about both affairs.

They even had my book laid out for sale, and I was signing each copy that was sold. It was truly an amazing night, and I felt loved by all who were in attendance. After the party, I started thinking it wouldn't be right to leave without saying something to my family. The day before I boarded the plane, I drove out to Jersey, and they were shocked to see me because I hadn't been there in a long time. I didn't tell them as soon as I got there, because I wanted to see how this visit was going to go first.

We had a good visit, and so I decided it was time to tell them before I left, heading back to Brooklyn. When I said I was moving to Texas, my sister Lorraine said, "You ain't going nowhere—stop lying." I looked my mother in the eye and said it again: "I'm leaving for real." My mother knew I wasn't lying, and she started to cry. Lorraine knew then that I was telling the truth, and so she asked, "When?"

When I said "Tomorrow," they all looked at me in disbelief. I told them I was all packed, and the movers had already come to get my things. They appeared happy for me because of the promotion, and they said they would visit me in Texas. I gave each of them a hug, and now I was officially ready to leave New York. It really hit me that I was leaving everything and everyone behind.

I'd watched enough movies in which the woman arrives in a new place, meets a wonderful man, and lives happily ever after. I was hoping that this would be my chance at trying to find love and happiness. I rented my apartment sight unseen, through the realtor I had planned to use for purchasing a house, at first. I had a two-bedroom, two-full-bathroom apartment in a brand-new complex.

I didn't realize how small this town was until I moved there. Being from New York, I guess I took for granted all the convenience that living in New York had to offer. In New York, there was always something to do, but in Beaumont, there was absolutely nothing to do. In this town, if you didn't watch sports, hunt, or fish, you were assed out. The main hang-out spot was Buffalo Wild Wings. You can literally pull up to the mall and park directly in front of the store, on a Saturday afternoon.

This wasn't the worst part of Beaumont. Closer to the institution, it smelled like sewer almost all the time, because the plants were constantly releasing strange gases into the air. The bugs in this town were twice the normal size of the average bug. This town was my new home, and I had to accept it, but I hated it. Once my car and household items arrived, I realized I didn't have much. I was sleeping on an air mattress until I purchased a new full-size bed for the smaller of the two rooms. Although Saint said the Dirtbag had been lying about sexing him on my bed, I couldn't trust his words, so I left that bed in the basement, and also because it smelled moldy from the black mold that had started growing down there. I had to throw out a lot of my clothes and shoes because of the mold in the basement.

I had to purchase a dining-room set, a living-room set, and my first king-size bedroom set, for my master bedroom. I slept in the smaller room until my king-size bed arrived. I was happy to have a second room for the people who said they were going to come visit me in Texas. My place was cozy and comfortable for me and Missy, once I had things all set up. I also had to purchase a new computer, and, the day I set it up, the Dirtbag almost made me regret it. When I saw all the messages she had posted on Lifestream, I could only shake my head in disbelief.

One evening there was a knock at my door, and it was Papa John's Pizza, saying they had a delivery for me. I said I hadn't placed an order for any pizza, and I asked, "Are you sure you have the right apartment?" The delivery guy repeated my full name and number, and I said, "Yes, that's me, but I didn't order anything." He left just as confused as I was.

Later that night on Lifestream, the Dirtbag posted, "That black gorilla is eating pizza alone with the damn dog." After the post, I started receiving phone calls on my house phone from blocked numbers, and, when I answered, I would hear her say "black gorilla" and start laughing. I would hang up, and she would call right back. Wow—I'd thought this would all stop now that I wasn't in New York anymore. She had to have gone to some extremes just to find out my phone number and address.

I would never go that far for someone I didn't care about. Her obsession with me was borderline scary. I called Saint to let him know what was going on and that his honey bunny just won't stop this foolishness. He was offended that I referred to her as his honey bunny, but I didn't care. That was the nickname I'd heard him call her on the phone call she'd let me listen to.

"Saint, you'd better talk to your little friend before she ends up in jail again—and this time, I will make sure the charges won't get dropped."

He said, "Sharon, I know you don't believe me, but I don't talk to her like you think I do."

I wasn't trying to hear his bullshit. I just wanted him and that girl to leave me alone, so I could move on with my life.

A few nights later, she did the pizza thing again, and I called Saint once again. I took my anger out on him, because none of this bullshit would be happening if he hadn't screwed the devil. I could block her on Lifestream for the most part, but because I was totally bored in Beaumont, I would unblock her every now and then. I think her vagina got a little moist whenever she saw I was online. I could have become drunk with the power I had over this girl. I literally could make her react whenever I wanted her to. The messages would be non-stop the moment she realized she was unblocked. I guess she felt that she had to get them all in, before I put her ass on block again.

Shortly afterwards, I started receiving emails from BlackPeopleMeet.com, but I didn't understand why I was receiving emails from an online dating website, because I hadn't signed up for it. When I read the profile information, I knew it was the little idiot. She said my hobbies were singing, writing books, and cum facials. Once again, I unblocked her on Lifestream just to confirm it was really her, and I got the proof I was looking for.

Like clockwork, once she saw I was online, she couldn't help herself and posted something about me having better luck finding a man on BlackPeopleMeet.com. I made a few phone calls—one to BlackPeopleMeet to see if they could close that account and get the IP Address for the computer that had set up the account. My second was to the local precinct to see if I could file charges against her for this.

Both phone calls were met with negative results. BlackPeopleMeet said they couldn't give out that information, and the local precinct said there was nothing they could do from there and for me to call Nassau County Police to see what they could do. I did just that and was told the same thing—nothing could be done. At work, the control-room officer would call me on the radio to say I had a call from an outside line, but when they would transfer the call, the person would hang up. When I asked who it was, they would simply say, "It was a girl who sounds just like you"—meaning my New York accent. I didn't even know the number to the institution to give to anyone, so it was safe to say that it was the Dirtbag.

My and Saint's conversations were all about her and her crazy behavior. In between the arguments, he managed to tell me that he'd gotten a lateral transfer to another institution, which was about four hours from me. The little asswipe heard that Lurchette was going to another institution as well and assumed he was going to the same place, because he wouldn't tell her where he was going. Of course, this, too, was posted on Lifestream. Just another example of how she would make up anything to try to get under my skin. I'd learned from a crazy inmate never to let anyone know that they'd hit a nerve. None of her keyboard-warrior antics ever fazed me, and that touched a nerve in her. She was pathetic, and she proved it with every message. I just put her back on block and left her there.

I began to focus on the thought of Saint being closer to me and the fact that there were absolutely no male prospects for me in this town. I considered the thought that maybe we could start over. Once he finally made the move, we agreed to meet at a midway point between our two states. It was good to see him, and I could tell he was happy to see me as well. I think Missy was even happy to see him. There wasn't much to do in that town, so we just got something to eat and went to the movies.

Sexing him felt unnatural and awkward. Normally, I would perform oral sex on him, but I couldn't do it now. The thought of him being with the Dirtbag and knowing that she'd had him in her mouth, plus knowing that he was with the new girl, Mia, I just couldn't do it. He was upset, and I couldn't get certain images out of my head; it was just a weird sex session.

Once we got back to our new hometowns, the fights and arguments began again. He would hang up the phone on me, and I would refuse to call him back. Hanging up the phone is something that I find to be very disrespectful, and because we were a good distance apart, I couldn't just jump in my car and be at his front door. So I just wouldn't talk to him until he apologized. The apology could've been sent via text or voice mail, but I was very serious about someone hanging up the phone on me. It started out with up to two weeks of not talking to each other, and before I knew it, it had been a month.

He was very aware that I had made it my birthday tradition to go somewhere exotic, and because this was going to be my 40th birthday, I decided on Cabo San Lucas. Although Saint and I weren't really on speaking terms, he wanted to celebrate my 40th birthday with me, so I received what I believed was an insincere apology via text.

I booked the trip for myself, and I sent him my itinerary, so he could do whatever he wanted to do with the information. I arrived in Cabo a few hours before Saint, and, because I'd booked the trip for one, when he arrived, they charged an additional $300 for him to be in my room. When asked by the hotel staff if he was staying in the room the entire trip, I said "Yes," and he said "No." I guess he saw the confused look on my face, and that's when he told me that he had to leave early.

This trip was different because we hadn't really been speaking and we hadn't had sex since the one midway point visit. On the day of my birthday, he just wanted to lie on the beach and soak up the sun. I absolutely hate being in the sun. He made me promise if I gave him some time to get sun, he would do whatever I wanted to do. However, when it came time to do something, he refused. I ended up walking down the beach alone and crying on the day of my 40th birthday. I was wishing that he hadn't even come on the trip.

When I came back toward him, he was up and writing in the sand, "Happy Birthday, Sharon. Love, Saint."

This one gesture turned the trip around for me. I will admit he won the dress competition on this trip. We wore all white, but I didn't really like my dress, although I got compliments. I made him go parasailing on this trip, and we went riding on the quads. I ended up flipping my quad over and scratching up my elbow, but I still had fun. We went for a boat ride to a little island in the water. There were calm waters on one side of the beach, and when you walked through what looked like a cave, the water was very rough. The guy called it "Lovers Beach" on one side and "Divorce Beach" on the other side.

The waves on the Divorce Beach side were amazing to watch. We sat there and talked for a little while, and, for a brief moment, I forgot about all the grief and pain he'd caused me. Later that night we went to a club in downtown Cabo and watched the most rhythmically challenged people ever. The alcohol consumption from the club that night lowered my inhibitions and made sex not seem so forced and uncomfortably awkward. I still refused to perform oral sex on him, and a condom was a must.

He left the next day, and I didn't feel anything. It was a strange feeling for me. There was a definite disconnect beginning to form. Normally, I would be sad, because I would be thinking that things are not supposed to be this way. This was not the life I'd dreamed of having with him. I still wasn't completely ready to give up on us just yet. I believe someone in love should do everything they possibly can, and fight to the finish, before walking away. I knew when things were good between us, they were really good, and to me it was worth fighting for. I thought I could regain that loving feeling I'd once felt for him.

After the Cabo trip, I knew our vibe was off. Saint would normally answer my calls right away, or if he couldn't get to the phone, he would call right back. I started noticing that I wasn't getting a call back, and I knew he'd seen that I'd called. I could tell when he was on the phone, because his phone would beep alerting me that he was on the other line. It had gotten to a point where I just didn't call him anymore, and when he called me, I would sit there and watch the phone ring. I felt that, if he could dish it out, then he should be able to take it.

I tried to do what I did in New York when Saint got on my nerves, which was spend time with my family. I made the two-hour trip to Houston twice, to see my brother, and then I decided to see if, at any point, he would try to make the trip to come visit me. Just like I thought—not even a phone call, so that last visit was my last visit.

I decided maybe I should make a better effort at meeting someone here in Beaumont or nearby. Because I was now a supervisor, dating an officer was not worth me losing my job. However, there was a guy who worked in the laundry room, who was the exact same skin complexion and height of Saint. I was very attracted to him, and one day, out of the blue, he called the lieutenant's office and just started talking to me. The conversation was going well, and he let me know that he was interested in me when he first saw me, but he wanted to see how I carried myself first. He told me that he finally decided to call because he noticed that I kept to myself, and he hadn't heard any rumor about me since I had been there, and he liked that.

I was flattered, because he was a very handsome guy, and he chose to pursue me. We spoke every day after he made that call. Talking to Todd made me not think about the fact that I wasn't speaking to Saint. I liked Todd, and he seemed like a good guy so far, but you just never know these days, so I Googled him. I also searched for him on social media, but he didn't have any social media pages set up. I knew that he didn't live too far from me, and the Todd that I found online was listed as having a spouse. I didn't want to jump to conclusions, but I was definitely going to ask him when we spoke again.

Just like with Saint, we kept it professional at work—strictly business. One evening, before he left work, he stopped by the lieutenant's office to have his outcount form signed, and I made it a point to look at his hand for a ring or any signs of a tan line from wearing a ring. It was a relief to see that he wasn't wearing a ring and didn't have a tan line from a ring. I knew he would call me at work later, so I just waited for his call. Although I didn't see a ring, I still wanted to ask him about the name that had popped up. After all, I could have the wrong person.

I am not the type to beat around the bush, and I don't have patience anymore for men, especially after all I had been through in the past years dealing with Mr. Saint. When he called that evening and I asked the question, I was hoping to hear, "No, I don't know who that is," but, instead, I heard, "Yes, that's my wife."

I wanted to hang up the phone immediately. I felt like I'd lost respect for him, and we hadn't been talking that long, but it had been long enough for him not to lie about being married. More than that, he was the one to initiate whatever may have taken place between us.

I had to ask him, "Why would you call me knowing that you are married, and why don't you wear a wedding ring?"

He said he found me attractive, and he and his wife were going through some things. I thought to myself, *Oh, my God—cue the violins. Here comes the bullshit.* That was the classic line for all married men trying to bait and catch new fish. I let him know that I was not interested in being anyone's side piece and that we could be cool at work. He tried to convince me that I shouldn't be that way, but my mind was made up.

His only other question was, "How did you find out about her?"

"Does that really matter at this point?" I asked. "At the end of the day, you are a very married man, and if you are looking for something on the side, then you should be upfront with that woman so she can make the decision if she wants to take the ride with you."

He apologized and said that it was not his intention to lie to me.

I had to ask myself, *Is God trying to be funny? He sent me a man who was almost the mirror image of someone who had put me through living hell for the past nine years, just to see what I would do.* For a brief moment, I almost fell for it.

Now that the Todd distraction was gone, I was focused on Saint again. I was wondering what he may or may not be doing, and why he wasn't calling like he used to. Because of my nightly conversation with Todd, I didn't realize it had been two months of us not speaking. I was determined not to call him, because I wasn't going to appear weak ever again. I had to find something else to occupy my time, so I started going to the high school track just to walk and listen to my music. When the lyrics of a song started speaking to my heart, I started running and singing out loud. I didn't care who was around—I had to let it out.

I sounded very winded because I was the heaviest that I had ever been in my entire life. I weighed in at 177 pounds of breast, butt, and back fat. I started out in the walk-run phase, but I pushed myself to make it around the track until I was able to complete one mile without stopping, all the while punching at the air, as I pictured Saint's face. This really helped me to relieve some aggression that I had toward him.

Saint finally called and began talking as if we had just spoken last night. I hated being phony, so I just cut him off and asked, "Who is she? And Saint, before you begin to lie, remember who you're talking to, because I know you. I know that, when you become distant and you start to snap at me for no reason, I know there's some new woman whispering sweet nothings in your ear."

He said, "You're right. I did meet someone. I met her in the airport, going to Jamaica. "She is from St. Thomas, and she is a nurse. You know I always said I wanted to marry a nurse or doctor," he said. "We have been talking for a while, and she has been looking into trying to move here permanently."

"Oh, so you plan on being a green-card husband?" I asked, sarcastically.

"No, Sharon. That's not fair; I think I really like her," he responded.

"She is just like everyone else who was new and not connected to you and all your women drama," I said. "How can you be in a relationship with someone a gazillion miles away?" I asked.

"That's not true. She has come here a few times—well, not here, but she has met me in New York. My sister, Donna, met her, and she really likes her," he said.

"How long have you been dealing with this one?" I questioned.

"We have been dealing for a while now; in fact, when I left Cabo early, I was going to meet her in St. Thomas."

I shook my head as I said, "I should fucking hang up the phone on you."

"Why would you want to do that?" he asked.

"How dare you sit on this phone and tell me that you left my 40th birthday celebration to go be with another girl? Does she know about me?" I asked.

"Yes, I did tell her about you, but I told her we were having a lot of problems and fighting all the time, which was true."

"Saint, let me ask you a question: Did you tell the Dirtbag about her?"

"Why would you ask me that?" he said.

"I have not been receiving any messages or phone calls as of late, so either she's started fucking someone new or she's found someone else to stalk."

"Well, to answer your question, yes, I did tell her, and she was upset and crying."

I cut him off right away. "I don't want to hear none of that shit. You can keep all of that shit to yourself," I said.

I was happy that The Dirtbag had finally found someone else to stalk. Evening after hearing this new information, I was still holding onto hope, because this new woman was far away, and I was still the closest person to him out of all the women. I did question myself whether I was holding on because there were no other prospects or because I still had love for him in that way.

Saint started calling more often, but the conversations were mostly about the job. I think I realized then that I was holding on because there were no other prospects. When I would call him, I would get a text message saying either, "I'm sleeping," "I will call you back when I get up," "I'm cutting the grass," or "I'm out having drinks." I heard these phrases so many times, I just gave up on calling him and waited for him to call me. I think I was just calling for the sake of having someone to talk to.

Because the phone calls weren't coming in like I'd hoped they would be, I found myself running up to three miles per day nonstop. I also realized that none of my friends from New York were calling, either. I knew my family wasn't going to call, because they'd proven themselves to me while I was in New York. Here I was in this town, behind God's back, with no family, no friends, and no man. The only thing I had was the dog I didn't want in the first place.

But Missy became my saving grace because I felt abandoned by everyone, and the despair of it all led to a deep depression. All I did was go to work, jog, and barely eat or sleep. I hated looking at myself in the mirror because of the ugly dark circles that had formed around my eyes. I never felt pretty before, but now I believed that I was as ugly as I felt or people had called me in the past. Sleeping was the hardest thing for me to do because my mind would not shut down. I constantly thought about how I went from someone surrounded by people and being invited to everything, to this person who had no friends and sat around watching television all day. I started drinking a bottle of wine a day, just to be able to sleep at night.

When the wine stopped working, I started taking sleeping pills along with the wine to put myself to sleep. I knew I was taking a risk by mixing these two together, and, at first, I didn't care. If I didn't wake up, then it would be OK, because I really didn't have anything to live for, and it would appear to be an accident anyway.

One day while I was sitting around drinking, Missy came from her room with her toy in her mouth, and she was adamant about me playing catch with her. She loved for me to shake it back and forth, while she still had it in her mouth. Then, when she would loosen her grip, I would snatch it from her mouth and throw it down the hall. She would do this nonstop until she tired herself out. I looked at her little face, and I thought, *Who is going to know how she likes to play? Who is going to know that she likes her chicken on the bone, hanging off the side of the plate for easy access? Who is going to take care of her if something happens to me?* Missy gave me a purpose again. She gave me the reason I needed to wake up every day. That feeling of hopelessness was lifted, just like that.

When I finally looked in the mirror, I saw all the weight I had lost from all that jogging, just trying to clear my mind. I went from 177 pounds to 144 pounds, and I felt good. More than that, I felt like I *looked* good. Reinforcement for me feeling this way came when I went to the supermarket, and, while I was loading my car, some man drove by and screamed out the window in my direction, "You sure is purdy," in his Texas country accent. I laughed at the accent, but I appreciated the compliment.

I decided I wanted to go home to New York and show off my new look. My mother's birthday was coming up, so I thought a surprise visit would be nice. She was shocked to see me at her door—and even more shocked because of all the weight I'd lost. She said, "Girl, you look *good*," and that made me feel good to hear it coming from her.

My mother was not known for giving compliments but was exceptional at pointing out someone's obvious flaws, and in the worst way. I do believe my mother contributed to my self-esteem issues. She would always compare my hair to my sister's hair texture. She used to make comments like, "That dress doesn't look good on you; it would look better on Lorraine."

I guess I was old enough now not to let her words get to me. She would have to answer for her shortcomings at the Pearly Gates. I swore her to secrecy about my presence in New York, because I wanted to surprise my sisters as well. On my way to see my sister, I decided to stop by the institution and say hello to a few people. As sure as the devil is a liar, the little Dirtbag was sitting front and center in the lobby as I walked through the door. She was shocked to see to me and probably a little jealous because everyone else was so happy to see me. They all made mention of how much weight I had lost and how good I looked. I hadn't gone home for the attention, but it damn sure felt great.

When I got to my sister's house, it was more of the same. I ended spending the night at my sister's instead of driving back to Queens to my mother's late at night. I was rudely awakened by a phone call from the Dirtbag, screaming into the phone, something about her car. I laughed at her and hung up the phone, but, of course, she called right back, yelling, "I know you did it."

"Did what, little girl?" I asked, laughing.

"I know you came to my house last night and keyed my truck. We have cameras, so your stupid ass is on video!"

"I don't know what you're talking about, little girl, so please stop calling my phone with this nonsense" I said, with laughter in my voice.

As expected, Saint was the next person to call my phone. He sounded frustrated as he said, "Sharon, did you key that girl's car?"

"Don't call my phone talking to me about that girl!" I yelled at him. "I don't know anything about her fucking car, so tell her to stop calling me with that bullshit!"

He said, "Sharon, if you did key her car, you could be in trouble, because she said she has you on video."

I had to stop him from talking because the sound of his voice was making me sick.

"And she would be lying, because I was in New Jersey all night, and I can prove it, so tell her to call the police. That girl could tell you anything, and you would believe her! Please get off my phone," I said to him and then disconnected he call.

I must admit, there was some petty satisfaction with knowing that I'd caused her such distress. Like I said before, I could control her every emotion with just my presence. Upon my return to Texas, I did receive a phone call from the Nassau County Police Department. The officer said he was given my number by the "The Dirtbag," as being a possible person of interest in the vandalism of her vehicle.

He asked, "Do you have any reason why she feels you had something to do with this?"

"Sir, I told her when she called me that I had nothing to do with her car."

"She called you?" he asked.

"Yes, she did call me, and I don't know why she is singling me out because she has a slew of enemies. She has been arrested several times for harassment, therefore, it could be anybody," I told the officer.

"Well, were you here when this took place?" he questioned.

I responded, "I was in New York visiting my family, but the night that she claims this happened, I was in New Jersey, and I have receipts to prove it."

"You can prove that you were in New Jersey?" he asked.

"I absolutely can," I replied.

He said, "Well, if I need anything else, I will contact you."

"That's fine. I will be here," I said.

Needless to say, I never heard from him again, but unfortunately for me, I heard from the Dirtbag again. I guess she found it necessary to let me know that her insurance had paid for whatever happened to her car, as if I cared. This, in fact, was my last interaction with the Dirtbag, and all I can say is, thank God for small mercies.

Months had gone by, and the only ones to call me were my homeboy, Twinkles, and my homegirl, Sosa. It was a very lonely life in Texas, and, although I could have put myself out there, I didn't believe in wasting anyone's time, because I wouldn't want them to waste mine. My goal was to leave Texas the first chance I got, so there was no point in going through the motions of meeting, getting to know, and dating someone. Besides that, if I was truly being honest with myself, deep down, I knew I was still in love with Saint. I wanted him to really give chase and show me that he was truly sorry for everything he'd put me through. If he would've done that, I would have freely given him my whole heart again.

I also knew that I'd developed major trust issues and that anyone who tried to come into my life would absolutely pay for what Saint had put me through. I wouldn't want to purposely do that to anyone, therefore, I knew I had work to do with resolving those issues, or, should I say, "baggage."

Saint knew that I wasn't dating and that I hadn't had sex with anyone. I think that thought gave him comfort. He felt secure knowing he had his ol' faithful on standby—he had that spare tire just in case. Here we were again, and my birthday was around the corner. It was time to plan my birthday trip. After talking to my homegirl, Sosa, I decided Costa Rica would be a cool place to visit.

Saint started calling more often around this time, trying to find out where I was going for my birthday. When I told him, he asked if he could come along, so I wouldn't have to be alone for my birthday. I figured, *What the hell could it hurt?* So I said "Yes."

We met at baggage claim in Costa Rica, and the first thing he said was, "Sharon, you lost too much weight."

"Well, damn—hello to you, too," I said, sarcastically. "I think I look great, by the way, so thank you very much."

His response was an attempt to try to clean up his initial comment. He said, "I'm not saying that you don't look good. I'm just saying you don't need to lose any more weight."

I just kept my thoughts to myself and left that conversation alone. I realized that everyone had their luggage, but my suitcase still hadn't dropped. We later found out that my luggage hadn't make the change when I switched planes. They said they would have someone bring my luggage to the hotel once it arrived. It was the beginning of my vacation, and two things had already pissed me off. The bus ride to the hotel was filled with a weird silence.

Once we arrived at the hotel and entered our assigned room, I saw that they'd given me a garden-view room. This was the third strike for this trip, because I paid extra for an ocean-view room, and that's what I wanted. Saint was trying to convince me just to take the garden-view room, but I was not having it. They eventually found an ocean-view room that had to be cleaned and prepped, so we ended up just walking around and checking things out until it was ready.

This reminded me of the cruise cabin situation. During our walk, I asked about Ms. St. Thomas, and he said that they were still talking but that she wanted to get married before she committed to moving to the States.

Hearing that, I had to ask, "Does she know that you're here with me?"

"No, I told her that I was going by myself," he said.

"Whatever, Saint—that's your business. Some things will never change, because you will never stop lying," I said. He never replied to my comment.

Things started to look up a little when we finally got into the room—it had the best ocean view ever, and then the front lobby called to say my luggage had arrived. The first night we just hung out in the room, played Scrabble, and talked. I was really considering having sex with him that night because he was familiar, and it had been such a long time for me.

But Saint put a nail in that coffin lid when he told me that he was dating a GS-8 officer, who worked in the Receiving and Discharge Department in the prison. He started with the same old description: she is tall with a big ass, and the only exception was that she was brown skinned. I was stuck on the fact that he would risk his job and position to mess with an officer. Although he wasn't her direct supervisor, she was still an officer. He said they kept things on the low, so no one knew anything. I'd learned firsthand that there are no secrets in jail. When you think no one is paying attention, there is always someone taking notes. When I finally admitted to being involved with Saint, so many people at work told me they'd suspected something between us for a long time. He said she was trying to get a case-manager position at another institution, so it wouldn't be a problem for them. He started telling me that she was very good with money, and she helped him to be smarter with his spending.

I truly hated when he said things like this about his other woman, as if I had never done anything to elevate him as a man. He also said her family had money. I guess that meant my family was too broke for him. The shock came when he said she had a son, because I know how he felt about raising another man's child. He had an answer for that as well.

He said, "I didn't see it as a problem, because he was older."

Again, I asked, "So, did you tell her about me?"

"Yes, I told her about you and everything that I'd put you through," he stated. "I told her that I couldn't imagine my life without you because you are a really good friend, besides everything else."

I repeated my earlier statement, and this time he responded, "Pumpkin, don't be like that."

"Seriously Saint, you have this girl, and St. Thomas, but you're here with me. You will truly never change."

I sat there there shaking my head in disbelief and disgust.

He said, "Let's stop talking about this and finish this game."

I agreed to change the topic, but then the room was silent, except for the television playing. We both agreed to take a shower and get ready for bed. When he came out of the shower, I had my pajamas on.

He asked, "Are you sleeping in that?"

"Yes, why?" I retorted.

"No reason," he said. "Can you lotion me?" he asked.

I said, "Sure." After I'd massaged the lotion over his back and the back of his legs, I told him to turn over so I could do his chest and the front of his legs. When I saw his penis, I remembered that, normally, this would end with me kissing it, but for the first time I thought with my head and not my heart. So I finished with the lotion and got under the covers. I am totally afraid of the dark, except when I have someone in bed next to me. When he turned off the lights, he grabbed me by my waist to pull me close, like we'd slept in the past. It felt good to have his arms around me. He started to kiss my neck and put his hands inside my pajama pants, but I stopped him.

"Saint, I am not having sex with you," I whispered.

"Why not?" he asked, sounding aggravated.

"Saint, you just sat in here and told me all about this girl that you like so much, plus you have this St. Thomas chick, and I just don't want to do this anymore."

"Why not? That's what you do," he uttered.

"'That's what I do,'" I repeated. "We are back to that again?" I questioned.

"Yes. I mean, it never stopped you before, so what's the problem now?" he asked.

"*That* is the problem, Saint. The fact that you can say that to me, is the problem."

He got out of the bed, put his clothes on, and left the room. I turned the television on and turned over. I didn't care where he went or what he was going to do, I went to sleep.

I think he came back into the room about 1:30 in the morning, and then he just got back in the bed. He still held me around the waist and whispered in my ear that he was sorry for what he'd said.

I said, "I'm still not having sex with you."

He said he understood, and we went to sleep. The next day was my actual birthday, and, as usual, I planned a day at the spa and dinner. The spa couldn't take us until later in the day, so we decided to go down to the beach, so he could get some sun. Costa Rica is such an amazing place; the beach was more like going to the zoo. While he was soaking up rays, I took a walk down the beach and saw beautiful, colorful crabs popping up out of the black volcanic sand. I was also scared to death because there were several large iguanas just cruising along the beach. I also saw a bunch of little baby turtles that were trying to make their way across the sand into the ocean water.

I had been to several places, but none with water like Costa Rica. You can walk out into the ocean as far as you can go and still see your feet the entire time, surrounded by an array of vibrantly colored fish. While relaxing in a lounge chair in the shade, because the sun felt like we were on the equator, I felt my chair rock as if someone were behind me rattling my seat. I turned around, but no one was there.

Then, as I looked toward Saint, he was looking back at me with the same puzzled look on his face. There was an elderly couple not too far from me, and they also had that look on their faces. When I surveyed the rest of the beach, all the other beach-goers didn't seem fazed at all by the strange shaking.

One of the hotel workers noticed us looking around bewildered, and he said, "It was just an earthquake."

My first reaction was, "Oh, *hell* no," as I jumped up from my lounge chair. I yelled over to Saint and said, "I am going back to the room."

He wasted no time getting up to follow me. That was the first experience with an earthquake for both of us. I think we were both amazed at how everyone reacted as if this were normal. This was the perfect segue for the full body massage we had scheduled.

That night, we got dressed, and I know I won our dress competition with the black and sequined dress I had on. He had on black and gray, basic top-and-bottom outfit. It was the cufflinks that I'd bought him that stood out the most in his outfit.

After dinner, we changed again and went over to the casino, where I won $50. We sat at the bar in the casino and talked like we were best friends who hadn't had a sexual relationship for more than 10 years. We laughed about so many of the things that took place in our situationship, and he apologized for many of the things he'd done during our situationship. When you're able to laugh at something that caused you so much pain, that's when you know that you're over it. You've made it through to the other side. I think we both knew there was no turning back for us. It was a ten-plus-year situation that just didn't work out. We both realized that we were meant to be just friends.

For me, looking back, I realized that I should have put an end to that situation a long time ago. I can't really say why I stuck it out so long. I guess, for the most part, my self-esteem played a major role—and my determination to win. Saint would have been the prize that I won in the face of all those people who'd called me ugly. In typical Saint fashion, he asked if it was OK for him to step away to call his ladies. We laughed about that as well.

Like most of my vacations, I have a things-to-do list, and in Costa Rica, I wanted to go zip-lining and be up close and personal with monkeys. Also, as usual, I had to convince Saint to partake in the activities. When putting on the harness to go zip-lining, Saint said, "Why do you always find things to do that always smush my package?"

I laughed and said, "That's my way of getting you back for always cheating on me."

By the time we got to the first lift, Saint was changing his mind as he looked down and saw nothing but jungle trees. The guide said this wasn't even the highest lift. I went first because it was my idea, and I was so glad I did, because watching Saint come across was one of the most comical things I'd ever witnessed, besides him on the horse, or maybe swimming. When he arrived on the first landing, he said he didn't want to finish the other lift. But the guide said he would have to go back across or climb down, so he gave in and kept going. I noticed a smile on his face after the second lift.

I, on the other hand, was second-guessing this idea. I somehow stopped short of the landing on the second lift and was literally dangling over the jungle of trees below. One of the guides had to zip-line across and crash into me to get me to the landing of the second lift. I was scared, but I still wanted to complete the zip-line experience. So when he asked if I wanted to try going across hanging upside down, I was all for it. That was one of the most exhilarating and scariest things I had ever done, and then to top it off, I couldn't stop the zip-line when I got to the third landing. I crashed into the tour guide standing on the third landing in order to stop.

By the fourth lift, I was ready to be done, and so was Saint. After zip-lining I tried so hard to get Saint to go in with me to see the monkeys, but he was having no parts of that adventure. The guide advised me to take everything out of my pockets and remove my earrings because Capuchin monkeys would take them. As soon as I entered the cage, four monkeys jumped on me. Two were playing in my hair, one was on my arm with his monkey paws down the front of my shirt, and the last monkey was searching my back pockets. I felt violated by those monkeys, but they were so cute. Overall, Costa Rica was not a bad end to a long-overdue breakup between me and Saint. We spoke only now and again after we got back home, mainly job-related issues.

For me back in Beaumont, life disappointments were coming at me from every corner. My tenants had stopped paying their rent, and I was bleeding money trying to keep up with all the bills. With having gone through all the failed relationships, there was one thing that I was able to take pride in, and that was my credit and my finances. I felt like I had hit rock bottom when I had to file for Chapter 13 bankruptcy in order to get rid of the house and save my job. As a condition of working for the Bureau, all staff must maintain good credit. The Bureau does consider filing bankruptcy as a form of taking responsibility for the debts.

That feeling of hopelessness was looming over me again. I had no man, no money, and no close friends or family near to help ease the depression I felt. I couldn't jog my way out of this feeling, so I started drinking a lot more. I was drinking until I would throw up. Because I wasn't really eating, there was nothing in my stomach to vomit up, and it was painful. I just wanted to stop the world and get off. When I left New York for Texas, that was supposed to be my fresh start, but instead it became my come-to-Jesus moment. I had daily conversations with God, probably making promises that he knew I wouldn't or couldn't keep. I had never prayed like I prayed while living in Texas. I started thinking about where I would want to live to start my life over, but I was afraid that, because my credit had taken a hit because of the bankruptcy, I wouldn't be able to leave because I wouldn't be able to get an apartment. I felt trapped in the state of Texas and in this tiny town of Beaumont.

I reached out to Saint, just to see if he would be willing to help me get a place if I needed him to co-sign or something, when I started putting in for transfers. He was happy to hear from me, because it had been months since we'd spoken. I didn't want to now be viewed as the other woman after all the years we'd had together, especially knowing that he was in a live-in relationship situation. He didn't hesitate to say "Yes," and it made me feel great to know that he still had my back.

It took a while, but I finally got selected for a lateral position to Terminal Island, California. Once again, God smiled on me because

Terminal Island offered staff housing, which would not require a credit check, and it was a paid move from Texas to California. I told Saint about the selection, and I also told him that, as soon as I got to California, I was going to start dating. I noticed a change in his tone of voice when I told him that. I guess, like most men, he suffered from the, "That pussy will always be mine" syndrome. He couldn't take hearing me say that I would eventually be having sex with someone else, so we went back to radio silence, no communication at all.

On October 31, 2012, I arrived in California, fulfilling a lifelong dream of living in oceanfront property. I can literally take 20 steps from my front door and fall into the Pacific Ocean. I was surrounded by lemon trees, an orange tree, a lime tree, and an avocado tree. I had a two-bedroom, one-bath apartment, more like a townhouse-style setup. The bedrooms and bathroom were upstairs, and the living room, kitchen, and dining room were downstairs. My bedroom had a balcony that faced the ocean, so I could sit and watch the cruise ships or cargo ships go by.

From the outside looking in, someone would think I had it going on, but in reality, I was broke. I was once sitting on six figures in my bank account, and now I had bad credit with only $2400 in the bank. As much as I wanted to be in a relationship, I couldn't afford to think about a man at this time in my life. I was a total failure, in my book. I didn't feel worthy of a man, because I no longer could bring anything to the table. The mere fact that I was not a ten in the eyes of most men rendered me useless goods, and now I would be viewed as a financial burden.

I thought California was going to be my do-over state. Instead it became the humbling phase of my life. I think God wanted to test me to see if I had learned anything from my past, so he sent Karter into my life. We'd first met at the prison when I took a tour of the institution during my house-hunting trip. The day after I moved in, he and his friend stopped by to reintroduce himself; he asked if I needed anything. I was so happy they stopped by because my car hadn't been delivered yet, and Papa John's pizza didn't deliver to the reservation. They took me to Target and a supermarket called Ralph's so I could buy some cereal and milk and a bowl to eat it from.

Later that night, Karter offered to take me to something called, "First Thursday," in downtown San Pedro, which is the name of the town I would now call home. It was November 1, the day after Halloween, and in Mexican heritage, they celebrate this day and it is called "The Day of the Dead"—*La Muerta*. They had all different types of food trucks with a stage set up for a band and dancers. It was a really cool atmosphere. As we were jaywalking across the street, he reached for my hand, and the feeling was so natural that he didn't let go. I had to ask for my hand back, and we both laughed about it. As we sat there eating and talking, he let me know that he liked to be able to hold my hand, because he couldn't do that with his wife anymore.

In my head I heard the sound of tires coming to a screeching halt. I said, "Wait a minute—you're married?"

He said in a calm tone, "Yes, but we haven't lived as a married couple in years."

I was having a tug of war with my thoughts surrounding what I'd just heard. I knew I was physically attracted to him, and because our conversation just flowed so easily, I envisioned myself in a full-on relationship with him after one evening together. Unfortunately, I knew I had to put him into the friend-zone.

For the next two weeks, while I was on annual leave from work and setting up my new apartment, we hung out every evening once he got off of work as friends. For my 42nd birthday, he took me to California's pride and joy, Rosco's Chicken and Waffles. Personally, I found it to be overrated. There was no way I was going to be able to travel somewhere for my birthday after making this move, so I was glad just to be able to go out to dinner and have company.

I looked forward to him coming over after work and telling me about his day. He looked forward to me greeting him at the door with a big hug and his favorite drink in hand. I loved listening to stories of him growing up in California. All I knew of California was what I watched in videos and the news of all the gang violence.

I was a little reluctant about opening up to him so soon, because I didn't really know him.

Nevertheless, we sat at the dining-room table, and I told him about the situation with my house and my tenants. That topic made me cry, because I was a good landlord, and it hurt me to know that my tenants had completely shit on me. When the tears began to roll down my cheeks, he pulled his chair close to mine and put his arm around me to let me know it would be OK, and then he kissed me. When I pulled away from him, he said he couldn't help it. He said he had been wanting to kiss me for a long time now. He tried to apologize, but I told him there was no need to, because I had been wanting to do more than that, but I didn't want to disrespect his marriage.

"Sharon, I am married, but I'm not in a marriage," he said.

"I don't even understand what that means," I said.

"It means that I don't sleep with her. It means we don't talk unless it has something to do with the kids. I feel bad because she has been living her life as a single mother for many years because I have not been there. I really like you, and I want to see where this can go," he said.

Listening to him explain the situation surrounding his marriage, I felt my guard being lowered. I knew that most men who were married always said that they were having problems within the marriage, but his situation was different. They were married young, and they lived in separate states for the majority of their marriage. I think I gave him a pass because his story was verifiable. I told him that I was not entertaining having sex with anyone until I could see some paperwork from a doctor saying they are free and clear of all diseases.

I held my ground that night and we said goodnight with a kiss on the cheek. He went to the doctor that weekend, and, by the following week, he had his paperwork from his doctor showing a clean bill of health. The problem with that was that my cycle had started, but we weren't close enough for me to tell him that, so I improvised. He was trying so hard to get my pants off because he wanted to kiss the kitty. I still laugh when I think about it. I was lying on my back, and he was straddling over me as he was removing his shirt. I caught him off guard by grabbing him by the thighs and pulling him up towards my face. He was stunned, and a look of shock came across his face, because it had happened so fast. Within an instant, he was now straddling over my chest, and the fully erect part of him was kissing my lips. I hadn't been with a man in so long that I thought I'd lost my touch, but that proved to be an unfounded fear.

It was like I was hungry, more like starving, and someone had given me a hot link sausage. To fully enjoy my meal, I had to switch positions, so I used the same technique and flipped him over on his back. He said he wasn't used to a woman being so aggressive, but he liked it. As he was on his way to reaching his peak, he screamed, "Shit, Damn, girl!"

After he caught his breath, he still wanted to please me, but I couldn't let him, so I said, "I'm good with just pleasing you."

We lay there laughing and making jokes about how everything had gone down, until he had to leave. The next day was my first day at work. We didn't pretend not to know each other, but we did downplay how close we knew each other. I paid very close attention to how he conducted himself inside the prison. What I noticed was that, when mainline was announced for the inmates, and staff would report to the compound in front of the chowhall, the women flocked around him like thirsty hens. It was like someone had put out a bowl of food for stray cats. The scene also reminded me of a movie when the pimp arrives at a party with his hoes in tow. The man looked great in a suit, and he always walked with one hand in his pocket, pimp-like smooth. When he stood still, he would jiggle the change or keys in his pocket. It was as if this was his secret call to the women. Only the women who were very much attracted to him could hear this sound.

Every day that I witnessed this secret mating call, I would bring it to his attention at night, and we would laugh about it. He finally admitted that these females were secretly sending him the signs that he could have them if he would just make the move. He said one female was more direct than others when she stated, "When are you going to let me suck your dick?"

Another female knew he had a foot fetish, so she constantly sent him pictures of her feet. I thought it was crazy watching females throw themselves at a man like this. He used to try to get me to come visit him in his office, but I refused to be seen as one of his institution groupies. Our time together after work was more than enough for me. The time had come for me to make a decision if I was going to cross the line and have sexual intercourse with him. I was still really torn because he was a married man, regardless of the status of the marriage.

I watched him at work, and I was convinced that he was not dealing with these women on that level, so I did develop trust for him. I had to ask myself the real question, which was, *What is holding you back? You've already performed a sexual act with him even though he is married.* I think I was trying to find another excuse because I had no confidence in myself sexually anymore. I really believed that my vagina wasn't working because it didn't get wet. I also thought that, after all this time without sex, I wouldn't remember how to move. I didn't want to go back to the virgin stage of just lying there. I was just scared to be embarrassed. I decided that I would just give him a disclaimer about my broken vagina plumbing, so I wouldn't be judged so hard if it wasn't any good.

He was such a sweet person; he tried to convince me that it was all in my mind. My vagina betrayed me and made me look like a complete liar. The faucet opened up and would not shut off.

He said, "I thought you said it didn't get wet?"

I said, "It didn't get wet for years." *Maybe because it has been so long since I'd had sex was the reason that it was getting wet now,* I thought. Long story short, the session was great, and I couldn't wait to do it again. I still didn't reach a climax, but I enjoyed going through the motions of trying to get there. I felt like he had woken the beast within.

One of our most memorable sex sessions was on the staircase. This was a totally spontaneous moment that turned out to be mind-blowingly great. We spent every evening together, talking, eating, and having sex, but he would never spend the night. The day finally came for him to leave Terminal Island and continue his career elsewhere. When I arrived at work, I saw all those women crying because it was his last day. I mean boo-hoo bawling tears, because he was leaving. I teased him a little about the river that was forming at Terminal Island, all in his name.

We talked that night, and we agreed that we would continue seeing each other. I made the first trip, and we agreed to meet at the mall. I knew then that this was not going to last long, because I drove two hours to walk around a mall for him to call and say he wasn't sure he was going to be able to make it. Lo and behold, he didn't make it, because he said he found out that his wife's family was going to be at the mall. I was pissed, and I let it be known. I'd sacrificed my morals and my standards to try to make it work with this man. I started feeling like a fool who should have known better than to deal with a married man.

The following weekend, he came over and tried to make up for the previous weekend. He told his wife that he was going to spend time with his mother, so whenever she called, he had to answer the phone. That gave me déjà vu of when Saint used to answer the phone for Lexus or Lurchette in order for us to have an uninterrupted night. I felt like I had taken a step backwards. I justified the feeling in my mind by telling myself that he was different and that things would be fine. He was also telling me that I needed to have a little patience.

The following weekend was my turn again to go see him. He decided that we would meet at a restaurant midway. It was a quaint little Italian restaurant, but when we went inside, he asked to be seated in the back. Something in my gut told me there was a reason for that. When I asked, he said, "A lot of her family live in this town, and they come to this restaurant."

That was my final mental straw. I would not drive hours in traffic to be treated like a child conceived by a mistress. I never actually told him that I wasn't coming back here again—I just simply never mentioned seeing him again.

A few weeks went by, and we hadn't spoken at all. I have to assume he felt it was OK to treat me as if I were a booty call, because he eventually called, saying he was coming my way. He said he was going to stay with his friend, but he would stay with me if I would have him. I told him that he should stay with his friend.

He seemed surprised by my answer, so I had to let him know that I didn't have time to waste. I told him that I realized that it was a bad idea getting involved with someone who's married. I said, "I brought bad karma upon myself by doing that." If he was serious about dealing with me, then he would do what he needed to do to be with me, free and clear.

Again, he started with the excuse of needing to be there for his kids. I had to remind him that he could be there for his kids and not sleep in the bed with their mother. I told him that he could get his own place and still be there for his kids. He told me that I was being too hard on him. I had to remind him that it had been a few weeks since I'd even heard from him, therefore, he was lucky that I was even talking to him.

He tried to tell me that his kids were young and that they liked seeing their parents together. I didn't give it a second thought, because I didn't have to understand anything. What he needed to understand was that he should go work on his marriage and not try to get involved with anyone else until he was a single man.

All he could say was, "If that's the way you want it to be."

My response was, "That's the way it has to be."

I went back on a sexual hiatus, and, out of the blue, Saint called. I hadn't spoken to him in a while, but because we were now friends, I told him about Karter. I noticed an uncomfortable silence over the phone as he said, "I didn't want to hear that. You did say that, when you got to California, you would start dating, and I wish you all the best," he offered. "I guess in the back of my mind, I just always hoped that you would be with me," he said.

During that conversation, he let me know that he would be transferring to another institution on his second lateral. I thought that was cool because my homegirl, Sosa, and her hubby were at that institution, and it would be like a mini-MCC reunion for them. Once he'd made the transition, I started receiving more and more phone calls from my homegirl. In every conversation, she would ask if I had spoken to Saint. She would also ask questions like, "How would you feel if you found out that he had a girlfriend?"

I would always reply with the same answer: "I wouldn't care. Saint and I are just friends, and I would never go back to him," I told her.

She would say, "OK. I just wanted to know how you would feel."

Shortly thereafter, Saint called me to say that he was married, and he'd gotten his wife the Unit Manager position at the same institution with him. I didn't feel anything hearing this news, because I honestly didn't care. I was all the way over him and wished him the absolute best.

He said he thought that I would take it hard. He told me that, when he told Lurchette and the Dirtbag, they both took it hard and started crying. He obviously didn't know me that well, because if he did, then he would know that once I close the book on that chapter, I do not go back for a reread. There was nothing for me to cry over. Besides that, I'd shed all my tears over him during the course of our situation. I just wanted to move on with my life and find someone for me.

My homegirl called again, and that's when it hit me that she'd known all along and was trying to feel me out. I put her mind at ease and told her that he'd told me about the marriage.

She said, "I didn't want to tell you because I didn't want to hurt you."

I had to let her know that would never hurt me, because I was done with that part of my life. He was the past, and I was looking toward my future. I had to give her a little insight into her friend's psyche. I am the type of person who, when I am done with something or a situation, it is truly over for me, mentally and physically.

She said, "I am glad that you are handling it well."

Her statement made me believe that she hadn't believed me when I'd said I really didn't care. For me, there was nothing to handle. I wanted to live in the moment and enjoy my new life in California.

I decided to drive down to San Diego. I knew that Lexus was living in San Diego, so I reached out to her through Facebook. I had never in my life reached out to any of my "Situations" women, but because this particular girl constantly reached out to me as if we were friends, I figured, *What the heck?*

She agreed to meet with me at her apartment. When she came outside, I couldn't believe the person who was standing in front of me. She'd literally doubled in size, and, although she now had a five-year-old, beautiful little girl, I knew that was not baby weight. We went out to eat, and we talked about a lot of the lies Saint had told the both of us. I took a picture of us together and sent it to Saint, but of course, he didn't reply. I thought Saint would have told her the news, seeing as how he'd told the rest of us ladies about his marriage. So when I mentioned "his wife," she was shocked. I felt bad that I was the one to break the news to her. She pretended to be OK with learning that he was married—at least, while I was there.

However, Saint called me a few days later, saying that she'd called him, crying over hearing the news. He sounded as if he had the attitude that I'd told her, and he also asked why I'd sent him that picture of the two of us.

He asked, "Did you think that you were being funny by sending that picture to me?"

I replied, "It was not supposed to be funny, but more so, ironic. Who would ever have thought that that girl and I would ever be in a place where we would be taking a picture together?" I asked, rhetorically.

Saint felt I was being petty or malicious with my intent, so when the conversation ended, I presumed that I wouldn't be hearing from him anytime soon. After my conversation with Saint, I noticed that Lexus had blocked me on Facebook. I laughed to myself because these people really thought that they could have an effect my life. My mindset was "F" them both.

After months of being in California, things were not working out like I thought they would in the Operation-find-a-good-man mission. Financially, I was still a hot mess. I thought if I met someone who would be there to say everything would be okay and that it was not that bad, things could appear a little better. I was very much old-school when it came to meeting people, and I was delusional to believe that I could meet someone in California the old-school way. People are so into their cell phones while walking in the mall, at the gas station, in the dog park, in the supermarket, and any place where back in the day you'd have been able to just strike up a conversation and exchange numbers. We are living in the age of technology, and everyone is dependent upon their computers, smart phones, and tablets.

So, I decided to give the online dating thing a try. I refused to pay for an online dating site, so I created a profile on Plenty of Fish, which was free. I started communicating with a white guy at first. I figured that, at this point in my life, I should be open to all men because I had no luck thus far with dating only the "Brothers."

This guy seemed very nice, and conversation was going well until this fool had the nerve to ask me for money. He said he'd just arrived in Canada for work and had left his equipment in California. He wanted to know if I could send him money to get new equipment, and he would pay me back when he got back. I let him know that I'd worked in law enforcement with the Bureau of Prisons, and I would see him behind bars before I would ever send him a dime. Needless to say, I never heard from that clown again.

I was giving up on that site, but before I removed my profile, another guy sent me a message. His name was Chris, and he was easy on the eyes. He, too, said it was his first time trying out online dating. We communicated for a few days, and he seemed very attentive. In the mornings, I would receive a message saying, "Good morning, beautiful," and, at night, I would get a "Sweet dreams" message. He would also check in throughout the day just to see how I was doing and how my day was going. When he finally asked to meet in person, I was cool with that.

We decided to meet at a Starbucks in Hawthorne, California, which was almost a middle ground between my home and his job at Universal Studios. I did notice that he drove a BMW, but when he stepped out of the car, he was a lot shorter than what I was hoping for, and very slender.

He did have a nice-looking face, but his wardrobe did give me pause. Although neither of us drank coffee, we sat at a table outside mentally checking each other out. I learned he was a single father of two teenage girls. At my age, I had to accept that the men I would meet were more than likely going to have children, so I had to adjust my attitude. My new exception to the rule was that the children were almost grown. Under no circumstances would I accept children in diapers.

Hearing that he was a single father, I was intrigued to find out what he was teaching his daughters about dating. I wanted to know if he had taken the time to show them how a man is supposed to treat them. When I asked the question, it almost felt as if I was also feeding him the answer. He didn't seem to know how to answer the question based on his own teachings. I had to ask, "Do you let them know if a man doesn't open the door for them, then he's not the one for them? Do you take your girls to dinner and pull the chair out for them to let them see how a man should treat them?"

He said, "Yeah, yeah. I teach them all of that."

It was good to hear, and for me, he scored a few points. We talked for a little while longer and agreed to meet up again. I received my usual "Sweet dreams" text message, and I looked forward to seeing him again. The next day, I received a text saying how beautiful he thought I was and that he really enjoyed talking to me. We agreed to meet at a sports bar/restaurant near the airport.

The restaurant parking was in the rear of the building, which was not very well lit. I actually arrived before him, and I waited in the car for him to arrive. He texted me as he was pulling up, but he parked on the other side of the lot. We met at the back entrance, and I asked him if he had been to this bar before, and he replied, "Yes. It's around the corner from my house." As we were being escorted to our table, I thought about that for a second—I'd driven 40 minutes to get there. I thought this was selfish as hell, but I pushed it to the back of my mind.

I had on a wedge-heeled shoe, and the table was a step up from the floor. I paid very close attention to the fact that he didn't try to lend assistance as I took that step up. This was mental note number two. We ordered our food, ate dinner, and when the bill came, the waiter placed the bill in front of him. I watched this man turn the tray with the bill in it toward me, so I could see how much it was. He then reached into his pocket and took out half the money for the bill and placed it on the tray. This was mental note number three.

Then he asked if I wanted to play pool, which was in the back of the restaurant. I agreed, and as I stood up to step down from the table, he was already at the beginning of the hall leading to the back of the restaurant. He didn't even try to hold my hand or hold my arm to assist me as I stepped down. This was mental note number four. As we reached the back of the bar, there was a wait for the pool table. We decided to wait for the table to be free and had a seat at the surrounding bar-top table with high chairs. I waited briefly to see if he would pull my chair out, but he was already seated in his chair. This was mental note number five.

As we watched two guys, a White guy and a Black guy, playing pool, we overheard that they'd made a $5 bet. The White guy won but refused to take the money from the Black guy. The Black guy refused to take the money back, so the White guy came over to our table and asked Chris if he could give the money to his lady—that would be me. I refused the money and said he'd won it fair and square and that he should keep it. The man put the money on the table anyway and refused to take it back. As the man turned his back to walk away, Chris picked up the $5 bill and put it in his pocket. This was mental note number six.

It began to rain, so I decided not to play pool anymore and just call it a night. He agreed, and we walked toward the back door. As we stepped outside, he gave me a hug and proceeded to walk to his car. As I made my way across the dimly lit parking lot to my car, I took my seventh and final mental note. *This man is an absolute fraud. There is no way in hell that he has taught his daughters anything about how a man should treat a lady.* I asked myself all the way home, *How in hell could he have made it to be our age and not know basic date etiquette?* Chivalry completely died on his doorstep. This man had no manners whatsoever, and he seemed to be OK with that fact.

While I was driving home talking to myself, I received a stupid text from him saying something about me being beautiful. As much as I longed to hear a man tell me I was beautiful, I didn't want to hear that shit, at least not from him. That was probably fake, also, just like everything else about him. I was totally appalled by his behavior, so I didn't reply.

When I arrived home, I wanted to see if he would get any part of the night correct, but I was wrong. I didn't even receive a text message asking if I made it home safe while driving in the rain. I guess in his mind the night had gone well, because I received the usual "Good morning, beautiful" text message. I didn't respond to that message, either.

Two days passed, and he was still texting but not receiving a response from me. He finally decided to call, and I couldn't let this opportunity pass me by without letting this grown-ass man know that his behavior was unacceptable. When I answered the phone, I purposely sounded like I had an attitude just to let him know that I was not happy to hear from him. He did pick up on the tone in my voice and questioned me regarding my tone.

I let him have it—I gave him the business, as some would say. He sincerely apologized and said he hadn't realized that he didn't do any of the things I'd mentioned in my mental notes. He asked if he could see me again to make up for the misunderstanding. I thought to myself, *How can someone refer to bad manners and lack of chivalry as a misunderstanding? You either have manners or you don't. It's as simple as that.*

But I believe in second chances, so, I agreed to meet again. Besides, he was acting like he really liked me, and that's all I wanted at this point in my life. Because I mentioned that he'd made me drive all the way over there to meet him last time, he decided to come to me this time. I cooked dinner, and when he arrived at my place, my attraction for him was over once I opened the door. I know it may seem shallow, and who am I to judge anyone, but his outfit made my head crazy. He had on "Dad Pants"—washed out, faded jeans, with no shape, that sit right on the ankles. He also had on old black sneakers with bright white tube socks.

After we ate dinner, we started watching the MTV Awards on television, and this fool fell asleep on my couch. I couldn't resist the opportunity to take a picture of his outfit, showing how the Dad Pants had climbed up his ankles and was now resting mid-shinbone. I sent the picture to my girls, and we could not stop laughing via text messages. I knew I was being petty, but I also knew that he had to go. After I finished watching the show, I woke him up to let him know that it was time for him to go. He had the nerve to ask if he could stay. I am sure my face said what my mouth didn't get a chance to, because he said, "Sorry for asking." I walked him to the door and said, "Text me when you get home." When I closed that door behind him, it was for good.

I went upstairs and closed out my profile on Plenty of Fish. The next day, he had the nerve to send me a dick pic, as if that was supposed to entice me. I had flashbacks of Morales, except it was brown. *Why do men with skinny pencil dicks love taking pictures of it? More than that, why do they feel like I'm the type of girl who enjoys receiving dick pics? Because*

I don't. In fact, I hate it. I was done with him and the entire situation. I could say that I'd tried online dating and that it was just not for me.

I made up my mind to refocus on getting my financial situation under control and not focus on dating. I spent the next year and a half living for me and enjoying California life. I went hiking, stair climbing, and to every pier in Southern California. I spent some days feeling sorry for myself and wondering why I was living the way I was. I outwardly blamed my mother for not protecting me when my father passed away. She displayed a character flaw that I detest, which is weakness. She allowed my father's sister to come in and take the will, and she allowed his daughter to cause us to lose our home.

I had to stop blaming my tenants for my current financial situation. I had to realize that, if I would have just hired a property manager instead of being cheap and irresponsible, I wouldn't be in this financial predicament. I looked back at the failed relationships/situations and accepted my role in each and every failure. I think I was too accommodating to the men in my life. I had no real deal-breakers—at least none that I truly enforced. I was the one who made it easy for them to cheat on me. I was the one who didn't hold them accountable for hurting me. I never wanted to be the nagging girlfriend, so I didn't check or I didn't question the obvious signs of trouble in a relationship.

I had to accept that, as much as I said that I'd learned to love myself, I was really lying to myself. I didn't know what it meant to love myself or how to begin to show love to myself. I allowed these men to use me in the name of love. I always blamed the men for not treating me right. The fact is that I'd played a part in that. I taught them how to treat me. The fact that I didn't like myself lowered my standards, and, therefore, they didn't have to do much. The bar I'd set for myself was extremely low, therefore, anyone who said they liked me was already ahead of the game and over the bar. I took their cheating on me to mean that I wasn't good enough.

It took a long while for me to learn that them cheating on me had nothing to do with me at all. I think each of the men in my life tried to explain that to me in their own backhanded way. Self-reflection doesn't work unless you are truthful with yourself. It meant taking responsibility for everything that had gone wrong in my life up until that point. My father's words were coming into focus: "Everything that happens to you in your life, you let happen." I had to own it.

I started praying to God to help me let go of these thoughts. I needed him to help me forgive myself for allowing these men to use me. I had to ask for help in learning how to truly love myself. I surely prayed the single-most selfish prayer of all time, which was for a financial blessing. I knew that there were people in the world in far worse situations than me, but I couldn't see past my problems to think about theirs. I thought maybe once God realized that I'd truly learned to love myself and accept responsibility for my life, then he would send me a good man to round it all out. I thought I could fool God, but he had another lesson for me, or should I say, another test.

I am the type of person to do random check-ins with my friends and people I'd met over the years in the Bureau. I was always the one to reach out to say "Happy Anniversary" to the people who started with me working for the Bureau. On August 1, 2014, I sent a random email message to Steve. Just a brief refresher: Steve was the guy from training in Glynco, Georgia. He was the one I thought I could see myself spending a lifetime with. That email led to us speaking every day, sometimes six times per day. He was saying everything I wanted to hear coming from a man. He wanted to be married and was dating with a purpose. He, too, believed that communication was the basic foundation for any relationship to work.

I felt completely validated in my belief that he could be the one. I always thought of him as the one who got away, but now, he was back, and I was determined not to let him get away again. I learned that, over the years, he'd had a couple of lady friends, but he'd never cohabitated with a woman. I found that to be really odd. A man of a certain age should have already experienced sharing a space with a woman.

I remembered how easy it was to talk to him back in Glynco, when I poured my heart out about Eddie, my sister Angela, and my childhood. I felt I could tell him all about my journey with Saint. I felt comfortable telling him about my financial shortcomings as well. He listened just as he did when we were in Glynco and offered this little piece of advice from an Arabic proverb, "I complained that I had no shoes until I met a man who had no feet."

I wanted to always remember that statement, so I wrote it down on a post-it note and stuck it to my bathroom mirror. Whenever I started feeling sorry for myself, I would go and read it. I was feeling a sense of relief to have someone to share my feelings with. My guard was all the way down with him. I felt safe with him, and I believed that he would not hurt or betray me. I was a little concerned with his career progress, because he was still just a GS-8 officer. I think that ambition and drive in a man is a very sexy feature.

It was a relief to learn that he had been trying to get a promotion. I offered my assistance with revamping his resume to ensure that he at least would start to make the Best Qualified list. He began to tell me of his hopes to renovate his house, but he didn't know where to find the money to make it happen. He was considering taking a loan from his Thrift Saving Plan (TSP) account but didn't know how he would make ends meet with an additional bill. I suggested he take a hardship loan, which was a withdrawal from his TSP that he didn't have to pay back. He submitted the request to withdraw some funds, and it was approved.

He was very appreciative of my assistance with obtaining the money to fund his renovation, but he had no clue where to begin. All my experience with renovation of my own house and Saint's house had qualified me to lend assistance. I took the reins and began searching the internet for local, reputable contractors in his area. He was trying to renovate the kitchen and two bathrooms, all within that budget. I started sending him pictures of flooring, countertops, sinks, and backsplash options. He was overwhelmed with all the decisions he had to make. He said it jokingly, but he suggested that I come there and take care of all that stuff.

I was already 100 steps ahead of him. I had already priced out the cost of the trip to Augusta, just in case. In fact, I started calling him "my husband" and telling him that he was going to marry me. I finally told him that I believed that he was the one who got away. I believe that we all have that person who comes into our lives, and either we weren't mentally ready and we pushed them away, or the timing was off. For me and Steve, I think it was timing.

He had made a trip to New York and reached out to me, but I was in a situationship with Saint at that time, and meeting up with Steve would not have been a good look. Steve took this opportunity to let me know that he'd held that against me for all these years. During our many conversations, I learned that he had very little trust in women. So, with the fact that I didn't meet up with him in New York, I thought he would notice that I was a different type of woman and loyal to the person I was with. I thought maybe he would see that I was the type of woman that he could trust.

Because that New York meetup never took place, somehow, we got around to planning a trip to New York. He wanted to go visit all the tourist places in New York. Even though I was a born-and-raised New Yorker, I never made time to see these sights. He also wanted to go see his aunt, who lived in the Bronx. The idea of going to New York and being a sightseer was intriguing to me. In October we were booked and ready to see the sights, but I was more anxious to see him. I wondered if he still had those beautifully shaped eyes and that gorgeous nose with that sexy walk. We discussed at length the possibility of engaging in sexual intercourse, and, just as with Karter, I was adamant about seeing paperwork showing clearance of any and all sexually transmitted diseases. My request wasn't one-sided, and, therefore, I made my appointment as well. I knew I would probably have sex with him—even without the paperwork—if he looked as good as he had when I last saw him more than 10 years ago.

When I saw him at the airport, it was a little awkward because I didn't know whether to just give a casual hug and kiss on the cheek or a full embrace with a kiss on the lips. I decided to follow his lead, and he opted for the casual hug—no kiss anywhere. We checked into our hotel in Manhattan, and I decided to break the ice. I went right into my bag and handed him my paperwork from my doctor showing I was free and clear and demanded to see his paperwork. I knew I wasn't going back to California without getting me some of him. He looked just as good as he had back in 2000, when we'd first met, except he was a little more distinguished. That's when men develop the gray hairs in just the right places that doesn't make them look old but gives the appearance of wisdom.

Once I saw his paperwork, I was free and clear to take full advantage. I pushed him down on the chair in the room and began to give him a taste of what was to come that night. One of the things that I liked about him was that, although he was from the South, he didn't have a strong southern accent. When he uttered, "Lady," I knew he enjoyed the preview, so I stopped. It was like a trailer to a really good movie. It lets you see just enough to pique your interest but leaves you longing to see the entire show.

I stood up and said, "Let's go." He had a look on his face that was priceless.

He said, "Why would you do that?"

I smiled and said, "I just wanted to—now let's go."

He said, "Lady, you play too much."

I had my friend's car for the first night in New York, so the plan was to take him to the Bronx to see his aunt, and I would go over the bridge to New Jersey to surprise my sisters. We ended up stuck in traffic, and I knew trying to get to Jersey in that traffic was not going to be good. He'd originally told me that his aunt didn't want anyone in her place because she had stuff everywhere. I agreed to wait downstairs so he could spend some time with her. He felt bad with that idea, so he called his aunt and explained the situation, and she agreed to let me come up.

There's just something about me and older people. I loved her, immediately. She was so full of life and funny as hell. Ms. Bernice told me that she would kick my ass if I didn't put my money away when I was trying to pay for the Chinese food. We had a great visit with her, and I promised that I would come back to see her when I came home to visit my family. We drove straight back to the hotel after the visit with his aunt, so I could finish what I'd started earlier. He was more of a gentleman when it came down to engaging in sex. I was a little disappointed that there wasn't any kissing, but overall, I enjoyed every minute of being with him.

I think we really had a good time in New York. Most of the activities we embarked upon I probably would have never done had I remained a New York resident. I bought tickets for the hop on/hop off double-decker tour bus. We were able to go to the Statue of Liberty, Ellis

Island, the World Trade Center Memorial, and walk across the Brooklyn Bridge. I had always hated taking the subway, but because it was on his things-to-do list, I sacrificed. During the trip, Steve was able to spend a little time with two of my friends, Angie and Twinkles. He seemed to be impressed with my friends, and they approved of him as well. My homeboy, Twinkles, now the proud owner of Vasid Luxury Vehicle Car Service, a business he started after being fired from the Bureau, hooked us up with a car to pick us up from the hotel and take us to the airport. I knew I really liked him, and because my friends liked him also, that made it easier for me to see myself with him long term.

Once we got back to our homes, he really began to focus on preparing for the renovation. He made the comment again about me being there to help him, and I booked my trip to Augusta, Georgia, before he could change his mind. I was en route to spend some time with my future husband for my birthday, in my mind at least. Augusta was exactly how I pictured it, very quaint and country. His house was nice, with the potential to be better. I tried to give him a sense of what it would be like if he had a live-in woman. I had dinner ready when he came home from work, and sex was available whenever he wanted it. He even allowed me to have company come over to his house. My old friend, Regina, lived and worked nearby, and we were able to catch up. That's what I love about the people I called friends: time never stops, and we are always able to act as if we saw each other the day before.

I daydreamed about moving here with him, and having a friend close by would be great. I was really building a life with this man in my head. He managed to hurt my feelings a bit when he referred to me as a stranger in his house. We were having general conversation, and he mentioned having anxiety about leaving me alone in his house while he was at work. That comment let me know that he was not viewing our reunion the same way I was. I was disappointed, but I had to respect his views. He needed more time to see that I was a genuine person and that I could be trusted.

When I left Augusta, I couldn't really tell if he'd enjoyed having me there or not. We continued to speak to each other several times per day, and I hoped he was getting to a point where he felt more comfortable with me. In December, he made his first trip to California. I was excited to have him share my space. His trip to California was also to see his long-time Army buddy, who also lived in California. I can't recall if it was the first night or second night in California, but his friend drove out to meet him in Long Beach. I told Steve that he could take my car to go meet his friend and catch up. My plan was to stay at home and cook. I also stayed true to what I was taught from my situation with Dave, which was that a woman should not be too friendly with her man's friends.

Steve didn't want to drive, so I had to drop him off. It was strange because he still didn't want me to leave once we'd arrived at The Pike. I guess he wanted me to meet his friend. I wasn't overly impressed with his friend. He came off to me as that Black man who'd never had anything and now he had something to prove to the world—and I mean right down to the style of clothes he wore. They were flashy and screamed, *I want to be seen!*

I stayed for a little while, and then I left to go finish cooking. They weren't gone that much longer before they came back to my place. We ate dinner, and I made apple crisp for dessert. While I was in the kitchen fixing the plates for dessert, his friend walked in. My kitchen was extremely small, but this man was infringing on my personal space. I had to back up in the corner between the washing machine, stove, and utility closet, and ask him to step back. I was really uncomfortable around this dude, but he was Steve's friend, and I didn't want to be rude. He kept talking about them going out and having drinks. I suggested the Rosco's Chicken and Waffles in Long Beach, because they had a small lounge connected to it. I didn't want to go because of that dude and how he made me feel. Steve told me, "When a man asks you to come out with him, it's because he wants you there with him."

I couldn't protest any longer after he said that, but I couldn't tell him what had happened in the kitchen, either. When we went inside the lounge and found a table, I made sure I sat on the opposite side of his friend. Overall, the night was really fun. I can still see Steve and his friend forming a sandwich on the dance floor with this older lady who thought she still had it. On the way home that night, I did tell Steve what his friend had done in the kitchen and how it made me feel. I don't recall Steve saying anything about what I'd told him. I felt like it may have been something planned between them to test me. I never mentioned it again, but it stayed in the back of my mind.

His friend invited us out to his house in Lake Elsinore, which was about one hour away from my house. I really didn't want to go, but Steve wanted to spend time with his friend. I felt like this trip wasn't really about me but more about him spending time with his friend. Nonetheless, we went to his friend's house, and he was less creepy. I figured that, because he was around his pregnant wife and child, he toned down the creep in him.

Just as I thought, he was very braggadocious. I thought the house was cool, but it literally looked exactly like every other house on the block. I would be confused going home at night, for fear I may pull into the wrong driveway. The view from his backyard was amazing. I just felt it lacked privacy for swimming in the pool. He was trying so hard for us to go swimming in his heated pool. I prayed for a large-ass ice cube to fall in his pool, so I wouldn't have to hear him say, "The pool is heated" again. He did cook some good food on the grill, and we did have a good time playing cards and listening to their Army stories.

We also had a good time at the bowling alley. One of the best moments for me was when Steve bowled a strike and just walked up to me and gave me a kiss in celebratory mode. Up until that moment, I felt I was just a homegirl who'd given him a ride to see his homeboy. The bad part about that moment was when we were driving home and I mentioned it to him, he didn't even remember doing it. In the moment he had kissed me at the bowling alley, I thought he was seeing me in a different light, but in fact, I could have been anybody standing there, and he probably would have given them a kiss.

The rest of the trip was spent doing the basic California tourist sightseeing events. His visit was during a time when African Americans were tired of the obvious police brutality and the police officers not being held accountable for their actions. In many cities across many states, there were marches and protesters lying down in the street to cause awareness. During our walk down Hollywood Boulevard, we actually came across the protesters in the process of stopping traffic and lying down in the middle of the Boulevard. It was a prideful moment—but also scary, because you didn't know how the police were going to react. Steve was happy to have witnessed the live protest.

I also took him to Beverly Hills, so he could take a picture in front of the Beverly Hills sign. While out there, Steve spotted actor Al Pacino walking down the street. He walked over to shake his hand, and then everyone else ran over there. Steve was happy that he'd had that moment. I thought it was a cool visit overall. I just wish he'd treated me more like a girlfriend instead of someone who allowed him to stay in their home while he was on vacation. He went home, and I never spoke to him about my true feelings on his first trip to California.

It was now February 2015, and I was preparing for my second trip to Augusta. This trip was all about reconstruction and renovation. We were meeting with potential contractors and electricians. I ended up talking him into getting the whole house rewired, with new lighting in the kitchen and bathrooms. He finally agreed to a choice for the floor and countertop material, but none of that could be done without additional minor work.

I showed him how to remove wallpaper without tearing up the sheetrock. I told him that most of the money spent in construction was spent on demolition work. To save money and cost, I suggested we do some of the work ourselves, but prior to me arriving, he'd already paid the guys from Home Depot to come in and take out the old kitchen cabinets. He later admitted that I was right after watching them remove the cabinets.

It was Steve's intention to keep the old tile backsplash to save money. For me, that tile had to go, and so I started to remove it myself. While he was at work, I went to Home Depot and brought home some samples of inexpensive backsplash options. I also came back with a piece of board to fix the dent in his bed that was causing it to sink. That night, when he got home, he helped me finish removing the tile from the wall that I had been working on all day. He was a little upset at first because he felt like I was costing him money, but he agreed that it would give the renovation an overall better look.

Steve didn't have much construction experience, and, so, when he tried to remove the first section of tile, he ended up taking a large piece of the wall with it. Needless to say, we ended up back at Home Depot getting sheetrock, sheetrock tape, and mud. While we were there, I suggested we buy the plywood to level the floor under the cabinets, because that would also save him money. We also purchased a circular saw to aid in cutting the plywood.

Once we got back to his house, I paid close attention to how we worked together. It was as natural as rain falling from the sky. We tackled the floor first. The only issue we had was how to work the circular saw. We worked together to figure it out, and it was smooth sailing after that. We fixed the first hole in the wall together, and he clearly stated that he wanted to do the next large hole by himself. We took a small break to eat, prior to him trying to take on the bigger hole in the wall.

When he finished eating, he began to work on the wall alone. I decided to let him try it on his own, and I continued watching television. The next thing I remember was hearing him say under his breath that I wasn't doing anything but sitting around watching television. I reminded him that he'd said he wanted to do it on his own. After that, he said to me, "Get the fuck out then." I got up, went straight to the bedroom, and began to pack my bags. I had no clue if that tiny airport was even open, but I knew that I was not staying in his house. I started frantically trying to Google a cab service to take me to the airport. There was no way I was going to tolerate someone talking to me crazy because I was in their house.

When he saw that I was preparing to leave, he came to me, hugged me, and said he was sorry. He then whispered in my ear, "Don't go. I want you to stay." We had a brief discussion about the misunderstanding over what I thought I'd heard him say. He explained that he hadn't said, "Get the fuck out" and actually had said, "Well get the fuck on, then." He tried to explain that it meant something other than what I interpreted it to mean. I guess, because I'm from New York and he was from the South, that our interpretation of whatever he'd said was different. All I cared about was that he apologized. What I learned was that he didn't want me to help him but that he wanted me to be in the kitchen with him as he did the work. When it was all said and done, he'd done a fantastic job.

Sex that night was really great. I even thought I came close to having a true orgasm. I think that night I'd convinced myself that I was beginning to fall in love with him. I was nervous about our sex session that night because we didn't use any protection, and he didn't pull out. When he left for work that morning, I called my friend Angie and told her all about that night. By this point in my life, I didn't even want kids, and the thought of possibly getting pregnant quite frankly made me sick. I used his car and drove to the nearest pharmacy to seek out Plan B, the morning-after pill. I decided I would take my chances and pray my way out of this situation, because I was not about to pay $40 for one damn pill.

I'd never believed that I was a lucky person, but it just so happened that Steve told me that night that he'd had a vasectomy. Hearing this was almost like hitting the lottery. It was the icing on the cake for me. I wanted this man even more after hearing that. I never thought the word "vasectomy" would make me so happy. I never told him about my little trip to the pharmacy, because some things just don't need to be said.

The next few days went well. We looked at some of his vacation pictures, listened to music, and did a little dance together. We went shopping for a new fridge, but with me being the savvy consumer that I am, he ended up with a brand-new stove, microwave, and dishwasher, all for a great price. Steve thought I was going to get us in trouble for stealing. Technically, it *was* stealing. The stove they agreed to give us was missing some parts, however, when the guy came to move the stove to the truck, I had already taken the parts from another stove and placed them on ours. Once we made it back to his house with a fully equipped stove, he was very grateful to me.

All the minor kitchen demolition work was done, and it was all ready to be put back together, complete with flooring, cabinets, and backsplash. There wasn't enough time to take on the task of bathroom demolition, but we did purchase a new sink-cabinet combo and a new mirror-cabinet for the wall. Steve still wasn't confident in his abilities to complete demolition on his own, so he hired someone to do the work.

My week there seemed to go by at the speed of light. Before I knew it, we were back at the airport, where Steve saw some guy and became really excited to see him. He was a former pro football player by the name of Lynn Swann. I don't watch sports, so I had no clue who he was. I'm also not star-struck or a groupie of anyone, but I saw how excited Steve became when he noticed Mr. Swann. I wanted to do something nice for him, so I walked up to Mr. Swann and asked if I could take his picture for my friend. I would have loved to say, " . . .for my husband," but all in due time. Mr. Swann insisted on taking the picture with me instead. I texted the picture to Steve and let him know that I'd done something I would never do, just for him. I wasn't sure if he truly appreciated the gesture, because I didn't get the feedback that I thought I would. In fact, he downplayed how excited he'd been to see Mr. Swann once he received the picture.

Anyway, I was back in California and still helping to assist with minor decisions regarding the reno. By March, the renovations were complete, and everything looked amazing. Steve sent me pictures of the finished product, and I couldn't wait to make this my new home and update a few more areas in his house. I daydreamed a lot about being his wife and loving him to the max.

In April, Steve made his second the trip to California. On his second day here, his friend came to pick him up from my house. I thought it was weird that he didn't ask for directions to come back to my house. The other weird part was that Steve didn't ask me to go with them this time.

When he came back, he was overly excited that his friend had taken him to drive a speedboat at Shoreline, in Long Beach. He had the nerve to say to me, "Why didn't you think of that?" I ignored his comment because he'd never once mentioned anything that he would like to do while in California. From that moment on, *I* decided to do what *I* liked to do in California, which was climb the stairs at Sand Dune Park and jog at the track in Redondo Beach. I did take him to Santa Monica Pier, Manhattan Beach Pier and Esplanade, because these are places that I like to go to clear my mind. I felt that, if he wanted to do something specific, then he would mention it or call his friend to take him there.

The vibe felt a little off with this trip. Since Steve put a lot of emphasis on sex in a relationship, I thought maybe that would change the vibe of this trip. Steve had mentioned a sexual position he always want to try. After I got out of the shower, I suggested we try it. I thought I'd given him something that he'd never had before and that he would always remember me for sharing that moment with him. He gave no signs that he enjoyed sharing that moment with me. I realized—again—that I was on page 10, and he hadn't even opened the book on a being in a relationship with me. I was still hopeful that he would get on the same page as me, sooner or later. Overall, I thought the visit was okay.

When Steve got home, our first conversation didn't go the way I thought it would. I was completely blindsided by what he said to me. His entire attitude toward me had changed. He yelled at me as he said, "I don't want to do this! I don't want to be in a long-distance relationship!" He said it would be too expensive traveling between two states. I told him not to worry about the finances—that I would make it happen.

I felt tears starting to form in my eyes. I hadn't cried over a man since Saint. I was beyond hurt because I'd put him on a pedestal. I felt like he would be the man who would never hurt me. I put on a brave face and told him that I understood his position. But then I heard myself trying to convince him to still give us a chance. I reminded him that, with our jobs, I could put in for a lateral to come there or someplace close to him. I felt I was losing any hope of ever having a husband if he rejected me. Steve was perfect in my eyes, up until this point.

He was adamant in his stance, and he became really mean with his delivery whenever I hinted at the idea of still trying to make it work. At times, I felt it was disrespectful, and that's where I drew the line. I had spent more than 40 years on this Earth allowing myself to be disrespected by men, and I was not going to take it from anyone ever again. This entire situation reminded me of Saint right after his house was completed, and he flipped the script on me. We went from speaking up to six times per day to not speaking at all over the course of a few months since his last trip to California.

I did miss talking to him every day. I also longed to hear his voice, but I refused to call. He needed to apologize for how he had been speaking to me and treating me. When he finally called, it was to tell me that he'd gotten selected to Memphis as a lieutenant. He was speaking to me as if he had apologized and I had forgiven him. I went along with the conversation but kept his hurtful words and treatment in the back of my mind. I wanted this promotion for him more than I think he wanted it for himself. I deemed myself his number-one cheerleader. To show him I was proud of him, I sent him a very masculine floral arrangement to his job. His response to the gift was, "Thanks, but don't do that again." I thought the comment was a little ungrateful, but I had to let it roll off my shoulder. *Maybe he just doesn't like flowers,* I thought.

We began to speak more frequently, because I was now helping him to find a property-management company to assist with renting his house. It felt good to be talking daily to him again, even if it wasn't the conversation that I wanted to have. Many times, I wished that he would just change his mind and ask me to come visit. I did notice that every time he did call, it was for his own selfish reasons. He always needed help with something, and I was always available to lend a hand. When he said his feet hurt in his boots, I bought several boots for him to try so his feet wouldn't hurt. When he said he needed a new uniform so he could look good as a new lieutenant, I purchased new uniforms.

As the time grew closer for him to make the move to Memphis, I learned that his co-workers were having a gathering for him as a going-away celebration. I thought for sure that he would invite me to come down and be a part of the celebration, but no such luck. He didn't even think to ask me. My mind instantaneously went back to the old days, when I felt the men in my life were ashamed of me. I looked back over our brief time together, and the similarities between Steve and most of the men in my life struck me. I did everything I knew how to show that I was a supportive friend/girlfriend, but it was all for nothing. I felt like such a fool, all over again. How could I let this happen to me again?

I was an absolute idiot. I was going down the road of being a doormat once again. I set myself up to be put out like old trash. I decided to accept the fact that we weren't going to be a couple, and I tried switching gears to becoming a homegirl again. That idea backfired also with Steve. He was not receptive to that idea at all, or he just didn't know how to transition. Again, he became disrespectful, and with every attempt at a regular conversation, I was told to stay out of his business. I couldn't understand his point of view because I came from a world where I had plenty of homeboys, and we always talked about their relationships. I was still close to many of my ex-situation partners, and we always spoke about their current relationship.

Steve said, in no uncertain terms, "I don't want that from you." He judged me for being friends with Saint, who was now a married man. He felt I was wrong for continuing to communicate with Saint, because he believed that his new wife wouldn't approve. I thought he was hung up on my relationship with Saint, because he always found a way to mention him during one of our heated conversations. I knew that my conversations with Saint were very innocent, and I knew that Saint did tell his wife when we spoke. I was sending Saint emails for job prospects for him and his wife, but Steve didn't know this. I realized that his maturity level was not in sync with mine. He still held onto the barbaric notion that men and women can't be just friends. Then he showed me that he was really not the person I'd made him out to be in my head, because he gave the ultimate insult-to-injury by referencing the fact the Saint used to beat me. He actually told me that I was the one constant in my failed relationships.

That night, I actually shed some tears while talking to him, and he didn't care. I knew I was a better friend to him than he could ever be to me. We didn't speak for a month or more after that night. Just like before, he called out of the blue and was acting like everything was OK between us. This time, I wasn't playing along, and I let him know that I thought he was a messed-up person for saying what he said. I told him that it was the equivalent of telling a rape victim that it was her fault she'd gotten raped. He couldn't see the parallel between the two, or maybe he just didn't want to. I was so disappointed in the person that he had become. Maybe this was the person he'd been all along and I met his representative back in Glynco.

I questioned everything he'd ever told me—from the beginning. Did he really want to be married? Did he ever like me? Did he have a girlfriend all this time? Was I the chick on the side? Did he really believe that communication was a key component in a relationship?

I would call him, and he wouldn't answer the phone. I would text him, and I wouldn't get a text back. When I asked "Why?" he would respond rudely, which would lead to me not talking to him again for a period of time. On those rare occasion when I knew he was going to have a drink and I didn't hear from him, I would worry. I have always been the type to worry when I don't hear from someone, so I would call several times until I knew they were alright. I didn't ask for much, just a text saying, "I am out" or "I'll call you later."

Steve didn't understand this, and he yelled at me as if I were a child. "Listen, lady—don't call my phone like that," he would say. I made a serious effort never to dial his number again. I felt myself losing respect for him, something I thought I would never do. At the same time, I wished him no ill will. I wanted him to succeed in his career and in life. He was now living in Mississippi but working at the prison in Memphis. I don't recall whether I received an invitation or if my dumb ass offered to help him unpack once his stuff arrived at his new home.

I don't even remember how we got to the point where I wanted to go. I just remember booking a weekend trip to Memphis to help him get situated in October 2015. We did have sex, but I made him use a condom because he was obviously doing his thing in Augusta, and I didn't know what he had been doing since he got to Memphis.

The only positive thing that came from this trip was the reinforcement of the fact that we worked well together. For a brief moment, I started to fantasize again about the possibility of "us."

When I got back to California, once again, I ended up feeling used, because he went right back to being disrespectful with his words. I needed a break. My birthday was coming up, and, although my money was tight, I booked a last-minute birthday vacation to Cancun, Mexico.

I really enjoyed myself. My crazy birthday adventure was to swim with the dolphins and do the jetpack thing in the ocean. I was turning

45 years old and still could not say that I'd had a *real* relationship—where I was number one, and everyone knew it. I'd had a lifetime worth of situationships. Even though I had an amazing time in Cancun, I knew I didn't want to take any more solo vacations. I was really tired of being alone and having to do these things on my own. I wanted to share these moments with someone, so that we could look back on the pictures and laugh together. I thought about Steve a lot on this trip, for several reasons. Whenever we were in each other's presence, things seemed to be fine. We had fun when we were around each other. I think that, because he was the last man that I was with, I was holding on to hope.

Going back home, I was expecting at least a birthday card from him, but no, nothing. I brought him back a few keepsake items from Cancun, and after not receiving a card, I thought about not sending them to him, but I wasn't that person. I'd bought them for him, and so he should have them. He did call to say thank you for the gifts once he'd received them, but that conversation turned into an argument, because I brought up the fact that he could have spent a dollar to get me a card. He said, "I didn't even think about it." My feelings kept getting hurt by this man who I thought was a gentleman. I asked myself on many occasions, *What am I missing?*

Our communication became even worse than it had been in the past. He began to annoy me when he would call and ask, "What's going on?" Beyond those words, he had nothing else to say. I would try to spark conversation about anything. I would talk about work and the fact that I worked with lazy and incompetent co-workers, but he would just tell me that I'm probably the problem or that I complained too much. I knew that he was a new lieutenant, and he didn't understand how officers can be or how draining it was to work with lazy lieutenants.

My issue was that he sat in constant judgment of me. Everything I said or did, I was wrong. Any feeling that I felt was because I was a woman. He was not supportive of me in any way, shape, or form. I told him about writing this book, and he told me that I shouldn't publish it because I mentioned the abortions. I had to consider the possibility that this was all a part of the real reason he didn't want to be in a relationship with me. The mere fact that he mentioned it made me believe this was a personal issue or concern of his. I think he judged me for making the decisions I'd made in my past. I wanted to believe that he was more refined and that he would be able to see beyond my past.

I asked him if that was that the real reason he didn't want to be with me, but he always stuck to the fact that it was the distance between us—but I never believed that. There had to be another reason, but he was not forthcoming with that information. Whenever I would try to talk to him on how I viewed him and his behavior toward me, he would shut me down. He made me feel like my thoughts were stupid and invalid—just something not worth listening to, like the current, 45th President. Every time I tried to give him a chance to have a decent conversation, I found myself standing before a single-person jury.

He talked about the fact that I watched certain television shows instead of watching the news. I hated the news because, to me, it is not news. It is some reporter's opinion about the story. I would rather read the newspaper than watch the news. In his mind, I didn't have a thought of my own. Everything I said had to come from me watching reality television. I watched reality TV shows because I had no drama in my life, except him, and, to me, it was funny most of the time to see the drama unfold on TV. I found it hypocritical that he judged me for watching *Atlanta Housewives*, but his aunt, whom he respected, watched the show also.

Speaking of his aunt, I did keep my word when I went home to New York to go see her. We formed our own relationship outside of Steve. In fact, we never spoke about him when we talked on the phone. Steve called me, very upset, accusing me of telling his aunt that I was his girlfriend. Now I was upset, because at no point did I ever refer to myself as his girlfriend, nor did I lead her to believe anything of that nature. I may have been desperate to be in a relationship, but I never claimed anyone who didn't claim me. She liked me, and maybe she liked me for her nephew, but that had nothing to do with me. He was upset that she was telling him that he should have gotten me something for my birthday. She told him that he shouldn't waste my time.

What hurt me more was that he said to me, "This is why I didn't want you to meet her." I had to remind him that I didn't ask to meet her. I was willing to wait in the car, and he was the one who convinced her to let me come into her house. He also said that he didn't like me talking to her. At first, I told myself that I was not going to call her again, but I knew that we never had any discussion about him, and I genuinely liked her outside of him, so I continued to call and check on her, as she did me. Once he told her that I was not his girlfriend, I did notice that she didn't call me anymore, but that was to be expected. I still called her because I did care for her, but I limited my calls out of respect for him—after all, it was his aunt. I never told her that he didn't want me talking to her. I thought that would be petty and distasteful.

I guess I was still holding onto hope that someday he would change his mind about me—that he would see that I was not this negative person he'd made me out to be in his head. He viewed me as a person who loved to fight and argue all the time. I thought it was the opposite—because he was the one who'd caused all the arguments. I knew that I was not that person, and it bothered me to think that's what he thought of me. I also wondered how he'd come to that conclusion about me. I would never start a fight, but I would never back down from one, either. I was used to dealing with individuals who talked things over in order for us to come to some understanding so we could move on. Steve never wanted to hear anything I had to say, so we never came to a resolution on anything. Once it was set in his mind, it became written in stone, like the Ten Commandments. I was tired of doing battle with that mindset. Although it bothered me, there was nothing I could do about it.

I'd known *of* this man for sixteen years, but I didn't *know* the man. He wouldn't allow me to get to know him on an intimate level. The person I'd gotten to know within these last couple of years, I didn't like. I believed he was a good person, but he just wasn't a good person for me. I felt like I constantly had to defend myself when trying to have a simple conversation, but in his mind, this was viewed as being argumentative and loving to fight. He had a passive-aggressive way of communicating, and I was a straight shooter. I told him on several occasions just to be direct with me, because I was not good at deciphering his sarcasm. I didn't understand when he tried to give examples, because none of it made any sense to me.

I would think that the average person would make a statement, and, if it were misunderstood, then they would rephrase or try another way to express themselves.

Not Steve. He would repeat the same example over and over again, even after I told him that I didn't get what he was trying to say. To me there was nothing worse than trying to explain yourself and give an example, just to have the other person get caught up in the example and not the big picture or the point of the example. I would like to have made a smooth transition from wanting him to be my man, to making him one of my closest friends. I don't think he had a clue what friendship could look like between two people who'd once had sex.

At this stage in the game, my mind had totally checked out from him, so I knew my body would no longer respond to him sexually. Over the years, I'd learned that sex for me was more mental and not just a physical act. I think that, because he'd never had a female friend, he didn't know how to interact with a female on a platonic level. I questioned whether Steve truly knew how to be a friend to anyone, period. I tried to explain that, sometimes, two people who had sex can have a healthy friendship, but he couldn't accept that idea. When a relationship is built on true friendship, it can withstand the test of time, including no longer having sex or sexual thoughts.

Steve was incapable of achieving this level of maturity. I had never encountered someone so close-minded. It was frustrating constantly trying to get him to open his mind. The only time you could have a conversation with him was if you were talking about sex. I hated talking about sex with him because it was more of the same comments based on lack of common sense and basic knowledge. Few men know longevity in a relationship may come with periods of not being able to have sex. When a man lets it be known that he has to have sex, he is also letting it be known that he would cheat to get it. Sex should be viewed as icing on the cake. For men like Steve, sex *was* the cake, and everything else was icing. He believed that women are ruled by the penis.

Now that I think about it, maybe some of his thoughts and theories stemmed from his own insecurities. For me, constantly talking about sex ruins the actual moment of passion. An unrealistic build-up to the sexual encounter can lead to disappointment for both parties. Steve managed to undermine my sexual abilities. I'd never had anyone complain about having sex with me—in fact, it was just the opposite. Steve let it be known that he didn't enjoy sex with me, because I couldn't climax. This was a prime example of the ignorant statements that he would make. Although I knew my situation wasn't uncommon, hearing him say that to me made me feel less than a woman.

I believed in my heart that he was a smart man, but a lot of things he said made me think otherwise. I believed that, over the years, some women had really hurt him and that he was still in the process of dealing with that hurt. Some men act out when they've been hurt, and any woman who comes after that pain suffers the consequences. If he would have been willing to open up about whatever it was, then we could have been on a different path. If only he could've learned to trust me and know that he could be vulnerable with me, I knew I could help him overcome whatever it is. My heart was still wishing he could be different, or just be the person I'd met in Glynco.

This situation with Steve was different from the others, because, with them, I didn't know how I ended up in love. With Steve, I made a conscious decision to try to love this man and was willing to do whatever it took to have him love me back. I wanted to love him because I didn't want to have to say that this, too, just didn't work out. I wanted to love him because I believed somewhere inside him was the person I'd met in Glynco.

Although he was disrespectful during most of our conversations, I still answered the phone every time he called. I guess I was hoping that one of these phone calls would be the call I was hoping for—where he would say, "Sharon, I don't want to lose you, and I want to give us a chance." Every now and then, he would call during the midnight hours, and, for some odd reason, those would be the best conversations we ever had. We communicated just as I hoped we would all along, but somehow, when we would try having a conversation during normal hours, it was right back to the same disrespectful and rude behavior.

This back-and-forth, on again-off again, speaking-not speaking, went on for another year. During this period, Steve briefly tried to step up to be a friend. On April 21, 2016, I learned that Saint had slept with my sister-friend, Deidra. I remember this day because it was also the day that the famed recording artist Prince died. Saint had called, and while going down memory lane, he said, "One of the things that I regret the most that I did during our time together was sleeping with your friend."

I played it cool, as if he'd already told me about this, but I asked anyway. "Which one of my friends?" I was thinking maybe he was going to say someone who was more of an associate than a true friend. When he said her name, I really felt faint. I could have literally passed out sitting on my couch.

Again, I played it cool, so that I could hear the full story of how and when this had all begun. Saint was just talking as if he were telling me the weather. He said that, after the death of his mother, Deidra showed up at his house during her lunch break to offer her condolences. A few days later, she came over again, and they just talked. The next day she popped in again and said, "Look, I just want to suck your dick and leave." Steve said that she came in and did what she wanted to do and then left. She told him also that she had a female lover and would be willing to have a threesome with him. Over the course of two months, they were having sex right under my nose. She was coming to the house visiting me, or so I thought, but now I know why she was really there.

Saint said everything ended when he asked about the threesome again, and she said that she couldn't go through with it because she'd started having feelings for him. The only question that came to my mind when he finished telling this story was, "Did you guys ever think about me?"

He said, "To be honest, we never mentioned you. Oh, wait. One time, I think she said, 'You know we shouldn't be doing this.'"

It was at that moment that I couldn't hear any more. I could barely get the words out, but I told him to go to hell and never to speak to me again. He couldn't understand why I felt that way because it was now 12 years later.

"Saint, Deidra was more than just a friend. We called each other 'sisters,' and you knew that," I told him. I said a few more disrespectful words to him and hung up the phone.

The first person I thought to call was Steve. All he had to offer me was, "I'm sorry that happened, but why would he tell you that now?"

I tried to explain that we were just talking as friends, and he interrupted me to say, "He's not your friend, and he would only tell you that now to hurt you."

I knew that was not true, even though I was pissed at Saint. I knew he would never purposely try to hurt me. When I said that to Steve, it caused us to start arguing. Again, I didn't feel supported by him. I wanted to hear anything but that. Why would he start a fight with me, when I was on the phone damn near in tears? He put me in a position of defending the man who had just hurt me to the core.

I got off the phone with him and called my homeboy, Twinkles, to tell him what had happened, and I got the response that I needed from a real friend. It was just as simple as asking, "Are you OK?"

To finish off that topic, I did call Deidra and asked her about it. She simply said, "Yes." I shed a tear, not because I didn't already know that it was true, but because at that moment, I knew I'd lost a friend—or someone I considered a friend. I hung up the phone and never spoke to her again.

Steve did call back to check on me, but I was just not feeling him after the first conversation. We went right back to status quo communication, which was none. When he did call, the conversation was limited to work-related issues. As much as I was disappointed in his behavior, I still didn't want anyone talking bad about him as a lieutenant, so I helped him out as much as I could, which was a lot.

It was now 2017, and his behavior over the years had totally killed any notions that I was holding onto for a future between us. He was still doing the work-related check-ins, and he would ask the same question with every phone call, which was, "When are you going back to New York?" My routine was to go home in February to surprise my mom for her birthday and get my taxes done. Since

Steve decided he wanted to meet me in New York again, I had to tell her I was coming home this time. When he suggested getting a hotel room, I let it be known that I was not paying for a hotel and that I would be staying with my mother. He was welcome to stay there if he wanted to, or he could stay with his aunt. I knew Mother wouldn't have a problem with letting him stay at her place, because she'd always opened her doors to anyone. He eventually elected to stay at my mother's with me.

Because I couldn't surprise my mother with a pop-up visit, I decided to gather all my nieces, sisters, nephew, and brother together for a surprise birthday gathering for her. The catch to it all was that she was going to be doing all the cooking. I felt good being able to take my mother to the supermarket and say, "Get whatever you want." Steve didn't want to go with us to the supermarket, so we left him in the apartment. My mother thought Steve was really nice, but the way she was referencing him, I had to make it clear that he was not my boyfriend.

Once we got back to the apartment, my mother began cooking. She thought that I was taking all this food back to California with me. What I did was take food requests from my family members and had her prepare that food item. While she was in the house cooking, I was able to take Steve to Long Island to Raimos Pizza, the best pizza ever, and drive by the house where I grew up. I am a very nostalgic person, so this moment would have been extremely special to me if he was that special man in my life, but he showed no interest.

I hated to compare the men in my life, but, for a moment, I recalled when I brought Saint to see that house, and he showed genuine interest. We sat in the car in the front of the house and just talked. Saint asked which window was my bedroom, and then he reminisced on his house in comparison to mine. He remembered some of the stories I'd shared with him about 99 Shonnard, and I was able to paint the full picture for him. It felt good to have someone to relive some of my childhood memories with. I wanted to have that same moment with Steve, but he was just a man cut from a different cloth.

We left Long Island and headed to the Bronx, to spend some time with his aunt, and, even then, she still made comments as if we were a couple. This time, I corrected her by letting her know that we were just friends. She was so funny. She replied, "I know, because his thing can't reach from Memphis to California." The last time I'd gone home to see her, I learned that she loved raw and smoked neckbones. This time, I surprised her by bringing her the neckbones. She thought it was so funny that I remembered, and she couldn't stop laughing. Steve was happy to see her smiling and laughing the way she was. I wanted him to see that she and I had developed our own relationship outside of him.

We had a good visit with her, but Steve still had more sightseeing, New York-tourist things he wanted to do. We ended up in Harlem on 125th Street, at the Apollo Theatre. I no longer cared about him judging what TV shows I watched, so when we were in front of the Black Ink Tattoo Shop, which is one of the reality shows that I loved to watch, I had to take a picture. While we were there, my mother called to find out what time I was coming back to Queens, because she was almost finished cooking. I told her that I also wanted some fried dumplings, and you could hear in her voice that she was tired but willing to do it for me. Because I was on speaker phone, Steve heard her tone.

He said, "Sharon, don't do this anymore."

"I know my mother—she will be so happy in the end once everyone begins to show up, and she won't even think about being tired," I replied.

In my mind, Steve was just not a thoughtful person, so he couldn't understand or see the big picture. On the way back to Queens, we finally had a real conversation, once more proving that we got along and communicated so much better when we were face to face. He actually told me that he realized I was a good woman and, more so, a good person. He also finally admitted that he had a lady friend back in Memphis. I suspected that he did, and I also suspected that it was someone he worked with. He would never confirm whether it was a co-worker, but I felt it was, because, whenever I made mention of putting in for positions in Memphis, there was an uneasy tone in his voice. It was disappointing, because he'd once told me that he didn't like to date people on the job, but I couldn't fault him, either, because the heart wants what it wants.

I also knew that, if I had any thoughts of sleeping with him on this trip, learning that little piece of information about his lady friend put an end to that deal. He did try to make an attempt to engage in sex, but I said "No."

The surprise birthday dinner for my mom went off just as expected. My family thought he was really cool and that we looked good together, but I had to reiterate that we were just friends. They all laughed at me because I called *everyone* "just a friend." So, to reinforce that we were only friends, I pointed out the long-distance relationship factor. I lied and said Steve and I both agreed that things would be different if we didn't live in different states, but that was my wish and not his words. They accepted that answer and left the topic alone, but at this point, I didn't believe that anymore.

Typical of our situation, as soon as we got back to our separate states, the arguments ensued. I didn't realize that he was really upset that I didn't have sex with him. I felt offended that he thought that I would want to have sex with him after all the arguing and fighting that we had been doing. Was he thinking that I was that hard up for sex that I would just do it with him? Was he thinking that I was that easy? This went hand-in-hand with my theory that he believed all woman are ruled by the penis. I refused to be ruled by the penis, so if that meant that I would have to do without sex until I find the right person—someone who was going to respect me, love me, and truly want to get to know me—then I would do without the penis. At this point in my life, I could care less about a penis. I learned that sex for me was between my ears—not between my legs. If I felt disrespected by him or anyone, sex was the last thing I was thinking about.

I had to self-reflect again. Was I putting something out there that men felt that they could say or do anything to me and that I would still spread my legs for them? On the other hand, I had to think, *Why would he be upset with me for not sleeping with him, when he has a lady friend?* Furthermore, he was the same person who told me that he didn't enjoy sex with me. It was painfully reaffirming that I didn't know him, and he was not the man I thought he was.

I just never pictured him as a cheater. I always thought of him as the husband type. I saw him as a man who would make a woman feel safe. It also proved that he didn't know me at all, no matter how many times he proclaimed that he did. How can you claim to know someone when you never take the time to listen or ask questions about that person or their life? He, himself, told me once that, if a man wants a woman, he would do what it takes to get to know her. I believe one of Steve's issues was that he is a terrible listener. He already anticipated his response in his head, before any of your own words could leave your mouth. There is no way that someone is listening if they are already thinking of a response to something that was never verbally spoken. I found myself constantly saying, "Just listen, and let me speak."

Another issue I believe he had was that he couldn't take responsibility for his actions. He fought and argued to be right at all costs. There was no need to find a common ground or basic understanding of any issue with him. The basic purpose in having a discussion or conversation about an issue always took a back seat to his need to be right or his belief that he had taught me something. Maybe he just had a problem with saying, "I'm sorry."

I can't say for sure what it was, but I grew very weary of trying to be his friend and then having to get over what I felt were disrespectful actions on his part. When I told him that I was adding him to this book, he told me that he would sue me. I thought about that for a moment and decided to add him anyway. Our story was deserving of being told because it shows that people should never be put on a pedestal, because no one is perfect. He had been a major factor in my journey of trying to establish a relationship while dealing with low self-esteem. He was the person who finally showed me that I still have a lot of work to do on myself before trying to get involved with anyone.

Outro

Dear God, it was difficult writing this book. There is no other word to describe me but "stupid." I don't have all the answers about dealing with a man, but if I have too many questions, then I won't deal with him. Most people who write this type of book always seem to have found that angel that God has sent for them. I am happy to say that I am still alone and content with being that way until my angel is sent for me. I believe that God still has me doing the work that I need to do for myself. That might be the ability to look in the mirror and love the physical being that reflects before my eyes, or learning to forgive myself for being so cruel to my heart. My plan is to just live life, and, if my future does not have a good man in it, then that is God's will, and I will accept it. I plan to live life to the fullest of my ability. I plan on going to dinner, movies, more vacations; if the mood strikes me, I will go to a lounge and dance by myself.

I once read, "Worry is the opposite of faith, and so is not going out. Standing up, getting dressed, and going out the door is an act of faith. You're telling the universe you believe there is a good person out there whom you could love and who could love you. Sitting home and watching TV is saying, 'I don't have faith.'"

I plan to enjoy myself. My mind, my body, and my soul will be OK with just *me*. I know God sent those men to me for a reason. My journey with them was much like parables in the Bible: you can interpret them as you wish. I either read or heard someone say, "God will always prepare you for what he has prepared for you."

I was busy trying to buy love, temporary love, at best, but I have come to accept that love of self is the only everlasting love. Looking back at my financial woes, I think God may have stripped me of my money so that I could find someone who will love me for me—and not someone I purchased through gifts. I have always been the type of person who tries to see the bigger picture, and I went through a lot trying to get there. Every man I dealt with might not have been the One, but they were the ones I was supposed to learn from while waiting to meet the One.

The men I wrote about sensed my weakness. I learned over the years to be very careful about whom I displayed my vulnerable side to. It's not meant for everyone. The men in my life didn't earn the trust that comes with being able to show vulnerability. They knew I had no self-worth, and whatever they gave, I was willing to accept. While I was busy fighting my own self-esteem issues, I never gave it a second thought that the men in my life may have been dealing with their own insecurities. Maybe they were taking all that I had to give to fill themselves up.

I realized that, although I hated that image of a woman on her knees in front of a man, that is not the only way that a woman can bow down to a man. I took my share of disrespect, and my share of being treated like a doormat, for as long as I could take it. I guess God decided it was time for me to remove the blindfold and see things clearly enough to put a stop to it. He gave me all he felt I could handle, and, at my weakest moment, he gave me sight, and I realized I wanted more. I realized I didn't have to settle for that kind of treatment.

Being alone wasn't that bad. I accomplished a lot in my life when I was alone. If a man can't add to what I have when I am alone, then I won't allow him the opportunity to take away from that, either. This statement is not about material things; it is much deeper than that. You cannot grow wiser as a woman in a relationship unless you have had at least one bad man in your life to help you learn what your deal-breakers are. I forgive myself and the men I wrote about in this book, because, if it wasn't for them, I would probably never have seen the bigger picture. Once you have love of self, you won't accept a lesser love than what you give yourself.

About the Author

Sharon St. John has enjoyed a 20-year career with the Federal Bureau of Prisons after earning her Bachelor Degree in Criminal Justice at St John's University. When she is not working, she enjoys writing, singing, playing with her dog and making people laugh. Sharon has the ability to utilize a situation from her real life to create an intriguing fictional novel. She is the proud author of the books, *Issues* and *Me, Myself, and Men*. She is currently working on her third book which will be another fiction novel.